Profiles and Critiques in Soci

Profiles and Critiques in Social Theory

Anthony Giddens
Fellow of King's College, Cambridge

Chapter 2 contributed by Fred Dallmayr

University of California Press
Berkeley and Los Angeles

University of California Press
Berkeley and Los Angeles

Printed in Hong Kong
2 3 4 5 6 7 8 9

Library of Congress Cataloging in Publication Data

Giddens, Anthony.
  Profiles and critiques in social theory.

  Includes bibliographical references and index.
  1. Sociology—Philosophy.   2. Hermeneutics.
3. Positivism.   4. Social structure.   5. Political
sociology.   I. Dallmayr, Fred.   II. Title.
HM24.G4483   1983   301′.01   82–20231
ISBN 0–520–04933–0
ISBN 0–520–04964–0 (pbk.)

Contents

Preface

The essays which comprise this book all date from the past five years. As with my previous collection of papers, *Studies in Social and Political Theory* (1977), the articles included here were written against the backdrop of a number of larger works.[1] This book continues and amplifies some of the main arguments in those works. At the same time, since most of the discussions contained herein concern specific thinkers or schools of thought, my own views are defined polemically in relation to those of others. The book thus has an overall unity that might otherwise appear to be belied by the diverse range of its contents.

The first and third essays provide concise discussions of some of the themes analysed in greater detail in the range of writings I have just referred to. Together with Fred Dallmayr's critique of my views, plus the dialogue between us which follows, I hope that these help to clarify my arguments in relation to those themes. In analysing the impact of hermeneutics upon social theory, I endeavour to demonstrate that, while problems of 'interpretation' are fundamental to the social sciences, they certainly do not exhaust their concerns. I advocate what I call, for want of a more elegant phrase, a 'hermeneutically informed social theory'. This implies integrating hermeneutics within a broader approach to social theory, that acknowledges the basic importance of the analysis of long-term institutional change, power and conflict – matters which have rarely been confronted within the hermeneutic tradition. In this context I indicate the main elements of the theory of structuration, the means whereby I want to provide the groundwork for approaching these issues.

Dallmayr's commentary, written as a response to the first article included here, 'Hermeneutics and social theory', offers an acute yet sympathetic diagnosis of possible shortcomings in my account of the notion of structuration, and other concepts connected with it. The theory of structuration has to be assessed in some substantial part in terms of how far it helps illuminate empirical issues in the social sciences. In this respect it is encouraging that the ideas involved have been taken up in a variety of contexts.[2] On a more abstract level, there seems to be a strong convergence between my standpoint and those worked out largely independently by other authors.[3]

As the fourth essay, 'Classical social theory and the origins of modern sociology', makes plain, in my writings I have consistently been interested in three overlapping areas of interest. One is that of metatheoretical reflection, of the kind represented in the opening essays. But such reflection, I think, has to be related to the analysis of the trajectories of development of the 'advanced societies', increasingly incorporated within a world system; and to the critical examination of 'classical social theory', which still today remains the basis of a great deal of contemporary social thought. These three concerns are unified in so far as each bears upon a single overall preoccupation – with the distinctive features of late eighteenth- and nineteenth-century European thought, confronted with the vast social changes that have transformed the world in the twentieth century.

'Classical social theory and the origins of modern sociology' thus serves as a bridge between the opening articles and those which compose the rest of the book. These can be divided into two broad sections. One is spanned by my discussions of Comte and Durkheim. Comte coined the terms 'positivism' and 'sociology', and incorporated these into an encyclopedic account of the development of natural and social science. His influence over Durkheim was considerable, although of course Durkheim distanced himself from some aspects of Comte's views. However, in the articles included here, I concentrate primarily on Comte's methodological ideas, while my analysis of Durkheim is focused more on the political implications of Durkheim's thought.[4] Between these two essays come critical discussions of more recent contributions to social theory. A brief account of some newly published interchanges between Schutz and Parsons is followed by two more substantive critical commentaries on Habermas.

The essay on Durkheim makes a transition to the third section of the book. The articles included here also take the form of 'profiles and critiques' of the works of various authors and traditions of thought, but have a more strongly defined political orientation. Some of the issues I discuss in relation to Durkheim are raised again, from various angles, in most of the essays which follow. Such issues include particularly problems of the modern state, power, and violence, in the context of transformations in class structure. Marxist thought, in its numerous contemporary versions, is inevitably directly involved with these problems. The work of Raymond Williams offers one perspective upon Marxism – a perspective which suggests interesting contrasts with that of Marcuse, the 'improbable guru' of the student movements of a decade or so ago. Each can in turn profitably be compared with the writings of Marx's critics. As I try to indicate in the four concluding essays in the volume, both Marxism, and socialist thought more generally, stand in need of radical reconstruction in the current era. I offer objections against the views of those who have trodden a path from Marx to Nietzsche – including, in an earlier generation, Max Weber, and, in more recent years, Foucault. But I think that some of the questions to which these authors draw attention undeniably must be confronted in a direct fashion by anyone concerned with social theory today. In approaching such questions, I close the circle, reverting to ideas introduced in the opening essays in the book.

Cambridge   ANTHONY GIDDENS
October 1981

References

1. *New Rules of Sociological Method* (London: Hutchinson, 1976); *Central Problems in Social Theory* (London: Macmillan, 1979); *A Contemporary Critique of Historical Materialism* (London: Macmillan, 1981).
2. See, for example, the very interesting discussion by Allan Pred, 'Power, everyday practice and the discipline of human geography', in *Space and Time in Geography: Essays Dedicated to T. Hägerstrand* (Lund: Gleerups, 1981), and other recent articles by the same author; cf. also Derek Gregory, *Social Theory and Spatial Structure* (London: Macmillan, 1982).
3. See especially Roy Bhaskar, *The Possibility of Naturalism* (Brighton: Harvester, 1979), and John B. Thompson, *Critical Hermeneutics* (Cambridge: Cambridge University Press, 1981).
4. Cf. 'Durkheim's political sociology', in *Studies in Social and Political Theory* (London: Hutchinson, 1977).

Sources

'Hermeneutics and social theory' was originally given as a lecture in a conference on hermeneutics sponsored by the Sociology and Philosophy Departments of the University of Kansas in April 1981. Fred Dallmayr's commentary and discussion derive from the same occasion. 'Action, structure and power' was prepared for a conference organised by Paul Secord at the University of Houston in December 1980. 'Classical social theory and the origins of modern sociology' was first published in the *American Journal of Sociology*, vol. 81, 1976. I should like to thank the University of Chicago Press and the Editor for permission to reprint this article here, plus 'Habermas's social and political theory', which was published in vol. 83, 1978, in the same journal. 'The high priest of positivism: Auguste Comte' first appeared in *The Times Literary Supplement*, 14 November 1975; my thanks are due to the Editor for permission to reprint it here. Similarly, I am indebted to the Editor of *Contemporary Sociology* for permission to reproduce 'Schutz and Parsons: problems of meaning and subjectivity' (vol. 8, 1979). 'Labour and interaction' first appeared as a contribution to John B. Thompson and David Held (eds), *Habermas: Critical Debates* (London: Macmillan, 1982). 'Durkheim, socialism and Marxism' was given as a lecture in Rome in May 1981, sponsored by Alberto Izzo, of the Institute of Sociology. 'Literature and society: Raymond Williams' first appeared in *The Times Higher Education Supplement*, 14 December 1979; I am grateful to the Editor for allowing me to reprint it here. 'The improbable Guru: re-reading Marcuse' was written for a projected memorial volume for Marcuse. 'Class division, class conflict and citizenship rights' was given as a lecture at a colloquium organised by Il Mulino in Bologna, in October

1981. 'Classes, capitalism and the state' was first published in *Theory and Society*, vol. 9, 1980; I am grateful to the Managing Editor, and to Elsevier, the publishers, for permission to reprint it here. 'Power, the dialectic of control and class structuration' was written for a book designed as a *Festschrift* for Ilya Neustadt, to be published by Cambridge University Press. 'From Marx to Nietzsche? Neo-conservatism, Foucault, and problems in contemporary political theory' was given as the William James Lecture at the Institute for the Humanities, at New York University, in March 1981.

1

Hermeneutics and Social Theory

'Hermeneutics' – the theory of interpretation – has only recently become a familiar term to those working in the social sciences, at least in the English-speaking world. On the face of it this is an oddity, for the hermeneutic tradition stretches back at least as far as the late eighteenth century; and the term 'hermeneutics' derives from the Greeks. But this neglect is less odd than it appears, since the hermeneutic tradition was most firmly established in Germany, and many of the key texts remain untranslated into English. The concept of *verstehen*, the unifying notion of the hermeneutic tradition, became most widely known in the English-speaking world through its adoption by Max Weber. As such, it was subject to scourging attack by those associated with what I shall call the 'orthodox consensus'.[1] The controversy about *verstehen* in the English-speaking literature,[2] however, largely by-passed some of the most significant questions raised by the hermeneutic tradition. Weber was only influenced in some part by that tradition, drawing his methodological ideas more strongly from the work of Rickert and the 'Marburg School'.

But the principal factor explaining the relative lack of influence of the hermeneutic tradition in the Anglo-Saxon world has been the dominance of views of social science drawing their inspiration from positivistic or naturalistic philosophies of natural science. Such views were one of the main foundations of the orthodox consensus, an orthodoxy which dominated sociology, politics, and large sectors of the social sciences in general in the postwar period. There are three characteristics of the orthodox consensus I think it particularly important to emphasise. First, the influence of positivistic philosophy as a *logical* framework. This influence was itself twofold. The conceptions of science portrayed by philosophers such as Carnap, Hempel and Nagel were accepted (often in simplified or inaccurate form) as adequate versions of what the natural sciences are like. But it was also emphasised that the social sciences should be modelled upon the natural sciences: that the aim of the former should be to parallel, in the study of human behaviour, the achievements of the natural sciences. The object was to produce what Radcliffe-Brown once called a 'natural science of society'.

Second, on the level of *method*, the influence of functionalism. In the writings of Comte, Durkheim and many others in the nineteenth and early twentieth centuries, functionalism stood in easy and close connection with the thesis that sociology should be a 'natural science of society'. The widespread use of organic analogies in social analysis encouraged, and in some part derived from, the conception that biology stands in direct line of association with social science. Functional conceptions of a similar kind seemed appropriate to both. In the more recent period, the affiliation between functionalism and the belief that sociology should adopt the same logical framework as the natural sciences has proved more ambiguous. Modern positivist philosophers have been suspicious of the claims of functionalism, and have examined its logical status with a sceptical eye.[3] But if the marriage between contemporary positivism and functionalism was not a case of love at first sight, the relation was at least consummated. From their side, the philosophers gave grudging recognition to functionalist concepts as legitimate parts of the apparatus of science. Many of those working in the social sciences saw such recognition as providing an up-to-date formulation of the traditional ties between functionalism and the advocacy of a 'natural science of society'.

Third, on the level of *content*, the influence of the conception of 'industrial society' and of 'modernisation theory' more generally. I shall not have much to say about these in this discussion. However I think it very important to bear in mind that logical and methodological debates in the social sciences can rarely if ever be severed completely from more substantive views or theories with which they are intertwined. The concepts of 'industrial society' and 'modernisation' belong to what can be called the theory of industrial society. By the theory of industrial society I mean a particular set of views concerning the development of the 'advanced' societies, affiliated to liberal political ideas.[4] According to proponents of the theory of industrial society, industrialism is the main motive force transforming the contemporary world. In the postwar period, at a time of apparently stable growth rates in the Western economies, the theorists of industrial society foresaw the prospect of an indefinite period of prosperity, equalisation of wealth and income, and the expansion of equality of opportunity. Industrialism provided the guiding thread for this progressive movement of history, both inside the West and in the rest of the world.

Combining these three elements, the orthodox consensus provided a body of 'mainstream' opinion for sociology, and in some degree for the social sciences in general. Of course, it would be easy to underestimate the diversity of views within this consensus, and it never went unchallenged. In particular it had its critics from the Left. Throughout the period of its ascendancy, the orthodox consensus was challenged by authors influenced by Marx – although many such critics, such as Mills, Dahrendorf, Lockwood and Rex, did not regard themselves as 'Marxists'. In retrospect, the influence of Max Weber on their work seems more pronounced than that of Marx. But whatever the disagreements of these critics with the orthodox consensus, it provided a terrain for debate. There was some sort of unity to sociology, if only in the form of a common series of battlegrounds upon which issues were fought out – and even if the results of such confrontations were hardly always decisive.

Today the orthodox consensus is no more. What was an orthodoxy is an orthodoxy no longer, and consensus has given way to dissidence and disarray. The dissolution of the orthodox consensus has been substantially brought about by the critical attacks which have been mounted against positivism in philosophy and the social sciences, and against functionalism.[5] But its demise is certainly not something to be explained solely in terms of intellectual critique. The changes which have swept through the social sciences reflected transmutations in the social world itself, as the period of stable Western economic growth was interrupted by fresh reversals, crises and conflicts. The seemingly secure domain staked out by the theorists of industrial society proved fragile indeed. Even though I shall not be examining the implications of this directly, in my thinking logical, methodological and substantive problems are closely bound up with one another. The issues discussed here can be related directly to the concrete analysis of transformations in society.[6]

Hermeneutics, positivism, social theory

An interest in hermeneutics is one – among various other – responses to the toppling of the orthodox consensus, on the levels of the logic and method of social science. The English-speaking reception, or recovery, of the hermeneutic tradition has been considerably facilitated by the post-Wittgensteinian movement within British and American philosophy. Writers influenced by the later Wittgenstein, most notably Peter Winch, have proposed views of the social sciences sharply contrasting to those of the orthodox consensus. In suggesting that there is a radical dislocation between the social and natural sciences, that the understanding of 'meaningful action' is discrepant from the explanation of events in nature, post-Wittgensteinian philosophy converged with themes that have been the persistent concerns of hermeneutics. Winch's short book, *The Idea of a Social Science*,[7] has been a focal point of debate among philosophers for some twenty years, since its first publication. Most of those working in the social sciences, however, for a long period either ignored it, or dismissed Winch's claims as untenable. Only relatively recently has the book been regarded in a more favourable light.

In *The Idea of a Social Science*, Winch argued that the subject-matter of the social sciences is above all concerned with discovering the intelligibility of human action. To grasp why human beings act as they do, we must understand the meaning of their activity. To understand the meaning of conduct, according to Winch, is to grasp the rules that actors follow in doing what they do. Meaningful action is activity orientated to rules, where knowledge of those rules provides the actors' reasons for the conduct in which they engage. Understanding meaning and reasons, for Winch, involves relating observed behaviour to rules. Rules are not 'laws', in the sense in which that term is applied in the natural sciences. Neither the formulation of laws, nor causal analysis, have any place in social science. Social science is thus an interpretative, or hermeneutic, endeavour; a logical gulf separates such an endeavour from the logic and method of the natural sciences.

Winch thus produced a contemporary version of the dichotomy, long established in the hermeneutic tradition, between *verstehen* and *erklären*. *Verstehen*, the understanding of meaning, and the foundation of what were often called the 'human sciences' (*Geistes-*

wissenschaften) was contrasted by Droysen, Dilthey and others with *erklären*, the causal explanation of natural phenomena. Several things separate Winch's account from the characteristic preoccupations of hermeneutics. Winch does not employ the terminology of *verstehen*. More important, he is unconcerned with history. One of the main differences between positivistic and hermeneutic traditions has been precisely the continuing involvement of the latter with history. For hermeneutic authors, history – not as the elapsing of time, but as the capability of human beings to become aware of their own past, and incorporate that awareness as part of what their history is – has always been at the centre of the social sciences.

I do not wish in this context to offer a critical evaluation of Winch's work, and that of post-Wittgensteinian philosophy more generally.[8] Neither do I want to consider at any length the differences between these and Continental hermeneutics.[9] I do want to claim that, in social theory, a turn to hermeneutics cannot in and of itself resolve the logical and methodological problems left by the disappearance of the orthodox consensus. Winch's views cannot be sustained as they stand, and it would be a mistaken route to take to attempt to revive the differentiation of *verstehen* and *erklären*. This latter point, of course, is agreed upon by some of the leading contemporary exponents of hermeneutics, such as Gadamer and Ricoeur. But I think it equally wrong merely to dismiss the relevance of hermeneutics to social theory out of hand, as positivistically inclined writers have tended to do. I want to argue instead for what I propose to call a 'hermeneutically informed social theory'. I think it is essential in social theory to pay attention to the revitalisation of hermeneutics in the hands of the post-Wittgensteinian philosophers, Gadamer, Ricoeur and others. But at the same time I want to counsel caution; the ideas of such authors have to be received critically.

In most of my discussion I choose to use the term 'social theory', rather than 'sociology' – or, even worse, 'sociological theory'. 'Social theory', in my view, spans social science. It is a body of theory shared in common by all the disciplines concerned with the behaviour of human beings. It concerns not only sociology, therefore, but anthropology, economics, politics, human geography, psychology – the whole range of the social sciences. Neither is social theory readily separable from questions of interest to an even wider set of concerns: it connects through to literary criticism on the one hand and to the philosophy of natural science on the other. The very importance of hermeneutics in social theory signals this state of affairs: contemporary hermeneutics is very much in the forefront of developments in the theory of the text, and yet at the same time has relevance to current issues in the philosophy of science.[10] There is something new in all this, in what Geerz calls the 'blurred genres' of modern thought.[11] Some years ago, it was commonplace enough to call for 'inter-disciplinary' studies that would seek to overcome the conventionally recognised boundaries of academic disciplines. Such studies rarely amounted to very much. Today, however, real and profound convergences of interests and problems are occurring across broad spectra of intellectual life. Social theory is at the very centre of these convergencies, having both to contribute to and to learn from them. To talk of the 'blurring' of erstwhile separate frames of reference, or contexts of discussion, is an appropriate term in more than one sense. For the occurrence of a convergence of approaches has not always provided clarification of the matters at issue; it has also fogged them. In the wake of the collapse of the orthodox consensus, so far as the social sciences are concerned, there has come about something of a centrifugal dispersal of vying theoretical approaches. I have argued elsewhere[12] that this seeming intellectual disarray should not lead anyone interested in social theory – as indeed I think we all have to be – to throw up their hands in despair. The current phase of development of social theory is one demanding reconstruction on several fronts. Such a process of reconstruction, in my opinion, is already under way, although it is unlikely perhaps to recapture the consensus of the old orthodoxy. Indeed, it would be foreign to the spirit of contemporary social thought to attempt to do so.

Under the somewhat ungainly heading of a hermeneutically informed social theory I would include a number of basic ideas. There are two sets of questions I want to concentrate upon here, however. Each represents a reaction to the first two elements of the orthodox consensus to which I have referred previously: positivism and functionalism. I wish to develop an approach to social theory in which the concept of 'function' has no place; in my view the notions of 'functional analysis' or 'functional explanation' should also be dispensed with altogether, as resting on false premises.[13] However, the contributions of functionalism (in its various guises) to social theory cannot be merely laid to rest in peace. It would not do heart-

lessly to forsake Merton in favour of Winch. One of the most significant limitations of Winch's 'hermeneutic social theory' is that it
makes no mention of what has always rightly been a primary concern of functionalism: the unanticipated conditions, and unintended consequences, of action. In this respect Winch's account of
the method of the social sciences is inferior to that of Weber, whom
on the whole Winch refers to in an approving way.[14] A hermeneutically informed social theory, such as I wish to propose here, and
have sought to develop in some detail in recent publications, would
recognise the need for connecting an adequate account of (meaningful) 'action' (which, I think, Weber did not manage to do)[15] with
the analysis of its unanticipated conditions and unintended consequences. In place of functionalism I want to offer what I call the
theory of structuration.

As regards the logic of the social sciences, I want to emphasise a
different aspect of the relevance of hermeneutics to social theory.
Modern hermeneutics has come together with phenomenology in
accentuating the importance of everyday beliefs and practices, the
mundane and the 'taken for granted' in the constitution of social
activity. The social sciences, however, or so I wish to argue, involve
a rather special type of hermeneutical phenomenon in the conceptualisation of their subject-matter. A major objective of the positivistic standpoint involved in the orthodox consensus was to replace
ordinary, everyday language with a technical vocabulary of the
social sciences – a technical vocabulary of a parallel kind to those
employed in the various areas of natural science.[16] However the
relation between ordinary language, the forms of life in which its use
is implicated, and the technical languages of the social sciences,
proves to be considerably more complex and significant than was
supposed in the pre-existing orthodoxy. Hermeneutics in fact enters
it in a twofold way here – which is why I refer to my second theme as
that of the *double hermeneutic*. The social scientist studies a world,
the social world, which is constituted as meaningful by those who
produce and reproduce it in their activities – human subjects. To
describe human behaviour in a valid way is in principle to be able to
participate in the forms of life which constitute, and are constituted
by, that behaviour. This is already a hermeneutic task. But social
science is itself a 'form of life', with its own technical concepts.
Hermeneutics hence enters into the social sciences on two, related
levels; this double hermeneutic proves to be of basic importance to

the post-positivist reformulation of social theory.

The theory of structuration

I have outlined the elements of the theory of structuration in some detail elsewhere,[17] and therefore shall offer only a brief outline here. In working out a conception of structuration, I attempt to meet several *desiderata* that have been brought to the fore in current debates in social theory. First, the demand for a 'theory of the subject', as posed primarily by those working within structuralist traditions of thought. The call for a theory of the subject involves a defined break with positivistic standpoints in philosophy, and with the Cartesian *cogito*. 'Consciousness', as a property of human beings, is not to be taken as a given, a phenomenon which is a starting-point for analysis. But while correctly posing the requirement for a theory of the subject, and in turn arguing that this involves a 'de-centring' of the subject, structuralist thought has tended to dissolve subjectivity into abstract structures of language. A de-centring of the subject must at the same time *recover* that subject, as a reasoning, acting being. Otherwise the result is an objectivist type of social theory, in which human agency appears only as the determined outcome of social causes. Here there is a strong similarity between structuralism (including most varieties of so-called 'post-structuralism') and functionalism – neither entirely surprising nor purely fortuitous, for each has its origins in some part in Durkheim.[18]

Second, the demand that a theory of the subject which avoids objectivism should not slide into subjectivism. A relapse into subjectivism was precisely one of the main tendencies in early reactions to the dissolution of the orthodox consensus. Subjectivist conceptions on the whole have not offered an *explication* of the origins of subjectivity, even while stressing the creative components of human behaviour. In the theory of structuration, I argue that neither subject (human agent) nor object ('society', or social institutions) should be regarded as having primacy. *Each is constituted in and through recurrent practices*. The notion of human 'action' presupposes that of 'institution', and vice versa. Explication of this relation thus comprises the core of an account of how it is that the structuration (production and reproduction across time and space) of social practices takes place.

The notion of action has been much debated by philosophers, and has given rise to considerable controversy. I take the concept to refer to two components of human conduct, which I shall call 'capability' and 'knowledgeability'. By the first of these I mean that, whenever we speak of human action, we imply the possibility that the agent 'could have acted otherwise'. The sense of this well-worn phrase is not easy to elucidate philosophically, and it would hardly be possible to seek to elaborate upon it here; but its importance to social analysis is very pronounced, since it connects in an immediate way to the significance of *power* in social theory.[19] By the second term, 'knowledgeability', I mean all those things which the members of the society know about that society, and the conditions of their activity within it. It is a basic mistake to equate the knowledgeability of agents with what is known 'consciously', where this means what can be 'held in mind' in a conscious way. An explication of subjectivity must relate 'consciousness' in this sense (discursive consciousness) to what I call 'practical consciousness' and to the unconscious. Lack of a conception of practical consciousness, I think, is again common to functionalist and structuralist traditions of thought alike. By practical consciousness I mean the vast variety of tacit modes of knowing how to 'go on' in the contexts of social life. Like 'knowledgeability', 'capability' must not be identified with the ability of agents to make 'decisions' – as is posited in game theory, for example. If it refers to circumstances in which individuals consciously confront a range of potential alternatives of conduct, making some choice among those alternatives, 'decision-making' is no more than a sub-category of capability in general. Capability, the possibility of 'doing otherwise', is generally exercised as a routine, tacit feature of everyday behaviour.

By institutions, I mean structured social practices that have a broad spatial and temporal extension: that are structured in what the historian Braudel calls the *longue durée* of time, and which are followed or acknowledged by the majority of the members of a society. In the theory of structuration, 'structure' refers to rules and resources instantiated in social systems, but having only a 'virtual existence'. The structured properties of society, the study of which is basic to explaining the long-term development of institutions, 'exist' only in their instantiation in the structuration of social systems, and in the memory-traces (reinforced or altered in the continuity of daily social life) that constitute the knowledgeability of social actors. But institutionalised practices 'happen', and are 'made to happen' through the application of resources in the continuity of daily life. Resources are structured properties of social systems, but 'exist' only in the capability of actors, in their capacity to 'act otherwise'. This brings me to an essential element of the theory of structuration, the thesis that the organisation of social practices is fundamentally *recursive*. Structure is both the medium and the outcome of the practices it recursively organises.

Thus formulated, the theory of structuration seems to me to depart very considerably both from the sort of viewpoint developed by Winch, in respect of human action, and from the objectivism of functionalist theories. The latter fail to treat human beings as capable knowledgeable agents. Winch makes these factors central to his version of social science (although not in a wholly satisfactory way), but institutions only tend to appear in his analysis – like that of Wittgenstein, his mentor – as a shadowy backdrop against which action is to be interpreted. However, we cannot leave matters here, for the discussion so far does not make it clear where the unacknowledged conditions, and unintended consequences, of action figure in this scheme. Among the unacknowledged conditions of action, there should be included unconscious sources of conduct. Unconscious sources of cognition and motivation form one 'boundary' to the knowledgeability/capability of agents. But the 'bounded' character of knowledgeably reproduced practices also necessarily implicates social analysis in a continuing concern with the prime focus of functionalist approaches: social reproduction via feedback relations of unintended consequences. Here the unintended consequences of action are simultaneously unacknowledged conditions of system reproduction.

It is certainly necessary to insist upon the importance of such feedback relations in social theory. But the concept of 'function' is a hindrance rather than a help in conceptualising them. The notion of 'function' only has plausibility as part of the vocabulary of the social sciences if we attribute 'needs' to social systems (or 'prerequisites', 'exigencies' or other synonyms). However, social systems have no needs, and to suppose that they do is to apply an illegitimate teleology to them. In the theory of structuration, 'social reproduction' is not regarded as an explanatory term: it always has itself to be explicated in terms of the bounded and contingently applied knowledgeability of social actors.

One consequence of the preceding arguments is that the personal, transient encounters of daily life cannot be conceptually separated from the long-term development of institutions. The most casual exchange of words involves the speakers in the long-term history of the language via which their words are formed, and simultaneously in the continuing reproduction of that language. There is more than an accidental similarity between Braudel's *longue durée* of historical time and the *durée* of daily social life to which Schutz, following Bergson, draws our attention.

The double hermeneutic

As I have mentioned previously, some of the leading hermeneutic philosophers of today are critical of the contrast between *verstehen* and *erklären* drawn by earlier writers in the hermeneutic tradition. One reason for this is that which Gadamer in particular concentrates upon: the tendency of Dilthey and others to represent *verstehen* as a 'psychological' phenomenon.[21] In other words, *verstehen* was taken to involve 'reliving', or 're-experiencing' the mental states of those whose activities or creations were to be interpreted. In place of the 'psychological' version of *verstehen*, Gadamer locates the concept squarely in language, language being the medium in which 'understanding' is fundamental to human life. Here there is a major point of connection between Continental hermeneutics and the philosophy of the later Wittgenstein. In so far as Winch follows Wittgenstein, he cannot be regarded as advocating a 'psychological' version of *verstehen*. None the less, he does produce a latter-day rendition of the differentiation between *verstehen* and *erklären* – as a result, not of his conception of the understanding of action itself, but of his view of natural science. In his own day, Dilthey was strongly influenced by positivistic notions of science, and derived his view of the logic of the natural sciences substantially from John Stuart Mill. Winch's conception of natural science, which really only appears in his book as a foil to his discussion of the social sciences, seems to be derived directly from positivist philosophy – including that of Mill, to whom he devotes some attention. He questions Mill's view that 'all explanations . . . have fundamentally the same logical structure' in both the social and the natural sciences.[22] But he does not place in dispute Mill's account of natural science.

   Current issues in social theory, however, cannot be divorced from the rapid changes which have affected the philosophy of natural science. The orthodox consensus, as I have pointed out, not only involved the supposition that the social sciences should be modelled after the natural sciences, but accepted what itself has been called the 'orthodox model'[23] of natural science – that is, the liberalised version of logical positivism worked out by Carnap and others. The orthodox model of natural science is now itself no more. The writings of Popper, Kuhn, Toulmin, Hesse, Feyerabend and many others have successfully broken away from the ideas which dominated positivistic models of science. The 'newer philosophy of science' seems far from resolving the issues which its leading figures have brought to the fore. But it is clear that these developments cannot be ignored in social theory, even if we no longer sustain the view that our objective should be to construct a 'natural science of society'. In the social sciences today we have to attempt, as it were, to rotate two axes simultaneously. In rethinking the character of human action, institutions, and their relations, we have at the same time to bear in mind the transmutations in the philosophy of science.

Positivistic conceptions of science emphasised the anchoring of theories in observation statements, verification and prediction as the elemental logical components of scientific activity. The writings of Kuhn and other contemporary philosophers such as those mentioned above are still, of course, in some degree concerned with these matters. But they have made it plain that science is as much about 'interpreting' the world as about 'explaining' it; and that these two forms of endeavour are not readily separable from one another. The relation between the 'paradigms' (a word which has been so abused that it surely should now be discarded), or the frames of meaning, in terms of which scientific theories are couched, involve translation problems close to those which have long been a primary concern of hermeneutics. The problems raised here are of direct concern to theories developed in the social sciences. But there are some issues that are specific to the social sciences: one is the question of the double hermeneutic. The hermeneutics of natural science has to do only with the theories and discourse of scientists, analysing an object world which does not answer back, and which does not construct and interpret the meanings of its activities.

The double hermeneutic of the social sciences involves what Winch calls a 'logical tie' between the ordinary language of lay actors and the technical terminologies invented by social scientists. Schutz refers to much the same issue, borrowing a term from Weber, when he says that the concepts of the social observer must be 'adequate' to those employed by actors whose activity is to be described or analysed. Neither author, however, gives an especially convincing explication of the relation to which they thus point. Winch's version, I think, is more accurate than that of Schutz, although its implications remain undeveloped. According to Schutz's view, technical terms in the social sciences are 'adequate' only if the mode of activity analysed in a 'typical construct' is 'understandable for the actor himself' in terms of that actor's own concepts.[24] But this is not a defensible standpoint. Consider the example Winch takes in his discussion: the use of the concept of 'liquidity preference' in economics. Why should we suppose that the 'adequacy' of such a notion is governed by whether or not a street-trader understands, or can be led to understand, what it means? How well would that individual have to grasp the concept for it to be declared an 'adequate' part of the vocabulary of economics? Schutz has actually got things the wrong way round. The 'logical tie' implicated in the double hermeneutic does not depend upon whether the actor or actors whose conduct is being described are able to grasp the notions which the social scientist uses. It depends upon the social scientific observer accurately understanding the concepts whereby the actors' conduct is orientated. Winch is right to say of 'liquidity preference' that 'its use by the economist presupposes his understanding of what it is to conduct a business, which in turn presupposes his understanding of such business concepts as money, cost, risk, etc'.[25]

The implications of the double hermeneutic, however, stretch much further, and are considerably more complex, than such a statement suggests. The technical language, and theoretical propositions, of the natural sciences are insulated from the world with which they are concerned because that world does not answer back. But social theory cannot be insulated from its 'object-world', which is a subject-world. Those influenced by the orthodox consensus, of course, were aware of this. But being under the sway of the idea that prediction, on the basis of laws, is the main task of the social sciences, they sought to duplicate such an insulation as far as possible. The double hermeneutic was understood only in relation to prediction, in the shape of 'self-fulfilling' or 'self-denying prophecies'. The tie between ordinary language, daily social life, and social theory was specifically regarded as a nuisance, something which gets in the way of testing the predictions whereby generalisations are validated.

Winch's discussion indicates the logical limitations of such a standpoint; but he fails to demonstrate its poverty as a way of expressing the relations between the social sciences and the lives of the human beings whose behaviour is analysed. The double hermeneutic entails that these relations, as Gadamer insists, are dialogical. The fact that the 'findings' of the social sciences can be taken up by those to whose behaviour they refer is not a phenomenon that can, or should, be marginalised, but is integral to their very nature. It is the hinge connecting two possible modes in which the social sciences connect to their involvement in society itself: as contributing to forms of exploitative domination, or as promoting emancipation.

Conclusion

Many problems are raised by the developments I have described in the foregoing sections. I shall conclude by indicating what some of these are.

First. There are still quite basic issues to be resolved in the post-positivistic philosophy of natural science. Substantial objections have been raised against the views of each of the major authors whose work has helped undermine the orthodox model. The attempt of Popper, for example, to draw a distinct line of demarcation between science and non-science, or 'pseudo-science', on the basis of his doctrine of falsificationism, has turned out to be untenable. In *The Structure of Scientific Revolutions*, and subsequent publications, Kuhn raised – but has not been able satisfactorily to cope with – fundamental issues concerning relativism and truth in science. A modified realist theory of science, such as proposed in variant forms by Hesse and Bhaskar, may have most to offer here.[26] The implications for the social sciences have yet to be fully explored, but seem compatible with a viewpoint that draws from hermeneutics without succumbing to the historicism of Gadamer. Bhaskar's 'transformative model' of social activity in particular arrives independently at a conception of the social sciences having a great deal in common with my account of structuration.

Second. We have to reformulate pre-existing conceptions of the significance of causal laws in the social sciences. The logical status of causal laws in the natural sciences is by no means an uncontested matter. However, neither the positivistic view that laws in natural and social science are logically identical, nor the hermeneutic notion that causal laws have no place in the social sciences at all, are acceptable. I have argued elsewhere[27] that there is a basic logical difference between laws in social and natural science. Laws in the social sciences are intrinsically 'historical' in character: they hold only given specific conditions of 'boundedness' of knowledgeably reproduced systems of social interaction. The causal relations involved in laws refer to conjunctions of intended and unintended consequences of reproduced action; these conjunctions can be altered by the dialogical application of social analysis itself. The type case here is Marx's analysis of the 'laws of the market' in competitive capitalism. The 'laws of the market' hold only given a lack of overall understanding and control of economic life by producers, in the context of the 'anarchic' conditions of capitalist production. The connections they express are mutable in the light of action taken on the basis of knowledge of those connections. This having been said, we have to avoid the error self-confessedly made by Habermas in *Knowledge and Human Interests:* knowledge acquired in the process of 'self-reflection' is not a sufficient condition of social transformation.[28] Knowledgeability plus capability – each is implicated in the continuity or change of social systems.

Third. If the traditional differentiation of *verstehen* and *erklären* must be abandoned, we have to recognise the distinctive features of social life singled out by hermeneutic philosophies. I have accepted that it is right to say that the condition of generating descriptions of social activity is being able in principle to participate in it. It involves 'mutual knowledge', shared by observer and participants whose action constitutes and reconstitutes the social world. Again, however, there are a variety of questions at issue here: how we are to decide what counts as a 'valid' description of an act or form of action, for example; or how the beliefs involved in alien cultures may be subjected to critique. In respect of the conceptualisation of action, nevertheless, one thing is clear: deterministic views of human agency, which explain human action as the result of social causes, are to be rejected. It should be evident, in the light of my earlier remarks, that this does not imply that causal laws have no place in the social sciences.

Fourth. Social theory is inevitably critical theory. I do not mean by this to defend either a version of Marxism in general, or the specific accounts of critical theory associated with Frankfurt social thought in particular. I do want to insist that those working in the social sciences cannot remain aloof from or indifferent to the implications of their theories and research for their fellow members of society. To regard social agents as 'knowledgeable' and 'capable' is not just a matter of the analysis of action; it is also an implicitly political stance. The practical consequences of natural science are 'technological'; they have to do with the application of humanly attained knowledge to a world of objects which exists independently of that knowledge. Human beings, however, are not merely inert objects of knowledge, but agents able to – and prone to – incorporate social theory and research within their own action.

References

1. For further discussion, see *Central Problems in Social Theory* (London: Macmillan, 1979) ch. 7.
2. See M. Truzzi, *Verstehen: Subjective Understanding in the Social Sciences* (Reading, Mass.: Addison-Wesley, 1974).
3. Cf. Carl G. Hempel, 'The logic of functional analysis', in *Aspects of Scientific Explanation* (New York: Free Press, 1965).
4. See 'Classical social theory and the origins of modern sociology', in this volume.
5. Cf. my retrospective analysis in 'Functionalism: après la lutte', in *Studies in Social and Political Theory* (London: Hutchinson, 1977).
6. See *A Contemporary Critique of Historical Materialism* (London: Macmillan, 1981).
7. Peter Winch, *The Idea of a Social Science* (London: Routledge, 1958).
8. See, however, *New Rules of Sociological Method* (London: Hutchinson, 1976) ch. 1.
9. CF. K.-O. Apel, *Analytical Philosophy of Language and the Geisteswissenschaften* (New York: Reidel, 1967).
10. Kuhn has accepted this. See T. S. Kuhn, *The Essential Tension* (Chicago: University of Chicago Press, 1977).
11. Clifford Geertz, 'Blurred genres: the refiguration of social thought', *American Scholar*, vol. 49, 1980.
12. *Central Problems in Social Theory.*
13. 'Functionalism: après la lutte'.
14. Winch, *The Idea of a Social Science*, pp. 111ff.
15. *Studies in Social and Political Theory*, pp. 179ff.

16. For one of the clearest statements of this position, see C. W. Lachen-meyer, *The Language of Sociology* (New York: Columbia University Press, 1971).

17. *Central Problems in Social Theory*.

18. Ibid, ch. 1.

19. Cf. 'Action, structure, power', in this volume.

20. 'Functionalism: après la lutte'.

21. Hans-Georg Gadamer, *Truth and Method* (London: Sheed & Ward, 1975).

22. Winch, *The Idea of a Social Science*, p. 71.

23. Cf. Herbert Feigl, 'The origin and spirit of logical positivism', in Peter Achinstein and Stephen F. Barker (eds), *The Legacy of Logical Positivism* (Baltimore: Johns Hopkins University Press, 1969).

24. Alfred Schutz, 'Common-sense and scientific interpretation of human action', in *Collected Papers*, vol. I (The Hague: Mouton, 1967) p. 37.

25. Winch, *The Idea of a Social Science*, p. 89.

26. Mary Hesse, *The Structure of Scientific Inference* (London: Macmillan, 1974); Roy Bhaskar, *A Realist Theory of Science* (Leeds: Leeds Books, 1975).

27. *Central Problems in Social Theory*, ch. 7.

28. See Habermas's 'auto-critique' in Jürgen Habermas, 'Introduction: some difficulties in the attempt to link theory and practice', in *Theory and Practice* (London: Heinemann, 1974).

2

The Theory of Structuration: a Critique

FRED R. DALLMAYR

My task as critical discussant is complicated by the circumstance that I am strongly impressed by Giddens's general approach. Being sympathetic to many of his arguments, I cannot generate drama by launching a broad-scale offensive against his views. To be sure, there are disagreements between us (as I shall try to indicate); but these disagreements have the character more of a domestic skirmish than of a battle between opposed camps.

First, a few words of praise. On the whole, I find persuasive Giddens's portrayal of what he calls the 'orthodox consensus' in the social sciences and also his account of its demise. As he shows, the orthodox consensus was held together by logical, methodological, and substantive commitments: with positivism supplying the logic of inquiry, functionalism the methodological apparatus, and the notion of 'industrial society' the vision of human and social development. The demise or disintegration of the orthodox consensus calls into question all three of these components and thus can be traced to intellectual as well as social-economic crises and counter-trends. Although, in his paper, Giddens concentrates mainly on intellectual or theoretical aspects, he surely cannot be said to ignore the broader social-economic transformations occurring in our world today. 'In my thinking,' he writes, 'logical, methodological and substantive problems are closely bound up with one another.' This kind of balanced outlook strikes me as eminently plausible and commendable (although, on other occasions, the relation between the components may have to be spelled out in greater detail).

Equally praiseworthy, in its general outline, is the proposal for a reorientation of 'social theory' – as this term is used in the paper. In my view, Giddens is one of the handful of social theorists today who are attentive not only to the 'post-positivist' but also the 'post-metaphysical' condition of contemporary thought – that is, to the progressive, though frequently subterranean, erosion of traditional 'metaphysics' seen as a 'spectorial theory of knowledge' rooted in human subjectivity or in an inner 'glassy essence' of man (to use Richard Rorty's vocabulary). In his recent writings – particularly in *Central Problems in Social Theory* – Giddens has taken to heart the problems surrounding modern 'humanism' and the attacks leveled at subject-centred philosophical premises by Heidegger and contemporary 'post-structuralist' writers (such as Foucault, Derrida and Lacan). At the same time, however, he realises that social theory must in some fashion deal with the role of human beings (viewed singly or in groups) as actors, and thus with the issues surrounding human agency and 'social action'. Agency, in turn, is broadly related to such notions as purpose, intentionality, and human responsibility (what traditionally has been termed 'freedom'). As a result, Giddens has seen himself faced with a momentous challenge: the challenge of incorporating the lessons of ontology and post-structuralism *without* abandoning concern with the 'knowledgeability' and accountability of actors; more ambitiously phrased: the task of moving beyond subjectivist metaphysics *without* relinquishing some of its insights, and especially *without* lapsing into objectivism and determinism.

As outlined in the paper and other writings, Giddens's response to this challenge takes the form of a 'hermeneutically informed social theory' – a theory which is neither purely hermeneutical in the sense of the traditional *Geisteswissenschaften* nor a refurbished brand of positivism dressed in interpretative garb. In his words, such a theory pays 'attention to the revitalisation of hermeneutics in the hands of the post-Wittgensteinian philosophers, Gadamer, Ricoeur, and others', while at the same time treating hermeneutical views 'critically' and with caution. Designed as a reply to the orthodox consensus, the proposed perspective provides antidotes to the two main ingredients of that consensus – functionalism and positivism – without cancelling their valid contributions (without, for example, 'heartlessly' forsaking 'Merton in favour of Winch'). On the level of methodology, functionalism is replaced by what Giddens calls the 'theory of structuration' whose chief aim is to link 'an adequate account of (meaningful) action with the analysis of its unanticipated conditions and unintended consequences'. In the domain of the logic of inquiry, positivism is corrected and overcome through the notion of a 'double hermeneutic' – an approach which recognises that social science is basically an interpretative enterprise dealing with social 'forms of life' which, in turn, are webs of meaningful, pre-interpreted activities and relationships.

In the following I would like to take a somewhat closer look at Giddens's 'hermeneutically informed social theory' and at its two main components: the 'theory of structuration' and the 'double hermeneutic. As the paper points out, the first component owes its inspiration to a number of demands or *desiderata* prominent in contemporary social theory: particularly the demands for a 'theory of the subject' and for a methodological strategy bypassing both objectivism and subjectivism. Taking its cues from structuralist and post-structuralist arguments, the 'theory of the subject' involves a break with the Cartesian *cogito* and with the modern focus on consciousness and subjectivity – but a break which simultaneously seeks to recover the human subject as a 'reasoning, acting being'. The methodological strategy connected with this outlook insists that 'neither subject (human agent) nor object (society or social institutions) should be regarded as having primacy', since 'each is constituted in and through recurrent practices'. Concerning agency and social action, the paper concentrates chiefly on the two aspects of 'capability' (option to act otherwise) and 'knowledgeability' – with the latter term comprising both 'discursive' and 'practical consciousness' and being differentiated from the Freudian domain of the unconscious. Elsewhere – in *Central Problems in Social Theory* – Giddens speaks of a 'stratification model' of human agency, a model connecting intentionality (or the 'reflexive monitoring of conduct') with unconscious motivational factors which in turn are tied to the 'unacknowledged conditions' and 'unintended consequences' of action. 'A "stratified" model of personality' he notes there, 'in which human wants are regarded as hierarchically connected, involving a basic security system largely inaccessible to the conscious subject, is not at all incompatible with an equivalent stress upon the significance of the reflexive monitoring of action, the latter becoming possible only following the "positioning" of the actor in the Lacanian sense' (p. 123).

In addition to human agency, structuration involves the role of social 'institutions' defined as 'structured social practices that have a broad spatial and temporal extension' – that is, as practices which, apart from operating concretely in time and space, also exhibit a paradigmatic 'structure'. In the paper, the term 'structure' is explicated as referring to 'rules and resources instantiated in social systems, but having only a "virtual existence"'. Helpful pointers regarding the meaning of these formulations can be gleaned from *Central Problems in Social Theory* (pp. 2–3). There, Giddens differentiates more clearly between 'system' and 'structure', portraying social systems as practices concretely 'situated in time–space', while depicting structure as 'non-temporal and non-spatial', as 'a *virtual order of differences* produced and reproduced in social interaction as its medium and outcome'. As features of concrete social systems, social institutions are basically practices through which the 'structured properties of society' – rules and resources – are instantiated and applied in the spatial-temporal setting of daily life. Against this background, 'structuration' signifies the continuous instantiation of the virtual existence of structure – a view which undergirds the paper's thesis that 'the organisation of social practices is fundamentally *recursive*', in the sense that 'structure is both the medium and the outcome of the practices it recursively organises'.

As it seems to me, the chief aim as well as the chief merit of the 'theory of structuration' lie clearly in the reinterpretation and novel correlation of agency and structure. The structural perspective championed by Giddens has distinct advantages over competing functionalist and systemic frameworks, while salvaging their main analytical assets. The accentuation of rules and resources as structural properties strikes me as potentially fruitful and as an advance over the well-worn 'sub-systems' familiar from functionalist analysis. Despite these and other accomplishments, however, I find Giddens's conception of structure and structuration somewhat vacillating and ambivalent; differently phrased: his approach seems reluctant at points to draw the full implications from the adopted perspective. As he has conceded in other contexts, his theory of structuration is indebted at least in part to Jacques Derrida's notion of the 'structuring of structure'; his portrayal of structure as a 'virtual existence', a 'virtual order' or an 'absent set of differences' is likewise reminiscent of Derrida's construal of '*différence*'. As employed by Derrida, however, the latter concept involves not only a factual differentiation of elements but also a more basic ontological (or ontic–ontological) difference; as a corollary, structuration in its radical sense injects into social analysis a profoundly non-positive or, if one prefers, 'transcendental' dimension. Against this background, Giddens's treatment appears at times half-hearted. In some passages, the notion of a 'virtual order' seems to imply no more than the contingent and essentially remediable constellation of 'present' and 'absent' factors – or at least a constellation in which absent factors can always readily be 'instantiated' or applied. Seen in this light, 'structure' tends to merge imperceptibly with 'system': the virtual order of structural properties shades over into Merton's distinction between 'manifest' and 'latent' functions.

Instantiation construed as the translation of latent into manifest properties is particularly evident in the case of 'resources' through whose application institutionalised practices are said to 'happen' or be 'made to happen' in the continuity of everyday life. In the case of 'rules' the translation process seems less evident or intelligible. The theoretical difficulties surrounding Wittgenstein's notion of 'rule-governed' behaviour are notorious (some of them have been elucidated by Wittgenstein himself). Giddens's portrayal of rules is not exempt from these difficulties. Viewed as ingredients of a virtual order, it is not entirely clear how rules can be 'both the medium and the outcome' of recursive social practices; at least further argument seems required to pinpoint the status of rules in the process of structuration.

Ambiguities also surround the notion of 'agency' and its relation to structuration – despite many attractive features of Giddens's perspective as articulated in his paper and elsewhere. In a formulation which (I think) can serve as a yardstick for future inquiries in this area, Giddens noted in *Central Problems* (p. 92) that the concept 'cannot be defined through that of intention, as is presumed in so much of the literature to do with the philosophy of action; the notion of agency, as I employ it, I take to be logically prior to a subject–object differentiation'. Depicted in this manner, 'agency' undercuts or transcends the customary bifurcation between subjectively intended activity and externally stimulated reactive behaviour – a bifurcation which in large measure permeates Weberian and post-Weberian sociology. Given this overall theoretical thrust, one is surprised to find in Giddens's treatment again an occasional half-heartedness or vacillation – manifest in his tendency of tying agency closely to everyday conduct understood as 'activity' or 'doing'. His paper presents the notion of action as referring mainly to 'two components of human conduct', namely capability and knowledgeability. As mentioned, capability is defined as the actor's possibility of acting or 'doing otherwise'. Practical consciousness, construed as one form of knowledgeability, is said in the paper to denote 'the vast variety of tacit modes of knowing how to "go on" in the contexts of social life'; in *Central Problems* (p. 57), the same concept is circumscribed as 'tacit knowledge that is skilfully applied in the enactment of courses of conduct'. In a similar vein, social institutions are described as structured social practices, that is, as modes of social interaction in which structural properties are implemented in a temporal or spatial setting.

What is obscured in this presentation is the claimed status of agency beyond the poles of intentional activity and reactive behaviour; more sharply put: what tends to be ignored is the peculiar nexus of action and non-action within agency itself. If the latter notion is really 'logically prior to a subject–object differentiation' and (as stated in *Central Problems*, p. 39) even adumbrates the 'connection of *being and action*', then social theory has to make room for a certain 'openness to being' and remain attentive not only to 'doing' but also to human 'suffering' understood as an experience actors undergo (and not merely in the sense of reactive behaviour). Against this background, one cannot completely assent to the assertion, put forth in *Central Problems* (p. 44), that social theory today needs 'a grasp of "what cannot be said" (or thought) as *practice*'. The mentioned difficulty or ambiguity, it seems to me, cannot entirely be resolved through reference to the 'unacknowledged conditions' and 'unconscious sources' of action: as long as such conditions or sources are depicted simply as 'boundaries' to the 'knowledgeability/capability of agents', reliance on functionalist types of explanation does not seem far-fetched or illegitimate.

So far I have pointed to some ambiguities or quandaries besetting Giddens's notions of structure and agency and their correlation in his theory of structuration. I would like to turn now to another feature of his perspective which is probably no less problematical: his conception of the 'double hermeneutic' and its relationship to structuration. As presented in the paper, hermeneutics serves mainly as a substitute for positivism on the level of epistemology or the logic of inquiry; seen in this light, its relevance is not restricted to the humanities and social sciences but extends to the philosophy and epistemology of natural science. In Giddens's words, 'the orthodox model of natural science is now itself no more'; in the wake of the writings of Kuhn, Toulmin and others, it is 'plain that science is as much about "interpreting" the world as about "explaining" it, and that the two forms of endeavour are not readily separable from one another'. What is distinctive about the humanities and social sciences is that hermeneutics operates, so to speak, on two levels: 'The hermeneutics of natural science are to do only with the theories and discourse of scientists, analysing an object world which does not answer back'; by contrast, 'the double hermeneutic of the social sciences involves what Winch calls a "logical tie" between the ordinary language of lay actors and the technical terminologies invented by social scientists'. In the latter case, hermeneutics thus signifies the interpretation of pre-interpretations – an aspect lacking in the study of nature: 'The technical language and theoretical propositions of the natural sciences are insulated from the world they are concerned with because that world does not answer back; but social theory cannot be insulated from its "object-world", which is a subject-world.'

The implication of these comments is that natural and social sciences are unified through their logic of inquiry, and differentiated only in terms of their diverse 'object-worlds' or targets of investigation. To be sure, unity is no longer predicated on the model of a 'unified science' extolled by logical positivism, but rather on the common adherence to hermeneutics seen as a framework of interpretation and intersubjective discourse. In stressing the linkage between natural and social sciences, Giddens seems to endorse, albeit hesitantly, the notion of a 'universal hermeneutics' as articulated by Hans-Georg Gadamer – and perhaps even the thesis of the 'unsurpassibility of hermeneutics' put forth at one point by Paul Ricoeur. Discussion about the relation between modes of inquiry, one might add, is not restricted to Continental thinkers. Something akin to the concept of 'unsurpassibility' seems to be involved in Richard Rorty's emphasis on 'conversation' as the common bond among disciplines – where 'conversation' is basically identified with hermeneutics. One difficulty conjured up by this accent on a common logic of inquiry is how it can be squared with Giddens's critical reservations regarding hermeneutics and his broader ambition to overcome the *verstehen–erklären* dichotomy. 'I do want to claim,' his paper asserts in one passage, 'that, in social theory, a turn to hermeneutics cannot in and of itself resolve the logical and methodological problems left by the disappearance of the orthodox consensus.' In focusing on the interpretative dimension of all disciplines, Giddens seems bent not so much on transcending the *verstehen–erklären* conflict as on resolving it in favour of understanding, particularly reciprocal understanding. Thus, assessing the relations between the social sciences and the concrete human agents under investigation he states: 'The double hermeneutic entails that these relations, as Gadamer insists, are dialogical.'

Another difficulty arising in the same context concerns the connection between logic of inquiry and methodology, that is, between hermeneutics and the theory of structuration. Given the claim that human agency – as a major ingredient of structuration – is somehow 'logically prior to a subject–object differentiation', it is not clear how, under the heading of the double hermeneutic, the object-world or target area of social science can simply be described as a 'subject-world'. More broadly phrased, it is far from self-evident how hermeneutical exegesis can penetrate to the 'virtual existence' or 'virtual order' of structural properties. The problems surrounding the relation between logic of inquiry and methodology affect also the status of history in Giddens's outlook and its relevance for social science. In his paper he affirms that 'laws in the social sciences are intrinsically "historical" in character'. The same point is stated more boldly in *Central Problems* where we read that 'there simply are no logical or even methodological distinctions between the social sciences and history – appropriately conceived' (p. 230). Whatever the import of the last qualifying phrase may be, the linkage between social science and history inevitably brings to the fore the age-old antimony between nature and history – and thus, in a new disguise, the contrast between natural science and hermeneutics.

The difficulties besetting the relation between hermeneutics and structuration are not unique to the reviewed paper. Actually, Giddens deserves praise for wrestling with the relevant issues in an imaginative manner and thus for bringing them into sharper focus. Readers of 'post-structuralist' literature cannot fail to be sensitised to the same issues. In light of the Nietzschean maxim that 'everything is interpretation' – a maxim endorsed by most post-structuralists – the question inevitably arises how interpretation can grant access to epistemic structures and, more generally, yield a 'theory of the subject' bypassing the *cogito* and traditional subjectivity.

*   *   *

Response to Dallmayr

Professor Dallmayr describes my views so accurately and sym-
pathetically that I feel uncharitable in disagreeing with some of the
criticisms he makes. I do not think my discussion of action and structure is quite as opaque as he implies, although he raises some points
of considerable interest and importance.

I argue that 'structure' participates not just in 'doing' – which is
the core of 'Being' – but in the constitution of subjectivity that
articulates Being as 'human being'. Like Dallmayr, I take this to be
one of the main contributions of structuralist and post-structuralist
thought. Structure is neither relegated to describing the consequences of activity, nor to a phenomenon which the individual
somehow confronts as a constituted self. But in my opinion it is not
'structure' as such, but the idea of the duality of structure which has
priority in examining both the nature of subjectivity and the constitution of action. I do not consider that I am 'half-hearted' in pursuing the implications of this, although I do disagree with Derrida's
version of the de-construction of metaphysics.

In distinguishing 'structure' and 'system' in social theory, I mean
to get at the intersection of two types of part – whole relationships.
One type, which I connect to the notion of system, refers to the 'patterning' of the relations between individuals or collectivities. This
has always played a leading role in functionalist theories. I differ
from most such theories in emphasising that such patterning implies
reproduction across time and space. But the patterning of social
relations can only be grasped, as reproduced events across time–
space, via a second conception of part–whole relationships. This is
the recursive connection between 'presencing', constituted of
human activities, and structural properties of social systems which
are the medium and outcome of such activities.

Let me refer briefly to two other points. Dallmayr mentions that I
do not give enough attention to the openness of being, and more
particularly to the Heideggerian theme of suffering and care. I think
in fact that I do acknowledge the openness of being, in my account
of temporality and human existence. I also believe that there is a
direct connection between what I have to say about structuration
and the moral frameworks of human existence. I accept that I have
not so far anywhere elucidated this connection in the detail it
demands. But although I am strongly influenced by certain aspects

of Heidegger's philosophy, I am not at all satisfied with his interpretation of human caring.

Regarding the social sciences and history, I do not really see why my standpoint reverts to a version of *verstehen* versus *erklären*, although it certainly echoes Vico in accentuating the reflexive character of human involvement in history. In saying that the social sciences and history are the same 'appropriately conceived', I mean conceived of in the context of the theory of structuration.

*   *   *

Rejoinder to Giddens

I think it is rather careless of Giddens to say that he does not care about Heidegger's caring! However, I am more concerned here with his formulation of 'structure'. How are actors constituted, in his view? Apparently by some sort of forces outside them – in other words, by some kind of structure. He has told us repeatedly that he wants to move beyond the so-called subject–object dichotomy, beyond a spectatorial view of knowledge. But I find that precisely at this point he reverts again to the subject–object dualism of actors constituting and being constituted. Similarly, when he links social science with history, I remain unpersuaded that he does not lapse into historicism.

3

Action, Structure, Power

Approaches to the theory of action

I think it rather obvious that an important dualism runs through the literature of both philosophy and sociology in respect of problems of human action. There exists, of course, a great deal of philosophical literature devoted to the explication or analysis of action, much of it influenced by the writings of the later Wittgenstein. The action philosophers have given a great deal of attention to the concept of action itself, and to intentions, reasons and motives. But they have paid very little heed to the *unintended consequences* of action, in the manner in which such consequences are of concern to social theory. Thus, in a well-known discussion, Donald Davidson analyses the following issue: I move a switch, turn on the light, illuminate the room, and at the same time alert a prowler. Davidson's concern, as in the case of other philosophers who have discussed this and many other similar examples, is confined to questions of action-description: do I do four things, or only one thing that can be described in four different ways? Without wishing to deny the interest and significance of problems of action-description, it can be pointed out that Davidson's discussion is characteristic of the vast majority of philosophical analyses of action, which limit their concerns to what might be called 'the production of action' on the part of actors. They have not been interested either in the consequences of acts that escape actors' intentions or purposes, or in what I shall call the *unacknowledged conditions* of action. Partly for these reasons, issues which have always rightly brooked large in the work of social analysts – problems of the nature of institutions, of social change, conflict and power – barely appear at all in the writings of the philosophers of action.

Much the same is found with those schools of thought within the social sciences which have given prominence to human action in some sense akin to that employed by most of the action philosophers. A good case in point is symbolic interactionism, as drawn upon, for example, by Erving Goffman. Goffman – in contrast to many sociologists – treats human beings as reasoning, intentional agents, aware of and capable within the social environment which they help to constitute through their action. Although it is by now a banal observation, it still seems to me true to say that Goffman's sociology lacks any sustained treatment of the phenomena mentioned above, especially of overall processes of institutional transformation. Symbolic interactionism, in the hands of Blumer, Goffman and others, has not successfully developed modes of institutional analysis.

Strong on action, weak on institutions: this theorem becomes reversed when we look at the other side of the dualism that has tended to prevail in the social sciences and philosophy. Those traditions of thought which have placed the unacknowledged conditions and unintended consequences of action in the forefront, and which have emphasised problems of institutional organisation and change, have by and large failed to develop theories of action at all. They have stressed the primacy of object over subject, of social structure or social system over the purposeful, capable social actor. Such is the case, I would argue, with the majority of writings associated both with structuralism in France, and with the varieties of functionalist thought which have been so influential in the social sciences in the English-speaking world. The latter claim might at first sight appear difficult to defend in light of the fact that perhaps the leading functionalist thinker in sociology in recent times, Talcott Parsons, has expressly couched his ideas in terms of what he calls the 'action frame of reference'. I should want to maintain, however, that Parsons's sociology lacks a concept of action – in the sense in which I want to use the term here, at any rate. A conception of action in the social sciences, I want to argue, has to place at the centre the everyday fact that social actors are knowledgeable about the conditions of social reproduction in which their day-to-day activities are enmeshed. The reasons people have for their actions – or what I prefer to call the 'rationalisation of action', as involved with the chronic reflexive monitoring of conduct that social actors routinely carry on – are crucially involved with how those actions are sustained. In *The*

Structure of Social Action Parsons tried to integrate what he called a 'voluntarist' viewpoint of human conduct with a resolution of the 'problem of order' in society. Although he claimed to have synthesised the ideas of several prominent nineteenth-century thinkers, the basic outline of the conception he ended up with is, in my opinion, a heavily Durkheimian one. Parsons connected 'voluntarism' with a recognition of the 'emergent properties' of collectivities via the notion of the internalisation of values: core social values are simultaneously the source of motivational components of personality and the source of social cohesion. What 'voluntarism' comes down to here is an emphasis upon incorporating an account of motivation within a scheme of analysis of social systems – an emphasis that the psychological study of the personality system must complement, via normative values, the study of social systems. The behaviour of social actors is regarded as the outcome of the conjunction of psychological and social determinants, with priority attributed to the latter because of the pre-eminent role played by normative elements. The actor does not appear here as a capable, knowledgeable agent: Parsons's actors are, in Garfinkel's phrase, 'cultural dopes'.

How, then, are we to conceptualise the knowledgeability of social agents? How are we to incorporate our own knowledgeability of this knowledgeability within a broad treatment of action in social theory? I propose to answer these questions – although only relatively cursorily given the current context of this essay – in terms of Figure 3.1.

In Figure 3.1 I outline what I call a 'stratification model' of action. The implications of this model, I want to claim, however, cannot be fully elaborated without reference to my subsequent discussion of the concept of 'structure' in sociology. By using the

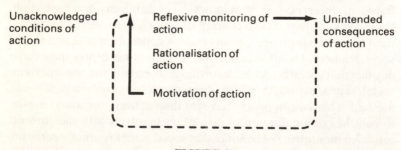

FIGURE 3.1

phrases 'reflexive monitoring of action', and 'rationalisation of action', I want to refer to the intentional or purposive character of human everyday behaviour. But I want to refer to intentional behaviour as *process*, as involved in the *durée* of day-to-day life. Too often philosophers treat 'intentions' and 'reasons' as discrete forms, somehow aggregated together in action. They ignore, or take for granted, what Schutz calls the 'reflexive moment of attention' which breaks into the continuing flow of action. Unlike many action philosophers, who often use 'motive' as casually synonymous with 'reason', I distinguish the two, regarding motivation as referring to the wantings that prompt action, and treating 'motivation' also as a processual term. I do not limit motivation to promptings available to consciousness, but wish to allocate considerable conceptual space to unconscious impulses – again, I think, unlike most action philosophers who have either simply left the unconscious aside or, following Wittgenstein's lead, have been suspicious of the logical status of concepts relating to unconscious processes.

In conceptualising the knowledgeability of social actors, it is not enough merely to distinguish between conscious and unconscious. It is important to differentiate two senses or levels in which agents are knowledgeable about the social environments they constitute in and through their action – between discursive and practical consciousness. The distinctive feature of human action, as compared with the conduct of the animals, I take to concern what Garfinkel labels the 'accountability' of human action. I think the notion of accountability to be a highly important one, meaning by it that the accounts which actors are able to offer of their conduct draw upon the same stocks of knowledge which are drawn upon in the very production and reproduction of their action. The 'giving of accounts' – or 'supplying of reasons' – for action refers to the *discursive* capabilities and inclinations of actors, and by no means exhausts the connections between 'stocks of knowledge' and action. What actors are 'able to say' about their activities is by no means all that they 'know' about them. Practical consciousness refers to tacit knowledge that is skilfully employed in the enactment of courses of conduct, but which the actor is not able to formulate discursively. The knowledgeability involved in practical consciousness conforms generally to the Wittgensteinian notion of 'knowing a rule' or 'knowing how to go on'. To 'know English' is to know an enormously complicated set of rules or principles, and the contexts of their application. To

know English is not to be able to formulate discursively those rules
or principles: linguists have devoted a great deal of labour to formulating what we already 'know'.

The knowledgeability of human agents, in given historical circumstances, is always *bounded*: by the unacknowledged conditions
of action on 'one side', and its unintended consequences on the
other. This is, as I have previously indicated, crucial to social
theory. For if writers who have produced 'objectivist' theories of
social life, especially the functionalists, have been unable to develop
adequate treatments of the knowledgeability of social actors, they
have nevertheless quite correctly stressed the escape of activity
from actors' intentions. History is not an intentional project, and all
intentional activity takes place in the context of institutions sedimented over long-term periods of time. The unintended consequences of action are of essential importance to social theory especially in so far as they are systematically incorporated within processes of the reproduction of institutions. This is why I have drawn
the dashed line linking each side of Figure 3.1: in so far as unintended consequences are systematically involved in social reproduction, they become conditions of action also. In recognising the
importance of this, however, I wish to avoid the teleological conno-
tations of functionalism, which substitutes 'society's reasons' for the
reasons of actors. In the terminology I shall suggest below, societies
have no 'reasons' or 'needs' whatsoever; only the actors whose
activities constantly constitute and reconstitute those societies do
so. Stripping the teleology from functionalism does not entail, I
shall try to show, abandoning the distinctively institutional emphases of functionalism in favour of some kind of 'subjectivism'.

Concepts of structure

In contemporary sociology, the term 'structure' characteristically
appears in each of the traditions of 'objectivist' social thought I have
mentioned earlier – structuralism, which has taken its name from it,
and functionalism (which in its modern versions is often referred to
in a rather cumbersome way as 'structural-functionalism'). Structuralist thought still remains fairly alien to most English-speaking
sociologists and philosophers, I would say, as do the post-structuralist writings of authors such as Foucault, Barthes, Derrida and

others. Although I think that structuralism has to be radically criticised in definite ways, I want to argue in what follows that certain ideas prominent in the structuralist tradition, to do with the notion of structure itself, are of some considerable importance to social theory.

A curious feature of the functionalist literature is the vast amount of ink expended on the concept of 'function', as compared with the virtually complete dearth of discussion of the notion of 'structure', a notion which is nevertheless continually used by functionalist authors. Consequently, the idea of structure typically figures in Anglo-American sociology as a received one, used in an unexamined fashion. Most English-speaking sociologists, when they use the terms 'structure' or 'social structure', have in mind some kind of connotation of structure as 'visible pattern' of social relations, as something akin to the girders of a building or to the anatomy of a body. In this kind of imagery, structure tends to be conceived as equivalent to *constraint* – a notion to which Durkheim perhaps gave the classic formulation, but which constantly crops up in the subsequent writings of sociologists.

The concept of structure which appears in structuralist writings is quite different from this – and, of course, in contrast to the fate of the notion in English-speaking sociology, has been much debated. To identify the difference it is perhaps best to return to the principal origin of structuralist thought, in Saussure's linguistics, although somewhat confusingly Saussure did not employ the term 'structure' but that of 'system', a matter to which I shall return shortly. Saussure's thought turns upon a relation between moment and totality quite distinct from that involved in functionalist writings, a dialectical relation between presence and absence. The relation between a sentence or an utterance and a language is not like that between an organ of the body and the totality which is the organism. When I utter a sentence, or make sense of an utterance of somebody else, I draw upon an 'absent corpus' of syntactic and semantic rules in order to do so. The syntagmatic relations between the words uttered exist in a temporal-spatial context, but the 'structural properties' of the language, as characteristic of a community of language-speakers, do not. These properties have a 'virtual existence' only.

I want to suggest a concept of structure in social theory which has affinities with this. I do not propose to abandon the notion that it is useful to conceive of social relations between individuals and collectivities – in so far as they are stably reproduced over time and space – as forming something like 'patterns'. But I wish to argue that this can most aptly be covered by the notion of 'system', freeing that of 'structure' for other conceptual tasks. I have already mentioned that Saussure used the term 'system' rather than that of 'structure'. In the subsequent structuralist literature, where the term 'system' appears, it is characteristically used as more or less synonymous with structure – or, as in Lévi-Strauss, as one among other defining elements of 'structure'. The concept of system here is largely a redundant one.

But the same is true of functionalist writings. If one looks at the writings of the leading functionalist authors, it is readily apparent that they either tend to opt mainly for one term at the expense of the other, or use the two interchangeably. Now this might initially appear strange, because there may seem at first sight to be a basis for sustaining a structure/system distinction in functionalism. For, employing the organic analogy, which is rarely far from the surface in most forms of functionalism, it might be supposed that the structure of society is like the anatomy of the organism; when the structure is 'working', we have a system. A system here is, as it were, a 'functioning structure': structure + function = system. If this equation is scrutinised more closely, however, it is apparent that the analogy does not hold for society. There is a sense in which the structure of a body can exist independently of its 'functioning'. The anatomy of a body can be studied, its morphology described, even though it has ceased to function, ceased to live. But this is not the case with society, with the 'patterning' of social interaction reproduced across time and space: a society ceases to exist if it ceases to 'function'. This is why even those functionalist authors who recognise some sort of distinction between structure and system tend in practice to collapse the two into one.

I propose to reserve the term 'social system' to refer to reproduced patterns of social relations. There is a great deal that can be said about the notion of system in sociology. I do not think, for example, that we can rest content with the idea of system which usually appears in functionalist thought, which often equates it simply with homeostasis. But I shall not attempt to discuss such issues here, limiting myself to the concept of structure. Figure 3.2 identifies the three basic notions with which I want to work.

STRUCTURE	Recursively organised rules and resources Structure only exists as 'structural properties'
SYSTEM	Reproduced relations between actors or collectivities, organised as regular social practices
STRUCTURATION	Conditions governing the continuity or transformation of structures, and therefore the reproduction of systems

FIGURE 3.2

Social systems, in this scheme, are regarded as relations of inter-dependence, involving the situated activities of human subjects, and existing 'syntagmatically' in the flow of time. According to the view I wish to develop (sketched in only in a relatively cursory way here), social systems are not structures; they have structures or, more accurately, exhibit structural properties. Structures are, in a logical sense, properties of social systems or collectivities, not of the situated activities of subjects. Social systems only exist in and through structuration, as the outcome of the contingent acts of a multiplicity of human beings.

The connotation of 'structure' I am suggesting here is much closer to that employed by Lévi-Strauss than it is to that which figures in functionalist sociologies. Lévi-Strauss's approach is ambiguous in a certain sense, in so far as it is not clear whether he regards structure as relations between a set of inferred elements or oppositions, or as rules of transformation that produce equivalences across sets. It seems that a similar ambiguity crops up in mathemati-cal notions of structure, where structure is usually thought of as a matrix of admissible transformations of a set: 'structure' could be seen either as the matrix, or the principles or rules of transforma-tion. However that may be, I shall treat structures, in social theory, as concerning the rules (and, as I shall elaborate upon later, the resources) which, in social reproduction, 'bind' time and space, rather than to the form of sets as such. Hence 'structure', as under-stood here, is a generic term: 'structures' can be identified as sets or matrices of rule–resource properties governing transformations.

An essential limitation of Lévi-Strauss's use of 'structure' (there are, I think, others) is that it has no notion of structuration, or at any rate a quite inadequate one. Lévi-Strauss treats processes of structuration as combinatory forms produced by an external agent (the unconscious, in his sense of that concept). A theory of structuration, however, which is concerned with all types of social processes, including the unconscious, must allocate a central role to discursive and practical consciousness – in the context of unintended consequences – in the reproduction of social practices. 'Structural analysis' in the social sciences, in my sense, then, involves examining the structuration of social systems: a social system is a 'structured totality', 'consisting' of reproduced practices. Structural properties exist in time–space only as moments of the constitution of social systems. None the less we can analyse how 'deeply layered' structures are in terms of the historical duration of the practices they recursively organise and the spatial 'breadth' of those practices: the most deeply layered practices in this sense are *institutions*. To give an example: some key structural relations instantiated in the capitalist economic system can be represented as the following set of transformations:

private property : money: capital: labour contract : profit

The movement from left to right represents a series of transformations crucial to the production and reproduction of a capitalistic economy. Money, the medium of 'pure exchange-value', provides for the convertibility of property rights into capital. The universalisation of money capital in turn is the condition of the commodification of labour-power, and hence of the nature of the labour contract in capitalistic production. The existence of property/money as capital in turn provides for the convertibility of capital into profit via the extraction of surplus value.

The duality of structure

In the light of the discussion in the preceding sections, how should we understand the relation between action and structure? My answer is already implied in what I have said so far. The dualism of subject and object of which I have spoken must cede place to recognition of a *duality* that is implicated in all social reproduction, the *duality of structure*. By the 'duality of structure' I refer to the essentially recursive character of social life: the structural properties of social systems are both medium and outcome of the practices that constitute those systems. The best way to illustrate this is by reverting to the Saussurian conception of the production of an utterance. When I utter a sentence I draw upon various syntactical rules (sedimented in my practical consciousness of the language) in order to do so. These structural features of the language are the medium whereby I generate the utterance. But in producing a syntactically correct utterance I simultaneously contribute to the reproduction of the language as a whole. This view rejects the identification of structure with constraint: structure is both enabling and constraining. The most revolutionary forms of social change, like the most fixed forms of social reproduction, in this conception, involve structuration. There is therefore no place for a notion of de-structuration, such as has been proposed by Gurvitch among others. The idea of de-structuration is required only if we continue to counterpose structure and freedom – which, in my opinion, both Gurvitch and Sartre do. Although Sartre has been strongly influenced by Heidegger, he does not seem to have incorporated one of the most basic elements of the latter's *Being and Time* into his own work. The counterposition of past and present in Sartre is what I seek to escape from here: for Sartre the past is 'given and necessary', while the present is a realm of free spontaneous creation.

To summarise: the 'differences' that constitute structures, and are constituted structurally, relate 'part' to 'whole' in the sense in which the utterance of a grammatical sentence presupposes an absent corpus of syntactical rules that constitute the language as a totality. The importance of this relation between moment and totality for social theory can hardly be exaggerated, involving as it does a dialectic of presence and absence which ties the most minor or trivial forms of social action to structural properties of the overall society, and to the coalescence of institutions over long stretches of historical time.

In case my overall emphases are not fully clear, let me at this point bring the discussion back to the knowledgeability of social actors. I intend it to be a major emphasis of the ideas developed here that institutions do not just work 'behind the backs' of the social actors who produce and reproduce them. Every competent member of every society knows (in the sense of both discursive and practical consciousness) a great deal about the institutions of that society: such knowledge is not *incidental* to the operation of society, but is necessarily involved in it. A common tendency of many otherwise divergent schools of sociological thought – but especially functional-ism – is to adopt the methodological tactic of beginning their analyses by discounting agents' reasons for their action, in order to discover the 'real' stimuli to their activity, of which they are ignor-ant. Such a stance is not only defective from the point of view of social theory, it has strongly defined and potentially offensive politi-cal implications. It implies a *derogation of the lay actor*. From this flow various important considerations – which again I do not have space to discuss here – about the status of social science as critical theory, and as implicated in practical social reform.

In conclusion I want briefly to revert to a consideration I deferred: the notion that the structural properties of social systems can be regarded as involving rules and 'resources'. By referring to 'resources' I mean to stress the centrality of *power* to social theory. This allows me to return to the theme by means of which I intro-duced this essay – the discrete treatments of common problems by philosophers and sociologists. I want to maintain that the concept of action is logically linked to that of power, if the latter term is inter-preted in a broad sense as the capability of achieving outcomes. Philosophers have talked about this under the headings of 'powers' or the 'can' of human activity, but so far as I know they have not tried to connect these notions to concepts of power developed in so-cial and political theory.

Philosophical discussions of 'powers' are concerned with the capabilities of individual subjects. Many analyses of power in the social sciences are also 'subjectivist', in the sense that they seek to define power as the capacity of an acting subject to intervene in the course of events in the world so as to influence or alter those events. I would include Weber's famous definition of power in this cate-gory, although the 'events' involved are the acts of others: power is the capability of an individual to secure his or her own ends even against the will of others. Quite distinct from this idea of power are those concepts, such as that formulated by Parsons, which see power above all as a phenomenon of the collectivity. What we see here, I think, is a dualism comparable with and related to the dual-ism of action and structure noted earlier. The same methodological tactic is appropriate: we should replace this dualism with a concep-tion of a duality, acknowledging and connecting each of these two aspects of power. This I try to do by means of the notion of resource. Resources are drawn upon by actors in the production of interaction, but are constituted as structures of domination. Resources are the media whereby power is employed in the routine course of social action; but they are at the same time structural elements of social systems, reconstituted in social interaction. Social systems are constituted as regularised practices, reproduced across time and space: power in social systems can thus be treated as involving reproduced relations of *autonomy and dependence* in social inter-action.

This leads me to one final concept that I want to talk about brief-ly, a concept that is very important in the scheme of social theory I am trying to develop. This is the notion of what I call the *dialectic of control* in social systems. It is one of the main areas in which the theorem that social actors know, and must know (in practical and discursive consciousness) a great deal about the circumstances of their action, can be most readily related to questions of power and domination. By the dialectic of control I mean the capability of the weak, in the regularised relations of autonomy and dependence that constitute social systems, to turn their weakness back against the powerful. My argument is that, just as action is intrinsically related to power, so the dialectic of control is built into the very nature of social systems. An agent who does not participate in the dialectic of control, in a minimal fashion, ceases to be an agent. All relations of autonomy and dependence are reciprocal: however wide the asym-metrical distribution of resources involved, all power relations express autonomy and dependence 'in both directions'. Only a per-son who is kept totally confined and controlled does not participate in the dialectic of control. But such a person is then *no longer an agent*.

4

Classical Social Theory and the Origins of Modern Sociology

My aims in this essay are both iconoclastic and constructive. An iconoclast, according to the *Oxford English Dictionary*, is a 'breaker of images', 'one who assails cherished beliefs'. I begin by taking to task a series of widely held views, relating above all to Durkheim's writings, of the past development of social theory. These views, as I have tried to show elsewhere,[1] are *myths*; here I try not so much to shatter their images of the intellectual origins of sociology as to show that they are like reflections in a hall of distorting mirrors. I do not, however, propose to analyse the development of classical nineteenth- and early twentieth-century social theory for its own sake alone, but wish to draw out some implications for problems of sociology today.

Some myths identified

There are obviously many different interpretations of the rise of social theory from its origins in nineteenth-century Europe to the present day; the views and controversies they express cannot readily be compressed within any simple analytical scheme. But at least certain influential ones are informed by a particular perspective which I call that of 'the great divide'. This is the idea that a fundamental watershed separates the prehistory of social theory, when it had not yet been disentangled from speculative philosophy or the philosophy of history, from its foundation as a distinctive and novel science of society. The most prominent of the cherished versions of this notion locates the great divide in the writings of certain European authors whose major works appeared between 1890 and 1920 –

especially in the writings of Durkheim and Weber, closely followed by those of Pareto, Michels, Simmel, and others. While it may be misleading to mention one particular secondary work developing this version of the great divide, since it represents an orthodoxy which crops up almost everywhere, it would be hard to dispute that Parsons's *The Structure of Social Action* (1937), perhaps the most influential study of European social theory published in English over the last half century, has played the largest part in establishing it *as* an orthodoxy.

It has often been pointed out that in the above work only minimal reference is made to the writings of Marx and Engels, which are cursorily relegated to limbo. But of course Marxism has its own rendition of the great divide, offering a very different analysis of the ideas produced by the writers of the 1890–1920 generation. Like the version mentioned above, the Marxist view has been stated with varying degrees of sophistication. Essentially, however, it supposes that the foundations for a science of society were established by Marx and Engels when they forsook the speculative philosophy of history, as represented by Hegel and Feuerbach. (Perhaps the most technically precise account of this nature is that offered by Althusser's thesis of the supposed 'epistemological break' in Marx's intellectual career, which separates philosophy from science in the development of Marxism as a coherent body of thought.) While I do not, in this essay, examine this sort of claim directly, I do discuss the view that considers the works of Durkheim, Weber and their non-Marxist contemporaries to be a response to the challenge posed by Marxism or by revolutionary socialism more generally. In its more extreme guise, the Marxist version of the great divide provides a rationale for dismissing the ideas of the 'bourgeois' writers of the 1890–1920 period as mere ideology. But, stated in subtler form, this kind of view holds that Marx's writings represent the great divide in the history of social thought because they are the axis about which the work of the subsequent generation of thinkers (and perhaps each later generation up to and including the present one) has turned. Such a perspective has been developed in a European context by Georg Lukács, Lucien Goldmann, and others, but has also found expression among certain American authors.[2]

I want to show that each of these competing versions of the significance of the 1890–1920 generation is mistaken and that the whole notion of the great divide as formulated by Parsons, and in a less sophisticated way by many others, is a myth. I do not suggest that major divides cannot be found in the history of social thought; nor indeed that there are no elements of truth in the accounts I shall analyse. But we must extract the rational kernel from its shell. Before specifying the elements of truth in the thesis of the great divide, I wish to discuss certain other notions about the history of European social thought which have been quite often closely associated with one or another account of the great divide, and which are particularly, though not exclusively, connected with Durkheim's writings: notions which also involve mythologies.[3] They are:

(1) *The myth of the problem of order.* According to this idea, the work of some or even most of the outstanding non-Marxist authors of the 1890–1920 period (but especially that of Durkheim) can profitably be understood as being preoccupied with an abstract 'problem of order' that was a residue of utilitarianism in social philosophy.

(2) *The myth of the conservative origins of sociology.* Although this theme has been developed in varying ways by different authors, it relies primarily upon the thesis that some, or most, of the principal intellectual perspectives in sociology today can be traced fairly directly to a group of early nineteenth-century authors who reacted against the changes resulting from two great revolutions in eighteenth-century Europe, the 1789 Revolution in France and the Industrial Revolution in Britain.

(3) *The myth of schism.* This in fact derives from attempts to effect a critique of the idea that a concern with the problem of order has played a vital role in the past development of social thought. According to this view, a preoccupation with order distinguishes only certain traditions in social theory; the history of social thought since the middle of the nineteenth century, it is supposed, can profitably be regarded as involving a persisting split between 'order theory' (alternatively called 'consensus' or 'integration' theory) on the one side and 'conflict' theory (sometimes referred to as 'coercion' theory) on the other.

More qualifications are in order. Although these four sets of ideas – the myths of the great divide, the problem of order, the conservative origins of sociology, and schism – have met with widespread acceptance, none of them has gone undisputed. Nor are they necessarily the most persuasive accounts that have been produced. I claim only that they have been sufficiently influential to be worth refuting. I do not attempt to trace out how far they have in fact become conventional wisdom, but address myself only to those authors whose writings have been most important in advocating the views in question. Also, it would be wrong to say that the four myths provide a unitary perspective on the past or that the proponents of any one of them have necessarily sought to defend the others. Nisbet, for example, who has probably done most to foster the myth of the conservative origins of sociology, has specifically questioned that of the great divide.[4] None the less there are important points of connection. The thesis that the problem of order was one, or perhaps *the*, major issue through which the concerns of contemporary sociology were shaped bolsters both the conviction that these concerns are connected in some privileged way with 'conservatism' and the belief that there is some definable historical counterpart to 'order theory' that can properly be labelled 'conflict theory'. Moreover, as I shall show subsequently, the myths of the problem of order and of conservatism, suitably interpreted, can provide ammunition for certain more naive Marxist versions of the great divide.

The problem of order

As a result of its frequent appearance in Parsons's major works, 'the problem of order' has become a catch-phrase in contemporary social theory. Introduced as an interpretative theme in *The Structure of Social Action*, it became firmly established as a key notion in Parsons's subsequent elaboration of his ideas. Below I comment briefly upon the ambiguity of the concept of the problem of order in his later writings; for the moment I wish to examine only its formulation in *The Structure of Social Action*, where it was introduced in relation to Hobbes. The problem of order, according to Parsons, 'in the sense in which Hobbes posed it, constitutes the most fundamental empirical difficulty of utilitarian thought'.[5] The rudiments of the 'Hobbesian problem', as Parsons presents it, are not difficult to express. In a state of nature, each person would be pitted against every other, in a 'war of all against all'; Hobbes supposes that by forming a compact with a sovereign authority, individuals in society escape from this prospect of unremitting struggle. This formulation is essentially inadequate, however, because it rests upon the assumption of social contract, as if actors at some point come to perceive that it is in their best interests to combine to recognise a sovereign authority. Inadequate though it may have been, Parsons says, it nevertheless was accepted unquestioningly as long as utilitarianism remained dominant in social philosophy – that is, until the late nineteenth century, when it was subjected to a massive re-examination and critique (above all in Durkheim's writings) in which the problem of order became of primary concern.[6]

On this basis Parsons incorporated into *The Structure of Social Action* and subsequent writings an analysis of Durkheim's thought which has met with widespread acceptance. But this analysis, influential as it has been, is not an accurate representation of the main thrust of Durkheim's work.[7] The textual evidence against the interpretation that Durkheim was concerned throughout his career with the 'Hobbesian problem of order', as formulated by Parsons, is overwhelming. First of all, at a relatively early stage of his intellectual development, Durkheim specifically, though rather casually, dismissed the 'Hobbesian problem' as being of no significance for sociology, saying that it depends upon a hypothetical state of affairs (man in a state of nature) which is of no interest to social theory, because it is wrongly posed in the first place.[8] Second, Parsons's account is based upon a misleading identification of the residues of prior intellectual traditions which Durkheim sought to criticise. As Parsons makes clear, the problem of order is tied to the utilitarianism of Hobbes and his successors. Now utilitarianism, not as represented in Hobbes's work but in the considerably more sophisticated guise of the writings of Herbert Spencer, was only one of the polemical targets at which Durkheim aimed his critical salvos in the early part of his intellectual career. Parsons's account concentrates almost exclusively upon utilitarianism as Durkheim's critical foil; but just as important – perhaps more so, since it supplied the main underlying parameters of *The Division of Labour* – was the latter's critical response to German idealism, both the 'holism' of Wundt and Schäffle, and neo-Kantian philosophy. These schools of thought preoccupied Durkheim in his very first writings, and various important ideas appear in those writings which Parsons supposes that Durkheim only arrived at much later, as a consequence of his struggles with the problem of order.

The Division of Labour itself is treated by Parsons as an early, and radically flawed, disquisition upon the problem of order. Two consequences flow from this. First, the work is severed from Durkheim's subsequent writings, which are regarded as successive, and progressively more acceptable, attempts to resolve the problem of order, culminating in *The Elementary Forms of the Religious Life*. By this time Durkheim is supposed to have made the full traverse from 'positivism' to 'idealism' (in the specific senses in which Parsons uses those terms). Second, *The Division of Labour* is exposed as hiding an essential, unresolved ambiguity. By showing that there is a 'non-contractual element in contract', Durkheim had, according to Parsons, demonstrated the inadequacy of the Hobbesian solution to the problem of order. But at the same time he had created a dilemma for himself, for where does the 'non-contractual element' derive from if the progress of organic solidarity, in terms of which contractual relations are formed, *ipso facto* entails the disappearance of collective values?

I deal with the second point first, since it relates to what I have already said about the intellectual traditions of which Durkheim sought to effect a critique. There is no ambiguity in the argument of *The Division of Labour* if it is viewed, not as an analysis of the problem of order, but as an attempt to reconcile 'individualism' (which from the beginning Durkheim disavowed in its original utilitarian form) with 'holism', on the basis of a critique of *both*. Durkheim sought to show – as he pointed out clearly enough in the preamble to the book – that the ideals of 'individualism', which set a premium upon the freedom and dignity of the individual, are themselves social products and therefore cannot, in the manner of utilitarianism, be treated as the premises of human society in general. Since these ideals are both the moral expression and the foundation of organic solidarity, they are not 'pathological' (as many idealist writers had suggested) but, on the contrary, represent the incipient moral order of the future.[9] This theme is further developed throughout Durkheim's writings.

It is true that there were important developments in Durkheim's work subsequent to *The Division of Labour*. One of the most significant was his discovery of the work of the English anthropologists which, together with that of Spencer and Gillen, prompted the researches culminating in *The Elementary Forms*. But although he came to have doubts about some of the views expressed in *The Division of Labour*, Durkheim continued to regard the general form of the framework set out therein as valid (adding a famous preface to the second edition in 1902), and drew upon it extensively in his later writings and lecture courses. If the central place accorded the problem of order in Parsons's exposition of Durkheim's works is abandoned, it becomes clear that Durkheim's main preoccupation, which of course he shared with many of his contemporaries, was with the contrasts and continuities between 'traditional' and 'modern' societies. The theory developed in *The Elementary Forms* both elaborates upon the idea of 'mechanical solidarity', as it was originally set out; and offers an account of the social sources of morality that is broad enough to include the emergent ideals of 'moral individualism', as well as connecting them to traditional theism.[10]

Finally, concentration upon the problem of order as Durkheim's guiding problem leads Parsons to represent the former's work as becoming more and more dominated by the notion of moral consensus, which thus almost completely blanks out his parallel concern with modes of institutional change. This aspect of Durkheim's thought is, however, highly important, not least because it constitutes a major point of connection between it and socialism. Although consistently resistant to the claims of revolutionary socialism, especially Marxism, Durkheim was equally consistently sympathetic to reformist socialism and specifically embodied some of its principles in his own theory. According to him, the moral regeneration necessary for the transcendence of anomie could come about only through a process of profound institutional change. In *The Division of Labour* this process was discussed in terms of the 'forced division of labour'; later Durkheim reshaped and expanded the idea as the theory of occupational groups (*corporations*) and the modern state.

I assess below some further implications of the 'problem of order'. For the moment it is sufficient to say that, far from supplying the guiding theme of Durkheim's sociology, it was not, in the terms in which Parsons formulates it, a problem for Durkheim at all. Since it was primarily on his interpretation of Durkheim's writings that Parsons rested his case for the significance of the problem of order in the evolution of modern social theory, we can make the further claim that the 'problem of order' was not of particular importance in European social thought in the nineteenth and early twentieth centuries. The implications of such a claim cannot be fully worked out without considering afresh the significance of utilitarian philosophy for the development of social thought in the nineteenth century, as I shall undertake to do, albeit briefly, later in my discussion.

The myth of conservatism

The notion that the origins of modern sociology are bound up in some special way with conservative thought has been advanced by various authors, including von Hayek, Salomon, and, nearer to the present day, Robert Nisbet.[11] Here I concentrate on Nisbet's account, again taking Durkheim's works as the main basis of my discussion, since the thesis of the significance of conservatism seems to be particularly persuasive when applied to Durkheim's views and has been taken up in this regard by other interpreters. But I also refer briefly to the writings of Max Weber.

In *The Sociological Tradition*, Nisbet formulates a powerful and comprehensive interpretation of the rise of European social theory, focusing upon the key role played by conservatism, especially by the 'counter-reaction' to the French Revolution as manifest in the doctrines of de Maistre, Bonald and Chateaubriand. 'Conservatism' here does not refer to directly political attitudes but to a series of major analytic concepts which, in Nisbet's view, became established as – and still remain – basic to the sociological tradition. As applied to the elucidation of Durkheim's thought, this is an altogether more subtle and interesting thesis than the one, occasionally expressed several decades ago, that Durkheim was a conservative in his immediate political attitudes and involvements.[12] If there was ever any doubt about the matter, it rested upon ignorance. Durkheim's sympathies never lay with right-wing nationalism or with its philosophy, and his work was (rightly) regarded by conservative Catholic apologists as highly inimical to their interests.[13] Although he normally remained distant from the day-to-day events of politics, his affiliation was above all to liberal republicanism (his influence upon Jaurès is well known); and he took an active role in support of the *dreyfusards*.

While acknowledging, then, Durkheim's liberalism in politics, Nisbet wishes to argue that none the less the main intellectual parameters of his social theory were formed through the adoption of a frame of concepts drawn from the conservative revolt against the legacy of the eighteenth-century rationalist philosophers whose ideas inspired the 1789 Revolution. This argument, however, can be taken in either of two possible ways, which are not separated by Nisbet. I call them the 'weak' and the 'strong' versions of the thesis of conservatism. We may, and ordinarily must, distinguish between the intellectual *antecedents* of someone's thought, the traditions drawn upon in forming his or her views, and the intellectual *content* of those views – what is *made* of the ideas taken from such traditions. For a thinker may draw upon a specific range of sources but may sculpture from them an intellectual system quite different from that or those whence they derived. It is entirely possible for a corpus of work to be 'conservative' in terms of the schools of thought on which it draws (the weak sense), without being 'conservative' as such (the strong sense) – and vice versa. I argue, in fact, that Durkheim's writings cannot be distinctively linked to conservatism in either sense. But I wish to make a further point which can be easily illustrated by reference to the works of other leading social theorists as well: that the work of any outstanding thinker – and this is what makes it outstanding – normally both *synthesises*, yet also thereby significantly *breaks with*, several apparently divergent intellectual traditions. With regard to the three European thinkers of the nineteenth and early twentieth centuries who did most to frame the development of social theory up to the present time – Marx, Durkheim and Weber – conservatism, in some sense, appears as an important fragment of their intellectual inheritance. But all of them also sought to transcend what they saw as its particular limitations by synthesising ideas drawn from it with ideas drawn from competing traditions.

I have already referred to Durkheim's intellectual inheritance, from the point of view of utilitarianism, with regard to the myth of the problem of order. This is not, however, the main focus of Nisbet's account, which concentrates upon Durkheim's indebtedness to the luminaries of the 'counter-reaction'. According to Nisbet, Durkheim was in a minor way – mainly in respect of his methodological position – influenced by the eighteenth-century rationalist philosophers. But his strongest debts were to critics of rationalism, such as Bonald, Maistre and Haller.[14] I think this is quite easily shown to be wrong if it is understood as the weak version of the thesis of conservatism. It is not accurate to say, as Nisbet does, that Durkheim's debt to the rationalism of the eighteenth-century *philosophes* was wholly a methodological one. Although he rejected major aspects of Rousseau's theory of the state, for example, his critical evaluation of Rousseau's philosophy was certainly not completely negative. It is evident enough, however, that within the spectrum of French social thought, the contributions of later authors, notably Saint-Simon and Comte, bulked larger on Durkheim's intellectual horizons, and it is through indicating Durkheim's debt to Comte that Nisbet seeks in substantial part to demonstrate the influence of the Catholic reactionary thinkers upon Durkheim's writings. Now Comte acknowledged the importance of the 'retrograde school', and there is a clear imprint of the ideas of the latter in the hierocracy envisaged as the corporate society of the future in the *Positive Polity*. But Durkheim explicitly rejected the basic features of this model; it was Comte's methodological writing, as manifest in the *Positive Philosophy*, which particularly influenced him – together with the more proximate influence of Boutroux. Evaluating and rejecting what he saw as the reactionary implications of the Comteian hierocratic model, Durkheim drew upon elements of the overlapping, yet distinctively different, analysis of the emergent society of the future foreseen by Comte's erstwhile mentor, Saint-Simon (while seeking to effect a critique of the latter also). This is of more than marginal interest, since Saint-Simon's works, inchoate and wild though they frequently were, are vital in the development of nineteenth-century social theory. Two paths open out from them, one leading to Comte and Durkheim and thence to contemporary 'structural-functionalism', the other leading to Marx. I have already alluded to the significance of socialism in Durkheim's intellectual background. This was also mediated through his early exposure, during a period of study in Germany, to the ideas of the 'socialists of the chair'; it was undoubtedly partly in response to their work that the underlying themes of *The Division of Labour* were elaborated.[15]

I conclude from this analysis that Durkheim's work was not conservative in the weak sense. But one further body of work from which he drew is worthy of mention and immediately relevant to the question whether Durkheim's writings may be regarded legitimately as conservative in the strong sense. This is neo-Kantianism, particularly as developed by Renouvier. One constantly finds Kantian formulations in Durkheim's works, often explicitly acknowledged as such by him. If there is any single problem with which Durkheim was preoccupied, rather than the 'Hobbesian problem of order', it was the Kantian problem of the moral imperative. From the early stages of his intellectual career up to and including the publication of *The Elementary Forms*, Durkheim was concerned with reformulating some of the key concepts of Kant's philosophy in a social context. He sought to show that both the moral imperative, and the very categories of the mind, are not to be taken as *a priori* but on the contrary can and should be explained sociologically. In conjunction with the other intellectual emphases that I have mentioned previously, this fact supplies the essential interpretative background for understanding how misleading it is to regard Durkheim's thought as having an inherently conservative cast. For Durkheim was concerned to show, first, that the forms of 'individualism' stressed in Kantian and in utilitarian philosophy were the products of an extended sequence of social evolution, rather than primitive and necessary assumptions of social analysis as such; and, second, that individualism is to be the moral counterpart of the emerging differentiated society founded upon a diverse division of labour.

One of the main props of the thesis that Durkheim's thought is inherently conservative is that, as Nisbet puts it, it constituted 'an all-out offensive' against individualism. But this view rests on a confusion of two senses of 'individualism' between which it was precisely Durkheim's object to distinguish: *methodological* individualism and *moral* individualism. One important strand of his writing is a critique of those forms of method – especially utilitarianism – which treat the individual as the starting-point of sociological analysis. But he wished to show that the rejection of individualism as a methodology does not preclude analysing the development of moral individualism sociologically – on the contrary, the latter process cannot be accomplished otherwise. The rise and significance of moral individualism cannot be understood via the ontological premises of methodological individualism:

> The condemnation of individualism [Durkheim says] has been facilitated by its confusion with the narrow utilitarianism and utilitarian egoism of Spencer and the economists. But this is very facile . . . what is unacceptable is that this individualism should be presented as the only one that there is, or ever could be . . . A verbal similarity has made possible the belief that *individualism* necessarily resulted from individual, and thus egoistic, sentiments.[16]

I do not say that Durkheim's attempt to distinguish between methodological and moral individualism was successful. Some of the main difficulties with, and ambiguities in, his work derive from unresolved dilemmas in this respect. But that it clearly distances his writings from conservatism cannot be disputed. The article from which the above quotation comes was written, in relation to the Dreyfus affair, specifically as an attack upon contemporary adherents of the sort of hierocratic reactionism prefigured in the writings of de Maistre and others in an earlier generation. In opposition to the conservative ideologists, Durkheim consistently argued that there can be no reversion to the sort of moral discipline that prevailed in former ages (which he sometimes referred to as the 'tyranny of the group', and under which there is only a feeble development of individual faculties and capabilities). Freedom does not result from escape from moral authority but from its transformation through the emergence of the values of moral individualism.

In *The Sociological Tradition* Nisbet differentiates between conservatism and two other 'ideological currents' that helped shape European social thought in the nineteenth century, 'radicalism' and 'liberalism'. He maintains that each of these also served to mould the thought of major thinkers of the period, for example Marx ('radicalism') and Mill and Spencer ('liberalism'). But as I seek to indicate below, if any such general labels are to be attached to them, Durkheim's writings are distinctively connected to 'liberalism' – although not of the utilitarian variety – rather than to 'conservatism'. One of the shortcomings of the thesis of the conservative origins of sociology is that 'conservatism' means different things in different countries and at different periods, as do 'liberalism' and 'radicalism'. Thus it would seem reasonable to hold that *one* of the traditions that shaped Marx's own writings was a conservative one: namely, Hegel's philosophy. Similarly, in the accounts of various interpreters, Weber is held to have been a conservative – in the strong sense – because of an irrationalism that ties his thought to that of the ideologist of National Socialism, Carl Schmitt.[17] In actual fact, I do not think this view to be any less partial and inaccurate than that which links Durkheim's writings in a privileged way to the 'counter-reaction'; irrationalism, particularly in the form of Nietzsche's ideas, is only one component of Weber's intellectual inheritance and of his thought, and one which he tried to synthesise with other, quite different, elements and thereby to transcend.

The myth of schism

Although it is perhaps even more pervasive than the others, the myth of schism can be dealt with more briefly, because in some part it depends upon them. It was invented, to put the matter crudely, by Dahrendorf, looking back over his shoulder to Parsons's 'problem of order'. According to Dahrendorf,[18] not one but two resolutions of the problem of order can be found in social theory. One is that which Parsons extracted from Durkheim, stressing the significance of consensus; the other, most clearly expressed by Marx, resolves the problem of order through the coercive control that a minority can exert over the rest of society. Dahrendorf compares Marx directly with Parsons; others, however, have looked back to Durkheim as the main founder of 'order theory'. Horton,[19] for example, traces the differences between Marx and Durkheim to divergent conceptions of man in a state of nature, linking Marx to Rousseau, and Durkheim once more to Hobbes. According to this sort of view, in the first such conception the evils in the human condition stem from the repressive effects of the incorporation of human beings in society. In the second, they originate in the opposite state of affairs: a lack of adequate social or moral regulation.

But it is not difficult to show how misleading this conception is. One cannot make sense of Marx's writings, even his early ones, by supposing that he was thinking in terms of an abstract contrast between 'human beings in nature' (non-alienated, free) and 'human beings in society' (alienated, unfree). Marx, like Durkheim, dismissed this from the outset as a residue of utilitarianism. Both saw the freeing of humanity from the limitations of bondage to nature and from self-ignorance as a product of social development. Human faculties are both produced and sustained by society. Alienation is maximised by the specific mechanisms of the capitalist mode of production and is transcended, neither by the destruction of society nor by reversion to a more primitive way of life, but by the transformation of society itself. Durkheim's vision was undoubtedly at odds with Marx's. The discrepancies do not derive, however, from two different versions of human beings in a state of nature but are anchored in divergent analyses of the development of a definite *form* of society due to the rise of industrial capitalism in Europe. For Durkheim, human beings in a state of nature would not be anomic because their needs, like those of animals, would then be wholly organic, and such needs are adjusted to fixed levels of satiation. It is precisely because most human needs are socially created that their limits, or their definition *as* bounded needs, must also be set by society. The correlate of this, obviously, is that the concept of anomie can only be properly understood, as Durkheim intended it to be, in the context of the destruction of traditional society and the emergence of moral individualism.

Some implications

It is time to take stock. In pouring cold water on the myths of the problem of order, conservatism and schism, I have talked mainly of Durkheim. The analysis could readily be extended to other authors, however, and I want to deny that these ideas illuminate the development of European social theory in the nineteenth and early twentieth centuries. Moreover, I shall seek to indicate that the false images of the past which they have fostered have had an unhappy influence on the contemporary debate about the present concerns and aims of sociology (and the social sciences as a whole). There can be few who do not have a sense of unease about the current condition of social theory, and it is not hard to see that the social sciences today stand at a crossroads. The difficulty is to see which path or paths to take, amid the welter of apparently clashing theoretical perspectives that have suddenly sprung into prominence. I accept that we are today at an important stage of transition in social theory – our own great divide, as it were. Within the confines of such a discussion as this, it is not possible to draw up a detailed proposal about the likely or proper future orientations of sociology; but undermining the myths of the past can help to illuminate some of the major tasks of today.

Broadly speaking, within 'academic sociology', as differentiated from 'Marxism', we can distinguish at least three responses to the current *malaise* of social theory: (1) a resurgent critique of positivism in the social sciences and an attempt to rework their foundations so as to escape from its toils; (2) the argument that sociology is tied to ideologies which legitimate the status quo, and hence a call for a new *radical sociology;* (3) the thesis that in the schism between 'order' and 'conflict theory', the former has won, and hence that new attempts should be made to develop conflict theory in a more adequate fashion.

I do not deny that certain advocates of one or another of these directions in social theory may have made valuable contributions. I do claim, however, that some recent versions – particularly within

American sociology as distinct from European social theory and philosophy – are in some part tied to the three myths criticised above and share their inadequacies. I shall first discuss the latter two of the trends I have mentioned above, which I shall relate to the theory of industrial society. I shall revert later to the problem of 'positivism', which I shall connect to the myth of the great divide in the context of the epistemological status of social theory.

The theory of industrial society

The myth of schism was originally fostered by critics whose attentions were directed at Parsons's mature theories, as set out principally in *The Social System*. These critics were mainly European (Dahrendorf, Lockwood and Rex); they sought to complement Parsons's ideas with others supposedly drawn from Marxist thought. Even though they rejected the problem of order as *the* problem of sociology, they tended to accept it in a relatively unexamined way as *a* fundamental basis for social theory, claiming that it should be complemented with notions of coercion, power, and conflict.

But the myth of schism not only rests upon misleading interpretations of the past; it is a wholly inadequate way of conceiving our present tasks. This is so for two reasons. First, it perpetuates an ambiguity in the idea of the problem of order itself – a dual meaning which Parsons himself pointed out when he first introduced the notion in *The Structure of Social Action* but which, because of the standpoint he wished to elaborate there, he treated as of no significance. 'Order' *can* refer, Parsons pointed out initially, to the antithesis of 'randomness or chance', where 'chance or randomness is the name for that which is incomprehensible, not capable of intelligible analysis' – a very general sense of the term indeed. In Parsons's formulation of the 'Hobbesian problem of order', on the other hand, the term 'means that process takes place in conformity with the paths laid down in the normative system'.[20] By suggesting subsequently, however, that for purposes of social theory these two formulations of order may be treated as one and the same, Parsons was able to develop the view that the 'Hobbesian problem' is the generic way in which 'the problem of order' *has* to be presented in sociology. But this second sense of 'order', normative integration or consensus, is a very special use of the term; and it does indeed appear the contrary of 'conflict', 'coercion', etc. We have to recognise, in other words, that while, in the first, very general, sense no one could deny that the task of social theory is certainly to account for 'order', the Parsonian formulation is *one specific approach* to this – and it is one that can be questioned in a much more profound way than is suggested by the critics mentioned above.

Second, the idea of schism is a crude and unsatisfactory way of representing the issues separating 'structural-functionalism' and 'Marxism'. The views supposed to be derived from the latter (stressing the primacy of 'conflict', 'coercion' and 'change') are purely formal and actually have no particular connection with Marxism at all. Thus it is quite mistaken to suggest that Marx was unconcerned with normative 'consensus', although of course he disliked that specific term. 'Common values' appear in Marxian theory in the guise of 'ideology', and what differentiates the latter concept from the former cannot be understood without reference to other concepts integral to Marxism: namely, those of modes of production and class interests. It is interesting to note that, although it originated in the writings of European authors, the idea of schism seems to have been more influential in American sociology subsequently than in Europe. One reason may be that, even though the bearing of conflict theory on Marxism is minimal, it has helped to supply in a somewhat covert way what is absent from the American intellectual scene but strongly developed in Europe: a vital and sophisticated tradition of Marxist thought itself.

The idea of schism is a sterile one and has to be abandoned. But because the call for a 'radical sociology' is tied both to it and to the myth of conservatism, it is appropriate to subject it to brief scrutiny. It is easy to see that, just as the notion that the chief focus of social theory should be the 'problem of order' calls forth the demand that this focus should be complemented by an analysis bringing conflict, coercion and change to the forefront, so the view that the roots of modern sociology are bound up in some special sense with conservatism tends to call forth the response that the conservative bias needs to be complemented by a 'radical' one. Now it may well be the case that some schools of social thought show elements of conservatism in either the weak or the strong sense (although I have already indicated the difficulties involved in the use of blanket terms like 'conservatism' or 'radicalism'). But this type of argument is quite different from showing that sociology is in some *intrinsic* way bound up with conservative views. Even if the latter view could be shown to be plausible, which I do not believe it can, it would still leave the epistemological basis of 'radical sociology' obscure. Marxism itself has always had trouble with its own epistemological status: that is, to what extent it is a neutral science and to what extent it is a critical theory linked to the interests of the labour movement. Such difficulties are surely only compounded by the diffusely expressed ideals of 'radical sociology'. I do not deny that social theory is linked in subtle and ramified ways to criticism, but only reject that sort of formulation of 'radical sociology' which I consider tied to the myths I have sought to undermine.

I can now move to the main point of this section. The acceptance of these myths of the past has generated a series of controversies, involving attacks upon 'structural-functionalism' which have concentrated almost solely upon its abstract or epistemological shortcomings. I refer to these again below. What I wish to show at present is that, since the debate has concentrated upon these issues, it has largely ignored what has been the substantive correlate of 'structural-functionalism': the theory of industrial society. This type of theory is, I think, expressed in the writings of Parsons himself, but the view is also broadly shared by authors as diverse otherwise as Dahrendorf, Aron and Clark Kerr.

Before I sketch in what I mean, some qualifications are once more in order. I do not wish to say that, even among non-Marxist authors, the ideas I describe immediately below have been without their critics, or that the alternative approach outlined subsequently has not already been partially anticipated by others. I do want to suggest, however, that the critics of the theory of industrial society have neither identified it exactly as I do, nor connected the elements of their critiques to an alternative programme.

The theory of industrial society runs roughly as follows. The fundamental contrast in the modern world, it is held, is between traditional, agrarian society, normally based upon the dominance of land-owning elites, sanctioned by religion, though in reality often deriving from military power and co-ordinated within an authoritarian state; and industrial, urban society, fluid and 'meritocratic' in its structure, characterised by a diffusion of power among competitive elites, where social solidarity is based upon secular exchange transactions rather than upon religious ethics or coercive military power, and in which government is transformed into a mass democratic state. The theory of industrial society recognises the phenomenon of class conflict but holds that it is characteristic of the *transitional* phase in the emergence of industrialism out of traditional society and that it becomes transcended (read 'regulated' or 'institutionalised') when the industrial order reaches maturity. In some versions – including the original Saint-Simonian ones – it is held that the very concept of 'class' loses its relevance once the transition to industrialism has been achieved. Further, an end of class conflict in the contemporary era means an end of ideology, save in a few industrialised countries, such as France or Italy, where the continuing existence of an archaic, peasant sector means that the old class conflicts and ideological movements have not yet dropped away. Conceptually, the theory of industrial society involves a polar typology of forms of societal organisation made familiar under a variety of names: 'status' versus 'contract', 'mechanical' versus 'organic' solidarity, '*Gemeinschaft*' versus '*Gesellschaft*', and so forth.

The theory of industrial society, as it has come down to us today, must be *abandoned*, or at least *dismantled*, and its assumptions and premises subjected to scrutiny. In so far as we apply it, in some guise or another, to the patterns of development of the industrialised societies in the present, we are operating within the sorts of assumptions made by most of those in the classic tradition of social theory when they sought to encompass theoretically the encounter of the post-feudal world with the coruscating influences of political democracy, urbanism and industrialisation. But some or most of these assumptions are obsolete in an era when the main 'internal' divisions and strains in the advanced societies are no longer, as in the nineteenth and early twentieth centuries, based upon the tensions between urban-industrial centres and the still strong centrifugal pull of a rural hinterland. Moreover, and just as important, the theory of industrial society is time-bound within certain characteristic intellectual biases of nineteenth-century social thought. The most important of these is an *anti-political* bias. Throughout the nineteenth century one can trace the imprint of the view, or the covert assumption, that the state is subordinate to society, and that consequently politics can be explained, or, more accurately, explained away, by reference to more deeply layered social phenomena. This, to borrow one of Marx's phrases, was the 'illusion of the epoch', reflecting an optimism about the pacific and consensual implications of industrialism, as contrasted to 'military' feudalism, questioned only by the few (including, most notably, Max Weber) – and shared in no small degree by Marx himself. The affinities between Marxism and orthodox sociology on this point have been obscured by the tendency to compare them on the abstract level of 'conflict' and 'order' theory. The threefold scheme of feudalism–capitalism –socialism certainly differs in a fundamental way from the traditional society–industrial society dichotomy. The latter treats capitalism not as a distinctive type of society but, for reasons already mentioned, as merely a transitional phase between the two main types (thereby precluding the possibility of the transformation of society through socialism). But this should not be allowed to divert attention from the fact that in Marx's writings, as in the theory of industrial society, there is only a rudimentary and highly inadequate theory of the state, no theory of military power, and no anticipation of the resurgent nationalism which, not many years after Marx's death, was to ruin the hopes of socialists for an international socialist commonwealth.

From the assumption of the impotence of politics, shared by the theory of industrial society and by Marxism, other assumptions flow which must be placed in question:

(1) Social development or change can be conceived of above all as the unfolding of endogenous influences within a given society (or, more often, a type of society); external factors are then treated merely as an environment to which the society 'adapts'. But society has *never* been the isolated, 'internally unfolding' system which this abstract model implies. This lesson should hardly need teaching in the contemporary world, with its intimate and intricate interdependencies and tensions spanning the globe. Were it not for the dominance of the endogenous model in sociology, one would not need to emphasise the extent to which politico-military power has shaped the character of the advanced societies. Successive world wars have brought about what internal industrial development failed to achieve in Germany and Japan – the disintegration of the hegemony of traditional land-owning elites. They have also provided the theatre for the processes of political change which created state socialism, first in the Soviet Union, and then in the other societies of Eastern Europe.

(2) The characteristic nature of any society is primarily (read 'ultimately') governed by its level of technological or economic develop-

ment – specifically, in the theory of industrial society, by the level of maturity of industrialisation.

(3) Consequently, the most economically advanced society (however defined) in the world at any one point in time shows to other societies an image of their own future. As Marx wrote to those of his countrymen who might doubt that the analysis of *Capital* might apply to them, based as it was upon the most industrially advanced society of the time, Britain: '*De te fabula narratur!*' (it is of you that the story is told!). In the closing part of the twentieth century, it might appear somewhat curious to take Britain as offering to the industrialised world an image of its future. But the underlying idea is alive and well: today it is trends in the USA which are most often taken – by non-Marxist thinkers, however – as demonstrating the future in the present for the rest of the world.

A breaking away from these stale ideas, the residue of the nineteenth century, offers prospects of new perspectives and constitutes one of the immanent tasks of social theory in the present day. The need for substantial rethinking is, I think, evident in the rash of speculative ideas suggesting that we are in the throes of a major process of social transformation in the industrialised world: theories of 'post-industrial', 'post-modern', 'technotronic' society, and so forth, abound. By and large, however, such theories continue the assumptions of previous times, holding, for instance, that 'industrial society' is in the process of being superseded by 'post-industrial society' (a process which, it is suggested, has proceeded very far only in the USA!). I wish to propose that our rethinking must be more profound and must break with the covert assumptions I have previously mentioned. This, I believe, implies a whole new theoretical and research programme for sociology, informed by the following presuppositions:

(1) The differentiation between sociology (as the study of social structure) and political science (as the study of government or political power) which has grown up over the years and become institutionally sanctified should be repudiated. It should be one of the major tasks of sociology to create a theory of the modern state and to explore its significance for problems of social theory in general.

(2) Sociology should come to terms theoretically with the unitary yet diverse international community, which is a 'global community' in a literal sense: a world in which the industrial and political transformations of nineteenth-century Europe have become transferred

to the international plane in the confrontation of rich and poor nations.

(3) We should take seriously and explore the possibilities inherent in the idea that there are differing 'paths' of development among the industrialised countries which cannot be squeezed between the confines of the old theory of industrial society. It has been shown and is generally recognised that there are differing paths to industrialisation. In addition, however, these possibly establish differing, chronic patterns of industrial and political organisation within the general type of 'industrial society'. We should neither leave the exploration of *differences* between societies to the historian nor merely explain them away by some idea of developmental lag.

(4) We should abandon the practice, which would in any case scarcely be defended by anyone in principle, of constructing theories of development on the basis of single cases (Britain in the nineteenth century, the USA in the twentieth). This is a call for a revitalised comparative sociology of the 'advanced' societies.

The epistemological status of social theory

There is an apparent contradiction in what I have said so far. Although I have accentuated that we are in the middle of a major phase of transition in social theory, I have also argued that the idea of a 'great divide' in the development of social thought in the nineteenth century is a myth. In concluding, therefore, it is necessary to clarify the argument. To do so, however, I must first examine the principal versions of the great divide as they are conventionally advanced. I again refer principally to Durkheim and secondarily to Weber, since no other thinkers of the 1890–1920 period have exerted a comparable influence upon the later development of sociology.

We might well have some initial scepticism about the notion of the great divide if we consider the frequency with which the claim has been advanced in the past that in the study of society science has finally triumphed over philosophy. After all, Saint-Simon made this claim of his works as compared with those of the earlier eighteenth-century philosophers; Comte and Marx made the same claim in relation to Saint-Simon; Durkheim and Weber made it concerning Comte and Marx; and Parsons made it, one might go on to say, concerning Durkheim, Weber and their generation! But let us look again briefly at Durkheim's writings. Durkheim is frequently seen as the leading figure involved in laying the foundations of empirical social science, the first author to apply systematic empirical method to definite sociological issues. This is held to be particularly manifest in *Suicide*, which is often regarded as the first statistical and empirical monograph of its kind to be published. But such a view is simply wrong, and is held in ignorance of the prior history of empirical research, in this area especially, but in other areas too, in the nineteenth century. The idea of developing a 'social physics' (Comte's term also, until he coined the neologism 'sociology') involving the systematic use of 'moral statistics' in order to study social life in a supposedly 'objective' fashion dates back at least as far as Quételet. Most of the generalisations, in fact, whereby Durkheim sought to relate variations in suicide rates to social factors were in no way original; neither was there anything particularly novel in his statistical methods. The distinctive character of Durkheim's work, in other words, did not lie in his method or materials but in his theories; and these were worked out within the context of, and can only be fully evaluated against the background of, the broad spectrum of issues which occupied him in *The Division of Labour* and other writings.

Now it is true that, in his methodological writings, Durkheim often emphasised the slow and partial way in which scientific progress comes about. Moreover his efforts to define precisely the scope of the subject-matter of sociology had as their object the achievement of the break with philosophy that writers such as Comte and Spencer had advocated but, as he saw it, had failed to bring about. But we can no more accept Durkheim's programmatic statements at their face-value than he did those of the authors he took to task. We might admit that *Suicide* conforms to the methodological prescription that sociology should concern itself with restricted, clearly delimited problems. We should perhaps have more difficulty in reconciling this with the far-reaching claims made in *The Elementary Forms*, even though that work is based upon an intensive study of one particular form of 'religion': Australian totemism. But the distance between methodological prescription and the themes actually developed by Durkheim surely becomes embarrassingly wide when we consider *The Division of Labour*. If it is not actually a philosophy of history, it is none the less of a sweeping and all-embracing character that is by no means alien to the sort of evolutionary schemes produced by previous nineteenth-century thinkers. Much of what Durkheim wrote in his work as a whole, in fact, hovers over that ill-defined borderline between moral philosophy and social theory. To be sure, he tried to show that age-old philosophical questions could be seen in a new light and thereby transformed; but this, after all, is no more than was claimed by many of his predecessors, including both Comte and Marx.

I shall not deal in detail with the technically elaborate version of the great divide set out in Parsons's *The Structure of Social Action*; some of my earlier comments obviously bear directly upon it. The Parsonian account of the unacknowledged 'convergence' of ideas in the thought of Durkheim and Weber (and others whose writings are discussed in the book) has little plausibility, if at any rate it is read as any sort of historical interpretation rather than as a documentation of Parsons's own formulae for the future development of social theory. Durkheim's methodological ideas, as I have already mentioned, are in direct line of descent from the *Positive Philosophy*, however critical he was of Comte in other ways. Weber had no such immediately available tradition and would certainly have rejected much of it, as he did the views of Menger within economic theory. His methodological position represents an uneasy and brittle synthesis of the sort of views espoused by the latter and the anti-generalism of the Historical School. For Weber, sociology always remained in an important sense the handmaiden of historical analysis. The Durkheimian version of sociological method would have been abhorrent to Weber, and since we can be fairly sure that Weber was well acquainted with the works of Durkheim and some of his prominent disciples, it is reasonable to suspect that Weber's tirade against the use of 'holistic' concepts in social analysis was directed in some part against the *Année sociologique* school, although no specific reference is made to it. In order to explain the divergences as well as the parallels between the writings of Durkheim and Weber, we have to look at the socio-political background of their writings, conspicuously absent from *The Structure of Social Action*, but figuring prominently in Marxist or Marxist-inspired versions of the great divide, to which I now turn.

The cruder variants of the latter are scarcely worth bothering with. The dismissal of the writings of the 1890–1920 generation of thinkers as merely an 'ideological defence of bourgeois society' is

inconsistent with Marx's own method. For him, if bourgeois political economy was 'ideological', it none the less contained a good deal
that was valid, which he wrote into *Capital* and made the corner-
stone of his own economic theories. But that version of the thesis
which sees 'sociology' – in the shape of the writings of Durkheim,
Weber and their generation – as having been formed out of a massive confrontation with Marxism is less easily shrugged aside. Thus
Zeitlin has lodged the claim that 'the outstanding sociologists of the
late nineteenth and early twentieth centuries developed their
theories by taking account of, and coming to terms with the intellectual challenge of Marxism'. Some (like Weber) 'adopted a recon-
structed or revised version of "Marxism"', while others (like Durkheim) 'sought to mediate between Marxism and other systems of
thought'.[21] I think this claim is wrong. First, it was not just Marxism
which played a key role in this respect but socialism more generally,
both reformist and revolutionary. Second, Marxism was influential
not just as an 'intellectual challenge' but also as an active political
challenge in the form of the rise of militant labour movements
toward the end of the nineteenth century. Third, there was another
fundamental intellectual and political challenge which occupied
Durkheim, Weber and others of their time – that deriving from
ultra-nationalistic conservatism.

By means of the third point, we can start to sort out the elements
of validity in the myth of the conservative origins of sociology. The
'conservatism' of Bonald and his contemporaries in France was first
and foremost a response to the aftermath of the events of 1789 and
the political philosophy that had inspired them. In France, throughout the nineteenth century, including the period at which Durkheim
came to maturity, social thought continued to be dominated by the
legacy of 1789, which was manifest in a succession of revolutionary
outbreaks culminating in the Paris Commune almost 100 years
later. The 1789 Revolution sent shock waves through the compla-
cency of ruling groups in Germany and Britain, and provided the
backdrop to Hegel's philosophy in the former country. But
although the fear of revolution (later, in Germany at least, concentrated against the spectre of Marxism) continued to haunt the dominant elites in those countries for decades, other trends of development separated them quite decisively from the French experience.
In Britain, the burgeoning of industrialism took place within the
context of a mutual accommodation and interpenetration of landed

aristocracy and ascendant commercial and industrial leaders that was unmatched elsewhere. This relatively even tenor of development, disturbed only briefly by Chartism, produced a society which gave rise neither to a large-scale socialist movement of a revolutionary kind nor to its counterpart, an aggressive theocratic or irrationalist conservatism. Nor, significantly, did that society produce a global sociology comparable with that of Durkheim, Weber and their contemporaries.

Spencer's formulation of the principles of sociology did not break significantly with utilitarianism, and the latter remained the dominant form of social theory in Britain throughout the nineteenth century. But, even in the guise of political economy, utilitarianism never enjoyed a similar pre-eminence in France and Germany. In the former it was overshadowed by the writings of the eighteenth-century *philosophes* and the reaction to them. In Germany the strongly historical and speculative bent in social philosophy and economics blunted its impact. 'Conservatism' in Germany meant primarily a nostalgic and romantic attachment to an idealised village community; its French counterpart, by contrast, was always linked to Catholicism and to the claims of embattled but militantly tenacious landowners, rentiers and independent peasantry. For German thinkers of Max Weber's generation the overwhelming problem was that of the antecedents and consequences of capitalism (analysed above all in terms of the destruction of traditionalism by technical rationalisation). In France, the comparable debate centred upon the fate of the ideals of individualism for which the revolution had been fought, in the face of the continuing assaults of the Catholic hierocracy.

Both conservatism and socialism thus figure in the political and intellectual backgrounds of Durkheim and Weber alike. In this regard, the work of each is an attempt *to rethink the foundations of liberalism in conditions in which liberal individualism and its base in social theory, namely, utilitarian philosophy developed in the British situation, were manifestly inappropriate*. But this very task helped to distance the main themes of their writings from one another. Weber worked against the backdrop not of a successful revolution (1789) but of a failed one (1848) and in the shadow of Bismarck's unification of the German state through military triumph. The rapid period of industrialisation from the top which ensued took place in social and political circumstances very different from those in France. Durkheim's *Division of Labour* and the theory of the state which he later elaborated were directed towards resolving the 'legacy of the Revolution' as he saw it: the distance between the ideals of freedom and equality heralded in 1789, and the reality of social stagnation and resistance to change epitomised by the disasters of the war of 1870 – the very war which sealed German unity – and by the repression of the Commune. Durkheim, like Weber, sought to borrow elements from socialism (and Marxian socialism was more prominent in Weber's intellectual horizon during the formative years of his career than in Durkheim's) and conservatism, but in order to transcend both.

In making these points, I do not want to fall into the sort of view, which I have already rejected, that sees the validity or usefulness of social theories as dependent upon the context in which they are produced, but simply to claim that such analysis helps us to understand more fully the theories and their distinctive qualities. The writings of the 1890–1920 generation *did* differ from much of what went before; but the elements which in a very general way exemplify the contrast do not accord either with Parsons's account or with the more naive versions of the great divide between social philosophy and social science. What, then, does distinguish the writings of the above-mentioned generation from what went before?

First, as I have already tried to show, an attempt to rethink the foundations of liberalism in the face of the twin challenge of revolutionary socialism and conservatism.

Second, the successful beginning of sociology as an accepted subject in the university curriculum (one should remember, however, that Durkheim first came to Paris as a professor of education and that Weber never occupied a chair whose title included 'sociology').

Third, a greatly heightened sensitivity to the study of other cultures and a breaking away from European ethnocentrism.

Fourth, and not unconnected with the third point, a general resurgence of concern with the sources of unreason in human social existence.

These factors helped to give the writings of Durkheim, Weber and some of their more prominent contemporaries an intellectual power well beyond those of most of their predecessors in social theory. But social science, as we know it today, was brought into being not primarily by the 1890–1920 generation but by that earlier generation of nineteenth-century thinkers among whom Marx, Comte and Spencer may be distinguished as most prominent. They, more than anyone else, gave modern social theory its impetus under the impact of the rise of physical science. Sociology was created as an apparently direct extension of the realm of natural science which, beginning with mathematics and classical dynamics, had via the theory of evolution progressed to the gates of the human world itself. Comte gave this vision its most immediate expression in his formula of the historical sequence of scientific development, whereby science begins as applied to phenomena most remote from human involvement and control but is brought ever nearer to human society, culminating in sociology, the science of human social conduct. The modern philosophy of science, stimulated by a revolution in that bastion of classical physics, Newtonian mechanics, has radically overturned the view of natural science which inspired the rise of sociology. The implications for social science have yet to be worked out. They constitute a background to the recent attempts of English-speaking authors to follow Scheler, Schutz and Sartre in trying to marry ideas drawn from phenomenology and hermeneutics to those current in the more orthodox traditions of sociology, together with a resurgence of interest in Marxism. From this apparent turmoil new forms of social theory are emerging. But what is crucial is that they should not be allowed to foster a *retreat from institutional analysis*: that is to say, an abandonment of the classic concern of social theory with issues of macroscopic social organisation and social change. For here lies the challenge to those who would undertake a rethinking of social theory today: to break with the classical traditions in a double way, substantively on the level of the theory of industrial society, and abstractly on the level of epistemology.

References

1. 'Four myths in the history of social thought', in *Studies in Social and Political Theory* (London: Hutchinson, 1977).
2. See, for example, Irving M. Zeitlin, *Ideology and the Development of Sociological Theory* (Englewood Cliffs, N.J.: Prentice-Hall, 1968).
3. 'Four myths in the history of social thought'.

4. Nisbet's *The Sociological Tradition* (London: Heinemann, 1967) emphasises the continuity of European social thought throughout the nineteenth and early twentieth centuries. See Parsons's review (*American Sociological Review*, vol. 32, 1967) of the work, in which Nisbet is taken to task on this point.

5. Talcott Parsons, *The Structure of Social Action* (New York: McGraw-Hill, 1937) p. 91.

6. It should be pointed out that Parsons also identified a second major trend in utilitarian theory, resting upon the postulate of a 'natural identity of interests' of human beings in society, associated with Locke rather than Hobbes; this later became of particular importance in classical economics.

7. For a more detailed discussion, see my *Capitalism and Modern Social Theory* (Cambridge: Cambridge University Press, 1971) pp. 65ff.

8. Emile Durkheim, *The Rules of Sociological Method* (London: Collier-Macmillan, 1964) pp. 122–4.

9. Durkheim, *The Division of Labour in Society* (London: Collier-Macmillan, 1964) pp. 41–4.

10. Interesting glosses on this appear in Durkheim's discussion of the development of educational systems in Europe from the Middle Ages to modern times. See Durkheim, *L'Evolution pédagogique en France* (Paris: Presses Universitaires, 1969).

11. F. A. von Hayek, *The Counter-Revolution of Science* (New York: Free Press, 1964); Albert Salomon, *The Tyranny of Progress* (New York: Noonday Press, 1955); Nisbet, *The Sociological Tradition*.

12. See Marion M. Mitchell, 'Emile Durkheim and the philosophy of nationalism', *Political Science Quarterly*, vol. 46, 1931.

13. Cf. the bitter attack upon Durkheim in Simon Deploige, *Le conflit de la morale et de la sociologie* (Louvain: Institut Supérieur de Philosophie, 1911).

14. Nisbet, *The Sociological Tradition*, p. 25.

15. See Steven Lukes, *Emile Durkheim: His Life and Work* (London: Allen Lane, 1973) pp. 86–95.

16. Durkheim, 'L'individualisme et les intellectuels', *Revue Bleue*, vol. 10, 1898, pp. 7–8.

17. Cf. Wolfgang J. Mommsen, *Max Weber und die deutsche Politik, 1898–1920* (Tubingen: Mühr, 1959).

18. Ralf Dahrendorf, *Class and Class Conflict in Industrial Society* (Stanford: Stanford University Press, 1959). Another version of this idea appears in Alan Dawe, 'The two sociologies', *British Journal of Sociology*, vol. 21, 1970.

19. John Horton, 'The dehumanisation of anomie and alienation', *British Journal of Sociology*, vol. 71, 1966.

20. Parsons, *The Structure of Social Action*, p. 91.

21. Zeitlin, *Ideology and the Development of Sociological Theory*, p. 321.

5

The High Priest of Positivism: Auguste Comte

There can be few works whose form and style seem to contrast as radically with its author's temperament and experiences during its writing as Comte's *Cours de philosophie positive*. The first volume of the *Cours* was written in 1830; Comte completed five more in just over a decade subsequent to that date. The six volumes offer an encyclopedic conspectus of the development of the sciences, beginning with mathematics, moving through physics, chemistry and biology, and culminating, in the final three works, in an exposition of the nascent science of 'social physics'.

The tone of the work is sober, its style ponderous, its theme the evolution of social and intellectual order. Its author, however, the erstwhile protégé of Saint-Simon, led a life only slightly less bizarre and disrupted than that of his mentor. From 1817 Comte worked in close but increasingly acrimonious association with Saint-Simon, which ended in a public quarrel in 1824 (producing a chronic controversy over the true originality of Comte's *Cours*, which he claimed owed nothing to that 'depraved juggler' Saint-Simon). The history of Comte's life from that date onwards was one of bitter wrangling with a succession of other scholars, a despairing and frustrated search for academic employment and academic recognition in France, punctuated by periods of madness. He met and married a woman who had previously been on the official police register as a prostitute; at the ceremony, which Comte's mother insisted he undertake, an attendant from the psychiatric hospital was on guard, and the groom harangued the priest throughout the ritual. The union was from the beginning a strained one, with intermittent separations and a final parting in 1824; Comte's violent rages were not infrequently vented physically against his wife.

None of this emotional misery emerges in the *Cours*, which is a testament to the equilibrium of nature and of society. It is unquestionably one of the greatest works of the period, helping to place Comte alongside Marx as a dominant figure in nineteenth-century social thought. From their influence come the two opposed yet intermingled traditions that to the present day serve as a continuing focus of debate in the social sciences. Comte's writings, as filtered through those of Durkheim a generation later, connect directly with modern functionalism, until quite recently the leading perspective in orthodox sociology, anthropology and political theory; Marxism has long served as the main vehicle of critical opposition to this orthodoxy. However fundamental their differences, Comte and Marx shared the preoccupations of the nineteenth century with the crises unleashed by political revolution and the advent of industrialism; and each looked to the triumphs of natural science in seeking to develop the social understanding that would allow human beings successfully to harness the forces thus released to their own self-betterment. For Comte and Marx alike, the development of such self-understanding appears as a logical extension of the success of natural science, in which the demystifying of the physical world for the first time makes possible, and indeed necessary, a scientific understanding of the sources of human conduct itself.

Comte's 'hierarchy of the sciences', documented in massive detail in his *Cours*, expressed this in much blunter fashion than anything that appears in Marx. The relation between the sciences is shown to be hierarchical in both an analytical and a historical sense, the latter being explained in terms of the famous 'law of the three stages' of intellectual development. Analytically, Comte makes clear, the sciences form a hierarchy of decreasing generality but increasing complexity; each science logically depends upon the ones below it in the hierarchy, and yet at the same time deals with an emergent order of properties that cannot be reduced to those with which the other sciences are concerned. Thus biology, for example, presupposes the laws of physics and chemistry in so far as all organisms are physical entities which obey the laws governing the composition of matter; on the other hand, the behaviour of organisms, as complex beings, cannot be simply and directly derived from those laws.

The logical relation between the sciences, according to Comte, helps us to understand their progressive formation as separate disciplines in the intellectual evolution of human kind. The sciences which develop first – mathematics and then physics – are those dealing with the most general laws in nature, that govern phenomena most removed from human involvement and control. From there, science penetrates more and more closely to man, producing finally in social physics a science of human conduct itself. The process is not achieved without struggle; scientific understanding lies at the end of the progression of intellectual life through the theological and metaphysical stages which characterise all branches of thought. The 'theological stage', in which the universe is comprehended as determined by the agency of spiritual beings, reaches its apex in Christianity with its recognition of one all-powerful deity: this stage, 'l'état fictif' as Comte calls it, is 'le point de départ nécessaire de l'intelligence humaine'.

The metaphysical phase replaces those moving spirits with abstract forces and entities, thereby clearing the ground for the advent of science, 'l'état fixe et définitif' of human thought. The enunciation of the law of the three stages, Comte says, is enough 'pour que la justesse en soit immédiatement vérifiée par tous ceux qui ont quelque connaissance approfondie de l'histoire générale des sciences'. (Comte later claimed to have achieved personal verification of the law of the three stages in his periods of insanity, which he had experienced, he said, as a regression back through from positivism to metaphysics to theology on the level of his own personality, in his recovery retracting these stages forwards again.)

The task of the *Cours* is not only to analyse the transmutation of human thought by science, but essentially to *complete* it. For, Comte made clear, man's understanding of himself is still in its pre-scientific phase:

> Tout se réduit donc à un simple question de fait: la philosophie positive, qui, dans les deux derniers siècles a pris graduellement une si grande extension, embrasse-t-elle aujourd'hui tous les ordres de phénomènes? Il est évident que cela n'est point, et que, par conséquent, il reste encore une grande opération scientifique à exécuter pour donner à la philosophie positive ce caractère d'universalité indispensable à sa constitution définitive . . . Maintenant que l'esprit humain a fondé la physique céleste, la physique terrestre, soit mécanique, soit chimique; la physique organique, soit végétale, soit animale, il lui reste à terminer le système des sciences en fondant la *physique sociale*. Tel est

aujourd'hui sous plusieurs rapports capitaux, le plus grand et le plus pressant besoin de notre intelligence.

Social physics was above all to be directed to practical ends. If it is true that the strange extravagances of the immanent social future envisaged in the *Système de politique positive* are absent from Comte's earlier work, it is still the case that the main elements of his political programme already appear there. These are stated with greater clarity, in fact, in the *Cours* than they are in the later work. The overriding theme is the necessity of reconciling order and progress. As Comte saw it, his insistence on the conjunction of these two social conditions separated positive philosophy from both the 'revolutionary metaphysics' that had provided the inspiration for the events of 1789, and the political theory of the 'retrograde school' of Catholic conservatism, which had been formed as a reaction against the turmoil ensuing from the Revolution. The latter school wanted order, but was against progress; the former sought progress at the expense of order. As a consequence, Comte argued, the two ideas seem disconnected, even antithetical:

> On ne peut se dissimuler qu'un esprit essentiellement rétrograde a constamment dirigé toutes les grandes tentatives en faveur de l'ordre, et que les principaux efforts entrepris pour le progrès ont toujours été conduits par les doctrines radicalement anarchiques.

For the 'order' desired by the Catholic apologists was nothing but a reversion to feudal hierocracy; while the 'progress' aspired to by the revolutionaries was nothing less than a subversion of any form of government as such. The sort of society which Comte foresaw as guaranteeing both order and progress none the less placed a heavy enough emphasis upon the sorts of features that bulk large in the works of the 'retrograde school' – moral consensus, authority, and an antagonism to the 'chimera of equality' – even if stripped of their specific association with Catholicism.

The man who coined the neologism 'positive philosophy' also introduced that of 'sociology' – abandoning 'social physics' in order to separate his own enterprise from that of Quételet, who had independently applied the term to his studies of social statistics, which Comte looked upon with some scorn. In envisaging sociology as a science of society which would make possible the same kind of control over the social world that had been achieved over the material world, Comte portrayed the new science as a natural outgrowth of the progression of human rationalism. His most important precursors in the formation of sociology, according to Comte, were Montesquieu and Condorcet. The distinctive contribution of the works of these authors, Comte asserted, is the emphasis on social life as 'aussi nécessairement assujettis à d'invariables lois naturelles que tous les autres phénomènes quelconques'. For Comte, recognition that social phenomena are subject to the operation of invariable laws is not at all incompatible with freedom of action or moral dignity: for the first depends on discovering and utilising social laws, while the second is enhanced by the authority of rational self-knowledge, freeing men from 'l'automatisme social, passivement dirigé par la suprématie absolue et arbitraire, soit de la Providence, soit du législateur humain'.

Notwithstanding his lack of immediate influence in France (a bibliography published in 1828 by Quérard listed him as having died the year before), Comte did achieve a considerable following for positivism overseas, in other European countries, the USA and Latin America. In Britain, the *Cours* acquired a notable admirer in John Stuart Mill. Many such followers were alienated, however, by the drift of Comte's thought in the later part of his career, as expressed in his *Système de politique positive*, which appeared over the years from 1851 to 1854, and which Mill called 'this melancholy decadence of a great intellect'. If the *Cours* bore little of the imprint of Comte's personal life, the subsequent work was expressly intertwined with it in a way which Comte's rationalistic disciples found both shocking and vulgar. Following his final separation from his wife, Comte formed an attachment to Clothilde de Vaux, a young woman deserted by her husband; after she died of consumption Comte gave over the rest of his life to a worship of her memory. The cool rationalism of the *Cours* gave way to a passionate advocacy of the Religion of Humanity, the Church of Positivism, whose rituals were elaborately set out by its appointed High Priest.

As a social movement, which Comte had all along sought to make it, positivism died with the withering of the groups of followers who remained to celebrate the Festival of Humanity held in London in 1881. The influence of Comte's writings, however, derives not from their practical issue but, so far as modern social science is concerned, from their reworking in Durkheim's version of sociological method. Durkheim had little use for the grandiosity of Comte's later pronouncements; but he was much influenced by the earlier. Durkheim held more or less the same view of Comte as the latter expressed of Montesquieu and Condorcet: that while Comte had set out an acceptable general plan for establishing a science of society, he had failed to advance very far in putting that plan into practice. As Mill remarked: 'M. Comte, at bottom, was not so solicitous about completeness of proof as becomes a positive philosopher.' The 'law of the three stages', according to Durkheim, is proclaimed as by fiat, not corroborated empirically; and Comte's writings are still embroiled in that very style of philosophy of history that Comte claimed to have transcended.

This having been said, in setting out his own methodological scheme for sociology, Durkheim drew heavily upon Comte's *Cours*, and several of the major emphases in the latter reappear in *The Rules of Sociological Method*: the plea for a 'natural science of society', and the insistence that 'social facts' can be studied with the same objectivity as occurrences in nature; the differentiation of functional from historical analysis which, as a distinction between 'statics' and 'dynamics', plays such a basic role in the *Cours*; and even the belief that the science of sociology can rationally distinguish what contributes to moral order and is thereby socially 'healthy', from that which is disintegrative and 'pathological'.

Comte invented the term 'positive philosophy' as a direct counterweight to the 'negative' criticism fostered by revolutionary political theory. In the *Cours*, the lengthy analysis of the development of the sciences is presented as a necessary preamble to his practical programme via the thesis that the progressive yet orderly evolution of science provides a model for a parallel evolution of society as a whole. What would Comte say to the modern philosophy of science which, in the writings of Bachelard, Kuhn and others, has supplanted evolution with revolution in the very heart of natural science itself? The transformation is a profound one, but aptly expresses the distance of the contemporary world both from that which Comte knew and that which he confidently foresaw for the future.

It would not be correct to rank Comte among the more ingenuously optimistic philosophers of progress in the nineteenth century: he was too much preoccupied with the possibility of 'moral anarchy' for that. Comte's *Cours* is none the less a monumental declaration of faith in science, in each of several respects: as providing a moral philosophy that would supplant that of feudalism without dissolving the moral order altogether; as supplying the only possible criteria of truth, measured against which those claimed by religion and metaphysics appear as mere sham; and as providing the singular means in the form of social science whereby both human beings understand and rationally control the conditions of their own existence.

In the present day, none of these remain feasible, as Comte held them. We might well still agree that science, or at any rate the rationalising influences among which science ranks as pre-eminent, dissolve traditional forms of religion and morality. But few would maintain any longer that, in and of itself, science can generate a moral ethos that is able to replace what has been destroyed: an expanded scientific understanding of the world has not produced the solutions to the moral crisis that Comte diagnosed. Positivism, in the sense relevant to the second claim, reached its apogee in the twentieth century in the writings of the Vienna Circle in the 1920s and 1930s. But in this radical form it was short-lived; since that time positivism in philosophy has been increasingly on the defensive, so much so indeed that the term itself has become almost one of abuse.

For both Comte and Durkheim (as well as for Marx) sociology was conceived on a par with the natural sciences, as *revelatory* or demystifying. Sociology is to strip away the illusions and habitual prejudices that have prevented human beings from understanding the sources of their own behaviour, just as the progress of natural science has eradicated such illusions about the physical world. But this is itself an illusion, in the way in which it was formulated by Comte and Durkheim at any rate – and, indeed, as it continues to survive within sociology today. This is not only because the sort of 'invariant laws', whose discovery Comte anticipated, and of which he believed his law of the three stages to be one, have not come to light in sociology, damaging as this surely is for the programme that he mapped out for the positive science of society.

The point is that sociology stands in a different relation to the 'prejudices' of habit or common sense than the natural sciences. To the natural scientist, lay beliefs about nature may or may not be correct: no particular consequence follows, and all common sense is in principle corrigible in the light of the progress of scientific knowledge. Lay resistance to the findings of the natural sciences, where it occurs, takes the form of a rejection of claims which undermine cherished beliefs – e.g. that the sun moves round the earth rather than vice versa. But if this is not unknown in sociology, another lay response is at least equally common: the 'findings' of the social sciences are regarded with suspicion not because they question common-sense beliefs, but on the contrary because they only reiterate, in pretentiously technical language, what everyone already knows anyway. What finds no place in Comte's version of a natural science of society, and others subsequently influenced by him or advocating the same type of standpoint, is that, even without the assistance of sociology, human beings are already the creators of their social world, knowledgeable agents whose skills in making sense of the conduct of others are an integral element of the existence of society as such. The conditions under which sociological research can play a revelatory role are more difficult to establish than in the case of natural science, and cannot be appreciated at all within any account of the logic of social science such as that offered in the intellectual tradition stemming from Comte and Durkheim. It is a mark of its influence that modes of social theorising in which human beings are presented merely as objects to themselves, as merely acted upon, should have survive so long.

6

Schutz and Parsons: Problems of Meaning and Subjectivity

Even the severest critic of Talcott Parsons must recognise the extraordinary nature of his contributions to social theory over a period of half a century. More than any other single scholar, Parsons has been responsible for introducing an Anglo-Saxon sociological audience to a sophisticated reading of the works of Durkheim and Max Weber – in addition to translating important segments of Weber's writings. Parsons early on developed a critical stance towards positivism (in a certain sense of that term, at least) and behaviourism, and has always taken a firm stand against antitheoretical tendencies in American sociology. He has produced a continuing flow of empirically orientated contributions himself, while never deviating from an overall strategy of developing a systematic framework of social theory. This framework was first of all outlined in *The Structure of Social Action*, originally published in 1937. There are many (including myself) who would regard this formidably long and dense volume as a greater achievement than any other single work or essay collection that Parsons has published subsequently.

The Structure of Social Action was the fruit of study in Europe, and was evidently more steeped in European traditions of thought than in American ones: Parsons has since acknowledged the overlap of some central themes of the book with the ideas of Mead, Cooley and other American social thinkers. He has also pointed to the need for an extensive discussion of Freud, which he would have incorporated into the book had he written it at a later period. But to those who have also been trained in the European traditions from which Parsons drew, there are lacunae in *The Structure of Social Action* at least as marked as any of these. One is the lack of a sustained confrontation with Marx and Marxism: only a few pages in the book are devoted to Marx, and historical materialism is dismissed as 'essentially utilitarian, with the addition of the historical element'.[1] Another is the absence of a discussion of phenomenology. Husserl is mentioned, but only in passing. Heidegger is not referred to either in the text or in the bibliography. There is one work strongly influenced by a version of phenomenology mentioned in the bibliography, although it is not referred to in the text: Schutz's *Der sinnhafte Aufbau der sozialen Welt* (1932), which is listed under 'secondary sources' relevant to the study of Max Weber.

Schutz read *The Structure of Social Action*, when it appeared, with much more attention and excitement than his own work had awoken in Parsons, as the exchange of letters between the two reveals.[2] Parsons read Schutz's book, he says, 'shortly after it appeared', but 'did not find it of primary significance' for the issues he was working on in his researches for *The Structure of Social Action*. Schutz acquired a copy of Parsons's book early in 1938 and 'realised immediately the importance and value' of the system of thought which it outlined. The events which led to the exchange of a series of letters, and a meeting between Parsons and Schutz, were then set under way. Previous to coming into contact with Parsons's work, Schutz had been invited by Hayek, who was then editor of *Economica*, to contribute a paper on his phenomenological sociology to the journal. Before beginning to write the paper, Schutz received and read Parsons's book; he then proposed to Hayek to include a discussion of Parsons's ideas in his paper, a proposal to which Hayek agreed. In the following year, Schutz spent the summer months studying Parsons's book 'again and again', finding 'new and interesting points of convergence with and divergence from my own thoughts'. The result was an article much longer than had been originally planned, consisting of 25,000 words rather than the 5,000 which Schutz had originally projected. Because of the expanded nature of his discussion, and because he still found some obscurities in Parsons's work, Schutz decided to send the paper to Parsons for his comments. The result was an interchange of some dozen letters between the two, from October 1940 to April 1941. The volume which collects these together includes Schutz's paper, and also a retrospective look at the debate by Parsons, written in 1974.[3]

The letters are as interesting for their absences, as the French would say, as for their manifest content. They were written when

Schutz was a newly arrived refugee in the USA in the early years of the Second World War. The only reference to the cataclysmic events in Europe, however, is in one of Parsons's letters, where Roosevelt's attitude towards the war and the possibility of decisive German victory is mentioned but only to illustrate a point on scientific truth. The letters are dry, humourless, and formal, but there are strong underlying emotional currents in them. The tone of Schutz's correspondence is unfailingly polite, even deferential, constantly emphasising the importance of Parsons's work. Parsons's replies, by contrast, are uncompromising and blunt. Schutz, he says, displays a 'complete failure to think in terms of the logic of theoretical systems'. He has, according to Parsons, 'seriously misunderstood my position': many of the things Schutz says may be plausible in their own right, but as criticisms of Parsons's work 'they are, in my opinion, overwhelmingly either wrong or irrelevant'. The exchange of letters terminates in an intellectual impasse, but also takes on a tone of slight bitterness. Schutz's reply to Parsons's defence of his point of view is one of rather hurt reproach. He sent his paper to Parsons, he says, only as a draft, in order to elicit Parsons's comments, and in the belief that most of his ideas were complementary to Parsons's own. But Parsons 'interpreted it exclusively as a criticism' of his work and, Schutz felt, rejected it in its entirety. Parsons replied in a conciliatory way, agreeing that his critical remarks 'were rather sharply formulated', but adding 'I did not in the least intend them to be derogatory but only to state my own position as clearly as I possibly could'. A short reply from Schutz, expressing relief that 'our "antagonism" in certain scientific questions' might 'have also affected our personal relations', terminated the exchange. In a letter written to Schutz's widow in 1971, in which Parsons gave his consent for publication of the Schutz–Parsons letters, he admits that he may have been 'unduly defensive' in his attitude towards Schutz's paper. *The Structure of Social Action*, Parsons says, 'had been unfairly criticised in a number of different quarters', and he accepts in hindsight that he might have been 'especially sensitive to critique coming from the German language, in which through my work on Max Weber I had become immersed'.

Why were Schutz and Parsons unable to forge a closer communication than they managed to do? A superficial, although not entirely irrelevant, answer would be that – at the time of the correspondence at any rate – Parsons had not read Schutz's work with the detailed attention which Schutz had devoted to Parsons's. In the 1974 postscript to the letters, Parsons seemingly accords recognition to the significance of the problems Schutz raised thirty years before. But he gives much more emphasis to the development and elaboration of his own writings over the period than he does to the centrality of the points Schutz attempted to bring to the fore. To my mind there are three major areas of disagreement between Parsons and Schutz that tend to differentiate the views of the two authors. One is the relevance of philosophy, or more especially epistemology, to the construction of theory in the social sciences. Another, not entirely dissociated issue is that of the status of 'science' in relation to the constitution of the life-world, or the 'natural attitude' – a major preoccupation of Schutz's existential phenomenology. A third basic question raised by the Schutz–Parsons correspondence concerns the nature of 'human action' itself, in relation to the temporal flow of human conduct and to its purposive character.

I fully agree with Maurice Natanson's judgement, expressed in his foreword written to introduce the Schutz–Parsons exchange, that 'its dominant albeit reluctant theme is the relationship between philosophy and social science'. Parsons wrote *The Structure of Social Action* in some part as a critique of positivism, but none the less he interpreted 'positivism' in the book in a somewhat idiosyncratic way. The positivism he set out to criticise was that involved in what he called 'the positivistic theory of action'.[4] Such a theory, according to Parsons, is one that involves 'the view that positive science constitutes man's sole possible significant cognitive relation to external (non ego) reality'.[5] The 'relation' involved here is that of the social actor with the surrounding world, not that of the social scientist or sociological observer. Parsons's critique of the 'positivistic theory of action' did not go far enough: his work, Schutz thought, lacks 'a radical analysis of social intersubjectivity', and fails sufficiently to differentiate the attitude of science from that of the practical actor in the life-world. For Schutz there is a considerably more pronounced discontinuity than there is for Parsons between the 'rationality' of science (natural or social) and the 'rationality' of day-to-day conduct, which is geared to different relevances or interests than those which concern the scientist.

Parsons's criticisms of the 'positivistic' conception that social actors behave like scientists led him to emphasise the normative character of action – an emphasis that continued through all the subsequent development of Parsons's system of social thought. The main defect of this conception in Parsons's view concerns its inability to account for the ends of action. For Schutz, on the other hand, to treat the social actor as like a scientist is to fail to grasp the creative and knowledgeable character of the constitution of society by its component members. This is precisely the insight later seized upon by Garfinkel, who effectively radicalised Schutz's contrast of 'rationalities' even further than Schutz himself did.[6] It is a point of some considerable importance in respect of the theory of action. As Schutz pointed out in his assessment of *The Structure of Social Action*, the whole weight of Parsons's analysis of action turns on the significance of norms or values in connecting 'voluntarism' to the resolution of 'the problem of order'. But this is a deficient conception in so far as it allocates little or no conceptual space for actors' 'rational' understanding of the social world they constitute and reconstitute in their activities. An understanding of human action, according to Schutz, must grasp the continuity of projects unfolding in time, in the context of various layers of relevances.

On each of the three points I have mentioned, I should personally be more on the side of Schutz than that of Parsons. At the same time I have to confess that the Schutz–Parsons correspondence is neither particularly compelling nor illuminating. Schutz's criticisms of *The Structure of Social Action* are not especially penetrating, and his presentation of his own views does not depart in any way from those familiar from the *Aufbau* and other of his writings. Parsons's responses to Schutz mainly just reaffirm views set out in *The Structure of Social Action*. Although I agree more with Schutz than with Parsons in regard to the three main problem-areas over which they diverged, I do not think Schutz's own position is at all satisfactory in respect to any of these. Schutz's epistemology is deficient in so far as he largely side-stepped, rather than resolved, the fundamental question left unanswered by Husserl: how intersubjectivity is to be derived phenomenologically from the experience of the ego. His discussions of rationality and of science are defective in several ways. He never satisfactorily resolved what the logical status of the rationality of everyday conduct is, as compared with the rationality of science; his conception of social science, as involving only the relevances of the 'disinterested observer', is open to numerous objections. Finally, Schutz's conceptualisation of social action –

although it is in my opinion superior to that of Parsons in treating human beings as skilled, knowledgeable agents – has serious weaknesses. Here, perhaps, we can reunite our two protagonists; for Schutz's social world, like that of Parsons's, is largely a consensual one. In this regard, both Schutz's and Parsons's portrayals of social life depart in a substantial way from that of the author whose conception of action influenced each of them: Max Weber.

References

1. Talcott Parsons, *The Structure of Social Action* (New York: Free Press, 1949) p. 493.
2. Richard Grathoff, *The Theory of Social Action: The Correspondence of Alfred Schutz and Talcott Parsons* (Bloomington: Indiana University Press, 1978).
3. Ibid.
4. Parsons, *The Structure of Social Action*, pp. 60–9. Parsons also discusses 'empiricism' on pages 69–72. Again he defines this in an unusual, and somewhat obscure way, as 'a system of theory when it is claimed, explicitly or implicitly, that the categories of the given theoretical system are by themselves adequate to explain all the scientifically important(?) facts about the body of concrete phenomena to which it is applied' (pp. 69–70). This conception seems to be influenced by Parsons's indebtedness to A. N. Whitehead, especially in respect to the so-called 'fallacy of misplaced concreteness'.
5. Ibid, p. 61.
6. Harold Garfinkel, *Studies in Ethnomethodology* (Englewood Cliffs, N.J.: Prentice-Hall, 1967).

7

Habermas's Social and Political Theory

Jürgen Habermas is the most distinguished, and perhaps by that token also the most controversial, social theorist and political philosopher writing in German today.[1] In the English-speaking world, to adopt a well-worn phrase, Habermas's works are well known, but they are not yet known well. In some part this is because of vagaries of translation. Four of Habermas's major writings have been translated into English under the titles of *Toward a Rational Society,*[2] *Knowledge and Human Interests,*[3] *Theory and Practice,*[4] and *Legitimation Crisis*. These, however, represent only part of a vast output, and they have not been published in a chronology which conforms directly to the development of Habermas's ideas. The original version of *Theorie und Praxis*, for example, was published in 1962, some years before *Erkenntnis und Interesse* (*Knowledge and Human Interests*), but these have appeared in reverse order in English. A more important reason for the relative lack of impact that Habermas's work has had among English-speaking social scientists is that he writes from the context of unfamiliar intellectual traditions: those of Frankfurt critical theory, hermeneutics, and Hegelian philosophy, as well as Marxism. To attempt a mix of all these sounds formidable enough, but Habermas's compass in fact extends much more widely. He is very familiar with the dominant trends in Anglo-Saxon social theory and philosophy and is considerably indebted to the latter in two particular respects. In the earlier part of his career, in conjunction with K.-O. Apel, he drew extensively upon the writings of Peirce; in his current work he makes a good deal of use of the theory of speech-acts, as developed by Austin, Searle and others. The extraordinary range of Habermas's writings defies easy analysis. In this review essay I shall concentrate my attention upon the works available in English but shall attempt to connect them to the overall development of Habermas's thought.

Two leading, and massive, themes recur throughout Habermas's writings and give his works their continuity. One is a concern with metatheoretical problems in social theory, especially in respect of the relation between theory and critique. The other is the objective of placing such a critique in the context of an interpretation of the main trends of development in Western capitalism since the rise of bourgeois society in eighteenth-century Europe. These were of course also the classic preoccupations of the 'older generation' of Frankfurt social philosophers, and Habermas's work preserves certain of their emphases. His reading of Marx, like theirs, strongly accentuates the Hegelian legacy, and he is highly critical of the more orthodox forms of Marxism; he tries to complement ideas drawn from Marx with others drawn from Freud; he accepts the theorem that 'organised capitalism' differs so profoundly from nineteenth-century competitive capitalism that some of Marx's central theories have to be radically reworked if they are to retain any relevance today; and he continues their concern with revealing the origins of the dominance of technical rationality in modern culture and politics. But these shared emphases at the same time serve to distinguish his views from the various positions taken by Horkheimer, Adorno and Marcuse, because the modes in which he develops this inheritance differ substantially from those of his legators.

A useful way of achieving an entrée into Habermas's metatheoretical writings is via his relation to the hermeneutic tradition or the *Geisteswissenschaften*.[5] Some of the ideas central to this tradition, especially the notion of *verstehen*, have become well known to English-speaking social scientists – principally through the methodological writings of Max Weber, who drew extensively although critically from this intellectual source. In Weber's writings, as in those of the early Dilthey, *verstehen* is linked to the reconstruction of the subjective experience of others, the grasping of the 'subjective meaning' of action, as Weber put it. Expressed in this way, the notion of *verstehen* gives rise to numerous objections, especially since both Dilthey and Weber wished to claim that the method of interpretative understanding is compatible with the achievement of objectively verifiable data. The 'psychological' version of *verstehen* has been effectively criticised and transcended by Gadamer in his *Truth and Method*.[6] Drawing extensively upon Heidegger, Gadamer develops a notion of *verstehen* in which understanding is seen not as a 'method' which the historian or social scientist uses to approach his or her distinctive subject-matter but as the characteristic property of human intersubjectivity as such – and as expressed above all in language. Language is the medium of social being and of self-understanding. *Verstehen* depends upon common membership in a cultural frame of meaning or what Gadamer calls a 'tradition'. The understanding of distant historical periods, or alien cultures, can be treated as involving the establishing of dialogue between discrepant traditions. Hermeneutics, Gadamer concludes, is the universal principle of philosophy, since understanding is the condition of all knowledge. Habermas accepts some of Gadamer's main ideas but sees them as partial, rejecting the latter's claim of the 'universality of hermeneutics'. Habermas opens his systematic discussion of logical issues in the social sciences, *Zur Logik der Sozialwissenschaften* (1967), with the suggestion that the major problem which has to be tackled is that of connecting two disparate philosophies which have largely developed in separation from one another: hermeneutics on the one hand, and empiricist philosophies of science on the other. Certain elements of each have to be accepted, but in order to supersede both.

The arguments underlying this view are fully developed and clarified in *Knowledge and Human Interests*, which culminates the first phase of Habermas's career and remains perhaps the most hotly debated of his works. *Knowledge and Human Interests* covers a sweep of intellectual history from the late eighteenth century to the early nineteenth. In the beginning sections of the book, Habermas discusses Hegel's critique of Kant's philosophy of knowledge and Marx's critique of Hegel, proceeding thence to discuss hermeneutics and positivism as two contrasting types of philosophy, exemplified by Comte and Mach, and by Dilthey, respectively. The line of development from Kant to Hegel to Marx forms a key period in the elaboration of epistemology or the 'theory of knowledge'. Hegel's writings mark a high point in the development of epistemology in so far as they make central the self-reflection of the knowing subject. Marx was correct, Habermas proposes, in holding that Hegel's philosophy was inherently limited by its idealism; but in attempting to formulate a materialist critique of Hegel, Marx himself slips into a basic error. What Marx does is to tend to assimilate two strands of Hegel's philosophy in his own conception of historical materialism:

the self-reflection of the subject and the material transformation of the world through labour. The thesis that history is the expression of the expanding consciousness of human beings of the circumstances of their action is thus merged with, and reduced to, the theme that human beings transform the material world and themselves through labour. Habermas also sets out this argument at various points in *Theory and Practice*, especially in the context of a lengthy discussion of Marxism in the chapter entitled 'Between philosophy and science: Marxism as critique'. To the degree to which Marx col-- lapses the idea of the self-formation of the human species through reflection into that of its self-formation through productive activity, Marxism merges with the rising tide of positivistic philosophy which dominates the latter part of the nineteenth century. Positivism is a philosophy which eclipses the philosopher: that is, the subject reflex-ively investigating the grounds of his or her claims to knowledge. Epistemology, as Habermas puts it, is replaced by the philosophy of science, based on 'the conviction that we can no longer understand science as *one* form of possible knowledge, but must rather identify knowledge with science' (*Knowledge and Human Interests*, p. 4).

The tradition of the *Geisteswissenschaften*, Habermas goes on to say, offers a contrasting viewpoint to positivism, but dissociates itself from the latter rather than developing a direct critique of it. Hermeneutics becomes concerned with the primacy of meaningful understanding, but only in spheres of activity disconnected from science. Hermeneutics and positivism are thus both partial philo-sophies, flawed by their incomplete character. A viewpoint that attempts to transcend both, which it is Habermas's aim to set out, has to recognise that they are (unknowingly) directed to different types of 'knowledge-constitutive interest': different logical forms which the disclosure of reality can take, whether this be natural or social reality. Hermeneutics is orientated towards an interest in understanding, at the level of ordinary language communication, in the context of the practicalities of day-to-day social life. Positivism, on the other hand, implicitly assumes an orientation to an interest in prediction and control in the production of instrumental or 'techni-cally exploitable' knowledge – mistakenly claiming that all know-ledge which is to *count* as knowledge is of this type. The knowledge-constitutive interests in understanding and in technical control are not, for Habermas, transcendental categories of a quasi-Kantian type; rather, they are presupposed as aspects of the human self-formative process. They thus connect to two major concepts that Habermas introduces which occupy a central place in his thought: 'interaction' and 'labour' (*Arbeit*). Labour, or 'instrumental action', is based upon empirical knowledge, yielding predictions that can be tested in accordance with technical rules (*Toward a Rational Society*, pp. 91–2). It is the object of what Habermas calls the 'empirical-analytical sciences' to develop knowledge which can be used instrumentally, to realise an interest in the prediction and control of events. The empirical-analytical sciences include not only the natural sciences but also the generalising social sciences, such as sociology. (Habermas also sometimes refers to these as the 'nomological sciences'.) Interaction refers to the saturated context of everyday life, involving ordinary language communication and governed by social norms. This is the concern of the 'historical-hermeneutic sciences'. Hermeneutic inquiry, in Habermas's words, 'discloses reality subject to a constitutive interest in the preservation and expansion of the intersubjectivity of possible action-orienting mutual understanding' (*Knowledge and Human Interests*, p. 310).

In *Knowledge and Human Interests*, Habermas identifies Dilthey and Peirce as the two figures who came closest to uncovering the roots of knowledge in interest, in regard of hermeneutics and natural science, respectively. But, as a result of the decay of epistemology in the nineteenth century, neither was able to connect his insights to a conception of the self-formative process of human history, such as had earlier been attempted by Hegel. In the context of the spreading influence of positivism, a return to this type of conception would have appeared as a regression to metaphysics. But such a reappropriation is just what is necessary for us to be able to grasp the significance of knowledge-constitutive interests: that is to say, a reappropriation of the notion of the reflexive capability of human knowledge. What has become lost to philosophy since Hegel is 'the emancipatory power of reflection, which the subject experiences in itself to the extent that it becomes transparent to itself in the history of its genesis' (*Knowledge and Human Interests*, p. 197). Recognition of an interest in reflexively comprehending the conditions of our own action is thus shown to be the condition of acknowledging the interest-bound character of knowledge in general. Self-reflection is connected to the interest in achieving autonomy of action through self-understanding, and hence is an emancipatory interest. The emancipatory interest provides the guiding inspiration for critical philosophy, or critical theory, which has as its aim the liberation of human beings from their domination by forces constraining their rational autonomy of action. In Habermas's meta-theoretical scheme, we thus have three elements of the self-formative process (labour, interaction, domination), connected to three knowledge-constitutive interests (technical control, understanding, emancipation), relating in turn to three types of disciplines (the empirical-analytic sciences, historical-hermeneutic sciences and critical theory).

At the turn of the twentieth century, there emerged a programme of research which mobilises each of the knowledge-constitutive interests and which, therefore, in Habermas's view provides something of a model for critical theory: psychoanalysis. Freud himself regarded psychoanalysis in a positivistic way, as a form of natural science. Looked at in terms of the theory of knowledge, however, psychoanalysis can be seen to incorporate an emancipatory aim within a framework which relates the hermeneutic and the nomological. Psychoanalytic theory is a dialogue between therapist and patient, and in that sense proceeds on the level of ordinary language communication. It is a hermeneutic endeavour in the sense that it investigates the character of such communication as an expression of an unconscious symbol-system. But this 'depth hermeneutics' is complemented by an interest in the causal conditions influencing the behaviour of the analysand, via mechanisms of repression. Hence we find in Freud a mixture of terms that are interpretative in character with others that borrow the terminology of natural science, such as 'force', 'energy', etc. These are related to one another through the emancipatory project of analytic therapy: the elimination of distorted communication through the enhanced self-understanding of the analysand, whereby he or she is able to expand autonomy of action. The dialogue between analyst and patient simultaneously furthers the progress of emancipation and expresses it, since it makes possible the growth of mutual understanding between the two parties.

Habermas has pursued the theme of distorted communication in a series of writings, only some of which are available in English.[7] He has continued to defend, in the face of some considerable attack, the thesis that psychoanalysis provides an exemplar for critical theory. But a concern with distorted communication obviously presupposes an idea of what a situation of 'undistorted communication' might be like – a notion of what Habermas calls an 'ideal speech situation'. In some part this is already latent in *Knowledge and Human Interests*, and it seems that Habermas has drawn upon Peirce's account of science in formulating the conception of an ideal speech situation. Peirce argued that scientific truth concerns not the relation between an isolated observer and a subject-matter, but a consensus arrived at through the discourse of many observers, where that discourse is not constrained by anything other than the canons of logical procedure or rational argumentation. Habermas in effect generalises this, since Peirce's argument refers only to one aspect (instrumental rationality or the technical interest) of the three dimensions of the human self-formative process. An ideal speech situation – the 'baseline' against which distortions in empirical circumstances of social conduct can in principle be determined – involves not only the rational attainment of consensus but also complete mutual understanding by participants and recognition of the authentic right of each to participate in the dialogue as an autonomous and equal partner.

The ideal speech situation is an analytical construct but, Habermas argues, any actual circumstance of communication anticipates it implicitly. Communication in interaction, he has tried to show in his current discussions of 'universal pragmatics', raises four types of 'validity-claims': those of *Verständlichkeit* (intelligibility), *Wahrheit* (truth), *Richtigkeit* (adequacy or correctness), and *Wahrhaftigkeit* (veracity or 'truthfulness'). Consensual interaction can be carried on only to the degree that participants credibly sustain validity-claims in each of these respects (which are usually taken for granted but can always be 'problematised', either by those involved or by the sociological observer): that what each speaker says is intelligible or meaningful; that the propositional content of what each says is true; that what each says is normatively legitimate; and that each is speaking honestly and without guile. *Verständlichkeit*, Habermas proposes, is the condition of all symbolic communication whatsoever; it has a different status from the other validity-claims, since communication must be intelligible before the others can be problematised at all. *Wahrhaftigkeit* also has to be separated out in a certain sense, because genuineness of intention can only be really demonstrated in how a person actually behaves. The other two are open to discursive justification, yielding two major types or parameters of discourse: 'theoretical-empirical discourse', concerned with the sustaining of truth-claims, involving appeal to empirical observation, and couched in terms of law-like generalisation; and 'practical discourse', concerned with justifying normative claims, involving appeal to interpretations of values, and couched in terms of appeal to moral principles.

In his current writings, Habermas is attempting to relate the mastery of these two forms of discourse to the psychological development of the child (using Piaget and Kohlberg) and to the major stages of human social evolution. What will emerge from this work still remains to be seen. It is clear enough, however, that Habermas's current concern with these issues links directly not just to the metatheoretical problems I have sketched so far, but also to more substantive themes which have preoccupied him from the earliest part of his career onwards. In his first major work, *Struktur-wandel der Öffentlichkeit* (1962) Habermas undertook a historical study of the rise (and subsequent decline) of discursive politics in bourgeois society from the eighteenth century to the present day.[8] The book was much debated in Germany and had an important influence upon the student movement, although Habermas himself eventually came to a position of sharp dissension from the views of some of the student leaders.

A 'public sphere', in which political life can be discussed openly in accordance with standards of critical reason, Habermas tried to show in the study, emerges for the first time in the eighteenth century. 'Public opinion' becomes differentiated from mere 'opinion', prejudice, or habit: the former presupposes a reasoning public. The bourgeoisie promoted the development of the public sphere in opposition to the traditionalist and hierocratic forms of authority of feudalism. This development reflects the division between civil society and the state characteristic of the emerging bourgeois order: the formation of rational public opinion mediates between society and the state. The spread of newspapers and journals, which both express and help fashion public opinion, played a major role in this process. The bourgeois or liberal idea of the public sphere was always at some distance from reality, but has been more and more undermined as a consequence of the social changes which have occurred from the early part of the nineteenth century to the present day. Today state and society increasingly interpenetrate: the public sphere is squeezed or 'refeudalised' by the growth of large-scale organisations co-ordinated with government, and by the commercialisation of the media. The expanding influence of science, and more generally the technical rationalisation of social life, accentuate this process.

The impact of technocratic consciousness in advanced capitalism is discussed by Habermas in several of the essays included in the English editions of *Theory and Practice* and in *Toward a Rational Society*. Since the latter part of the nineteenth century, he says, two major trends have become marked in Western capitalism: the burgeoning of state interventionism, directed towards stabilising economic growth, and the increasing mutual dependence of research and technology, as a consequence of which science has become a leading force of production (*Toward a Rational Society*, pp. 50ff). These changes mean that the relations between 'infrastructure' and 'superstructure' which Marx specified in relation to nineteenth-century competitive capitalism no longer apply. The idea that politics can be treated as part of the superstructure is adequate only so long as polity and civil society are separated, with the latter being 'autonomously' regulated through the operations of the market; and this is no more the case. The 'political' and the 'economic' are no longer easily separable. Hence the old form of legitimation, based upon the ideology of fair exchange, and expressed in its most sophisticated form in classical political economy, becomes increasingly obsolete, and is replaced by new modes of legitimation. There can be no return, Habermas argues, to the type of direct legitimation of power characteristic of the pre-capitalist order, and the legitimation system of advanced capitalism thus tends to become a technocratic one, based upon the capability of elites to 'manage' the economy successfully and sustain economic growth.

Because of the premium placed upon 'controlled economic development', science is more and more directly harnessed to the process of technological innovation. This situation, Habermas suggests, undermines the relevance of Marx's theory of surplus value; the labour power of the immediate producers now plays a relatively small role compared with the value generated by scientific-technical innovation. Critical theory can no longer be limited to the critique of political economy but must extend the critique of ideology to encompass the ramifications of technocratic power. Just as the traditional formulation of the theory of surplus value has to be abandoned, so do other basic formulae of Marxian theory, including that of class conflict. 'State-regulated' capitalism emerged in substantial part in response to the massive strains created by direct class antagonism. Class division, based on private property, still remains integral to advanced capitalist society. But it has become the area where the society can least admit the occurrence of open confrontation or struggle; hence direct conflicts tend to break out frequently in those sectors which have less transformative consequence for the system. Conflicts which reflect divisions at the centre become manifest at the periphery.[9]

At the core of the technocratic ideology of advanced capitalism, Habermas says, is the collapse of the distinction between the categories of labour and interaction, or the technical and practical: positivism, which also assimilates these categories, reducing the latter to the former, is hence a philosophical expression of technocratic domination. The growth of technical powers of control in contemporary society, he makes clear in *Theory and Practice*, can be analysed in terms of four levels of rationalisation. On the first two of these levels, the growth of technology is associated with the exclusion of normative elements from scientific discourse; on the other two levels, technical procedures become established as values in themselves, the pre-existing value elements having been defined as 'irrational'. The first level of rationalisation involves simply the use of nomological knowledge for the realisation of independently affirmed values. Rationalisation proceeds on the second level when choice is demanded between two or more procedures of equal technical effectiveness. One of the expressions of this is the development of formal 'decision theory', which attempts to rationalise the relation between goals and values, rather than being limited to providing technical means of reaching given ends. On each of these levels, values are treated as removed from the possibility of rational discussion, save in so far as some values are in part means to the realisation of others. When technical rationality is extended to values themselves, we have moved to the third level of rationalisation. The clearest example of this level, Habermas suggests, is game theory, where actors are treated as evaluating the consequences of their actions in terms of a calculus of preferences intrinsic to the postulated form of the game, without reference to any wider value-systems, which then disappear from view. The final, and most embracing, level of rationalisation is reached when the strategic decision-making framework, such as is characteristic of game theory, is generalised to cover all types of decision: where 'stability' or 'adaptability' becomes the basis of analysis of decision-making within self-programming feedback systems. On this level of rationalisation, decision-making can in principle be carried out through the computer: and it is this stage of rationalisation towards which modern technocratic politics is moving on a large scale. This, in Habermas's words, is a 'negative Utopia of technical control over history'. It is the most complete form of the reduction of the practical to the technical: hence Habermas's critical attitude towards systems theory, which he sees as the political economy of the contemporary era.[10]

In *Legitimation Crisis*, which first appeared in 1973 in German as *Legitimationsprobleme im Spätkapitalismus*, Habermas provides an extensive discussion of these and other issues. The language of systems theory is drawn upon and turned back against itself, and the theme of the displacement of strains from the 'centre', the class structure, is developed. Although the central conflict has been displaced, advanced capitalism is still riven by contradictions and open to persistent crises. The term 'crisis', Habermas argues, itself needs elucidation. The word originally comes from medical usage, and was from there imported into the social sciences. In its medical sense, it refers to the phase of an illness which determines whether or not the healing processes of the organism produce the recovery of the patient. A crisis in the context of illness is not just an 'objective' sequence of events; it is something experienced by the patient, having the form of powerlessness, and contrasts with his or her normal capabilities as an autonomous being. To speak of a 'crisis' is therefore to give a series of events a normative meaning, counterposing determinism to liberation. This is basic to the viewpoint which Habermas tries to develop in the book. There cannot be an adequate systems-theoretic (or functional) concept of crisis, simply treating 'crisis' as equivalent to 'threat to the stability of the social system'; the concept of crisis, in the context of critical theory at least, has to be understood as conjoining the 'subjective' and 'objective', as involving the *experience* of impairment of autonomy of social action in certain definite social conditions. We can grasp the relation between the subjective and objective components of crisis tendencies, Habermas claims, by distinguishing between social integration and system integration. Social integration refers to the 'lifeworld', 'in which speaking and acting subjects are socially related', system integration to abstractly conceived social systems, which, however, are to be seen as rooted in a normative order of symbols. Crises can be regarded as unresolved 'steering problems', of which actors in the life-world are often not conscious but which express themselves on that level in normative strain and a diminishing autonomy of action.

The 'steering problem' of advanced capitalism, Habermas tries to show, can be illuminated against the background of a general theory of evolution. What Habermas seeks to achieve here is nothing less than a wholesale overhauling of Marx's historical materialism, based on the differentiation of labour and interaction. The evolution of human society proceeds in two separable but connected dimensions: the development of the forces of production (which can be thematised as instrumental knowledge, orientated to technical control), and the development of normative orders (which can be thematised as symbolic norms ordering communication). Each involves knowledge-claims which, as Habermas has indicated previously, are in principle open to discursive redemption. In respect of the first, the theory of evolution aims to reconstruct the formation of scientific and technical knowledge; and in respect of the latter, the opening of normative structures to discourse, via the movement through 'increased reflexivity of the mode of belief, which can be seen in the sequence: myth as immediately lived system of orientation; teachings; revealed religion; rational religion; ideology' (*Legitimation Crisis*, p. 12). The relation between the development of the forces of production and normative structures, Habermas claims, is a problematic one. The changes which occur in one sphere do not necessarily produce corresponding alterations in the other, and this is the source of steering problems. In every type of social formation, what Habermas calls a 'principle of social organisation' connects forces of production and normative structures; steering problems lead to crisis effects if the organisational principle of the society in which they occur is unable to accommodate them.

Habermas distinguishes several major types of society based on different principles of organisation. 'Primitive social formations' are organised around age and sex roles, co-ordinated through the kinship system. 'Traditional social formations' are organised in terms of political class domination: a bureaucratic state apparatus serves as the co-ordinating focus of the hegemony of a landowning class. In more modern times the two most important types of society are liberal capitalism and advanced or 'organised' capitalism. As regards the former, as he made clear in his earlier writings, Habermas accepts the main lines of Marx's analysis, although he attempts to reconceptualise it in his own terminology. In liberal or competitive capitalism, the organisational principle is centred upon the relation of capital and wage-labour, and involves the division of state from society. In contrast with the previous type of social formation, in liberal capitalism class relationships are depoliticised and made anonymous: class relations express the asymmetries of economic exchange, and the latter becomes the principal steering medium. This system greatly expands the range of the productive forces and furthers the secularisation of belief on the level of normative structures. The formation of the 'public sphere' corresponds to the drive of bourgeois ideology towards universal principles defended by reason rather than by tradition and by the 'anonymisation' of class rule. 'The socially dominant class,' Habermas says, 'must convince itself that it no longer rules' (*Legitimation Crisis*, p. 22). Since the organisational principle of competitive capitalism involves an 'unregulated' market, steering problems express themselves as economic crises of a periodic character. Liberal capitalism produces 'a crisis-ridden course of economic growth'.

The main differences Habermas acknowledges between liberal and advanced capitalism are familiar from his writings prior to *Legitimation Crisis*. The development of strong tendencies towards monopoly or oligopoly within the economy, coupled with the expanding interventionism of the state, co-ordinated by the spreading rationalisation of technical control, transform the organisational nature of capitalism. Advanced capitalism is still capitalism, but the central economic contradictions express themselves in novel and more complex form than previously. While class relations are 'repoliticised' in a certain sense, the directly political form of class domination characteristic of pre-capitalist societies is not thereby restored: because, as Habermas has reiterated throughout his writings, capitalism cannot retreat to the traditional forms of legitimacy based on religion or custom. Advanced capitalism really needs such a mode of direct legitimation but does not itself generate it; rather, it corrodes these older forms of legitimacy. In their place it is able to put only the administrative capability to control the economic system – to be able to overcome the economic fluctuations of competitive capitalism. To achieve this, Habermas reaffirms, the centre has to be controlled most firmly: overt, politicised class conflict is not the most typical form of social conflict in advanced capitalism.

Advanced capitalism is a crisis-ridden society but one in which, as a result of the partial success in stabilising economic fluctuations, crisis tendencies express themselves in various guises. Habermas finds four such types of crisis tendency, interwoven with one another. One type is economic crisis, but like class conflicts today, and for the same reasons, economic crises rarely appear in pure form. Economic steering problems have come to be treated largely as problems of rational administration; difficulties in resolving dilemmas of economic growth thus tend to become 'rationality crises'. A rationality crisis is a hiatus in the administrative competence of the state and its affiliated agencies, an inability to cope. Habermas has already argued that the ability to cope, to co-ordinate economic growth successfully, is the main element in the technocratic legitimation system of late capitalism. Hence it follows that rationality crises, if prolonged or pronounced, tend to devolve into legitimation crises, the potential of mass withdrawal of support or loyalty. Finally, crises of legitimacy can in turn become 'motivational crises': the motivational commitment of the mass of the population to the normative order of advanced capitalism is tenuous anyway, as the old moral values are stripped away. Technocratic legitimation provides little in the way of meaningful moral commitment, but only the provisional acceptance of a materially successful economic system; the threat of widespread anomie, Habermas says, is endemic in late capitalism.

Since organised capitalism remains a contradictory order, whose principle of organisation cannot satisfactorily reconcile the forces of production (more and more dominated by scientific-technological imperatives, but still resting on private property) with the normative structure (technocratic legitimation), its crisis tendencies cannot be overcome without major social transformation. But what chances are there of this occurring, and what form might such a transformation take? We find very little in *Legitimation Crisis* in the way of answers to either of these queries. Habermas mentions the possibility of the emergence of a 'post-modern' era at one point, referring to Daniel Bell's concept of the post-industrial society, but does not develop the comment. The other relevant remarks which he occasionally makes are cursory and tentative, and the concluding part of the work reverts to a high level of abstraction, raising again the general question of the redemption of validity-claims in 'practical discourse'.

As a consequence, whatever illumination readers may derive from *Legitimation Crisis*, they are likely to feel dissatisfied with its outcome. The book condenses and connects many of the ideas developed in Habermas's previous writings, but it raises as many dilemmas as it claims to resolve. It would perhaps not be too harsh a judgement to say that this is true of all Habermas's major writings. Certainly his work, since its beginnings, has stimulated a continuing chorus of criticism – 'critical theory criticised' as one author surveying the response to *Erkenntnis und Interesse* put it.[11] Habermas has been involved in a series of public controversies – with Albert, in relation to the writings of Popper, and with Gadamer, Luhmann and others – which have helped shape the direction of development of his thought as well as led him to modify some of his original ideas. I shall not attempt to survey these debates here and shall offer only a brief personal assessment of the strengths, and what seem to be some of the main shortcomings, of his work.

As for the former, perhaps it is sufficient to say that no one can approach basic problems in the social sciences today, in respect of either the philosophy of method or the more substantive theory of the development of the advanced societies, without confronting Habermas's writings in a serious and systematic way. Habermas has helped to forge closer contacts between Continental and Anglo-American philosophy and social theory; he has made it clear that traditional versions of the epistemology of the social sciences have to be radically overhauled; he has developed the main threads of a powerful analytical model for interpreting the major processes of development that have transformed, and are transforming, Western culture; and he has elaborated a scheme for grounding critical theory that departs significantly from those formulated by the earlier generation of Frankfurt philosophers. And yet I would be prepared to say that there is barely one of the major claims in Habermas's writings that I should be willing to accept as it stands.

On the level of metatheory, I think the differentiations which Habermas makes between the nomological, hermeneutic and critical sciences, and labour, interaction and power, which are tied into a whole series of other distinctions, are unsatisfactory. The logical status of the knowledge-constitutive interests, as many critics have pointed out, is obscure. Moreover, the contrasts drawn between the first two terms in each of these triads seem to me to preserve too much of the old *erklären/verstehen* distinction that has dogged the tradition of *Geisteswissenschaften*, even if Habermas does rework these notions very considerably. This polarity of 'explanation' and 'interpretation' or 'understanding', although not applied by Habermas to separate the natural and the social sciences, has two consequences. On the one hand, it obscures the degree to which knowledge aimed at technical control is interpretative in character: an 'explanation' in science often consists in locating an observation within a theoretical system so as to render it 'understandable'. In spite of his strictures against positivism, Habermas seems to preserve something of the logical empiricist view of scientific theory (as a deductive system of causal laws) in his own scheme. Conversely, 'predictability' and 'control' are integral features of interaction without being linked to nomology: the 'predictability' of human interaction is in some part a contingent accomplishment of lay actors. One result in regard of the distinction between labour and interaction is that the latter comes to be equated, implicitly or otherwise, with symbolic communication or 'communicative action', and it is difficult to recover conceptually the material interests (in the usual sense of that term) involved in interaction. Critique then tends to become identified with the critique of ideology; or at least, the abstract provisions of the latter exist at some distance from the practicalities of achieving real social change. Similar difficulties seem to exist in the appeal to psychoanalysis as an exemplar for critical theory. The emancipatory goal of psychoanalysis, the expanded autonomy of the patient, is achieved through a process of self-understanding developed through the analyst–patient dialogue. Here there is a pre-existing consensual system, since analysis is entered into voluntarily by both parties; the participants share a mutual interest in the outcome, the betterment of the patient; the process of therapy is organised purely through symbolic communication; the achieving of reflexive understanding is the very medium of the extension of the analysand's autonomy of action; and the 'domination' which the patient overcomes as a result of successful therapy is that of his or her own inner make-up, not the domination of others. None of these conditions seems to apply in the circumstances of actual social life, for example in situations of class domination.[12]

Similarly, there are various critical observations which one could make about Habermas's discussion of the rise and decline of the public sphere and the transition from liberal to organised capitalism. His reappraisal of Marx, in respect of the latter's analysis of liberal capitalism at least, seems to me to be both too revisionist and not revisionist enough. Not revisionist enough, because he accepts too readily that Marx's account was valid in the nineteenth century; Habermas's portrayal of competitive capitalism is a rather orthodox one in this regard. Too revisionist, because he writes off too completely the relevance of some central Marxian ideas today. One must surely accept that, in classical Marxian theory, the themes of the rationalisation of social and economic life, and its consequences for human freedom, are broached only very inadequately. But I am not convinced that technocratic consciousness has submerged pre-existing economic divisions and conflicts as pervasively as Habermas seems to believe.

References

1. Review discussion of the following works of Habermas: *Toward a Rational Society: Student Protest, Science and Politics*, trans. Jeremy J. Shapiro (London: Heinemann, 1971); *Knowledge and Human Interests*, trans. Jeremy J. Shapiro (London: Heinemann, 1972), *Theory and Practice*, trans. John Viertel (London: Heinemann, 1974); *Legitimation Crisis*, trans. Thomas McCarthy (Boston: Beacon, 1975).
2. A collection of essays taken from *Protestbewegung und Hochschulreform* and *Technik und Wissenschaft als 'Ideologie'*. A further work now exists in English, assembled from more recent essays: *Communication and the Evolution of Society* (Boston: Beacon, 1979).
3. Includes as an appendix Habermas's inaugural lecture at Frankfurt, originally in *Technik und Wissenschaft als 'Ideologie'*.
4. This abridgement of the fourth German edition of *Theorie und Praxis* includes the essay 'Arbeit und Interaktion', from *Technik und Wissenschaft als 'Ideologie'*.
5. Cf. my 'Habermas's critique of hermeneutics', in *Studies in Social and Political Theory* (London: Hutchinson, 1977).
6. Hans-Georg Gadamer, *Truth and Method* (London: Sheed & Ward, 1975).
7. For example, 'Toward a theory of communicative competence', in *Recent Sociology, No. 2*, ed. Hans Peter Dreitzel (New York: Collier-Macmillan, 1970); 'Some distinctions in universal pragmatics', *Theory and Society*, vol. 4, 1976; *Communication and the Evolution of Society*.
8. This book has been the subject of much commentary in Germany. See, for instance, W. Jäger, *Öffentlichkeit und Parlamentarismus: eine Kritik an Jürgen Habermas* (Stuttgart: Kohlhammer, 1973).

9. This idea has been developed in various publications by Claus Offe.
10. Jürgen Habermas and Niklas Luhmann, *Theorie der Gesellschaft oder Sozialtechnologie?* (Frankfurt: Suhrkamp, 1971).
11. Fred R. Dallmayr, 'Critical theory criticised: Habermas's *Knowledge and Human Interests* and its aftermath', *Philosophy of the Social Sciences*, vol. 2, 1972.
12. Habermas comments on criticisms of this sort in the 1971 Introduction to *Theory and Practice*.

8

Labour and Interaction

Labour and interaction: innocuous-sounding terms, but ones around which Habermas has consolidated some of the main themes in his work. It makes sense to see most of Habermas's writings as concerned with what he has come to call the 'reconstruction of historical materialism' – a critical reformulation of the dominant concerns of Marx, both on the level of philosophy or 'metatheory' and on the level of the development of industrial capitalism since Marx's day. Habermas uses 'reconstruction' in a very deliberate way, as he makes clear. He is not interested, as he says, in reviving or 'restoring' traditional Marxist ideas: his preoccupation with Marx is not a scholastic or dogmatic one. As a tradition of thought which is very much alive, Marxism has no need of renewal. Rather, it is in need of a wholesale overhaul. 'Reconstruction,' Habermas argues, 'signifies taking a theory apart and putting it back together again in a new form in order to attain more fully the goal it has set for itself.'[1]

The distinction between labour and interaction played a central part in Habermas's early attempts to gain a critical purchase on the shortcomings of Marx. It has not remained unmodified in his subsequent writings, and in the first two sections of this account I shall attempt to trace out the various contexts in which he applies the two concepts.

I

The origins of the differentiation Habermas draws between labour and interaction are to be found in his discussion of the relation between Hegel and Marx – in an analysis which is avowedly indebted to the ideas of Karl Löwith.[2] Habermas's account gives more prominence to Hegel's Jena lectures than is usually acknowledged by Hegel's interpreters, many of whom have regarded these lectures as a transitory phase in the evolution of that thinker's mature philosophy. According to Habermas, the two lecture courses Hegel gave at Jena[3] constitute a distinctive, if incomplete, perspective upon philosophy, which Hegel came to abandon, but which for Habermas marks certain close points of connection between Hegel and Marx (even though Marx did not know of the Jena manuscripts). In the Jena lectures, Hegel treated *Geist* in the process of its formation, as a phenomenon to be explained. *Geist* is understood in terms of the communication of human beings via categories of meaning comprised in language. Language is the medium of self-consciousness and of the 'distancing' of human experience from the sensory immediacy of the here-and-now. As necessarily implying intersubjectivity, of *interaction*, language has a definite parallel to the significance of *labour* in Hegel's writings. Labour is the specifically human mode of relating to nature:

> Just as language breaks the dictates of immediate perception and orders the chaos of the manifold impressions into identifiable things, so labour breaks the dictates of immediate desires and, as it were, arrests the process of drive satisfaction.[4]

Labour and interaction are hence the two key aspects of the self-formative process of human beings in society, or of the development of human culture. In Hegel's Jena lectures, according to Habermas, labour and interaction are presented as irreducible to one another: a matter which becomes a crucial focus of Habermas's attention in his critique of Marx. Interaction is organised through consensual norms that have no logical connection to the causal processes involved in transactions with nature. This is not to say, of course, that empirically they are two separate realms of human behaviour. All labour is carried on in a social and therefore communicative context.

Even in the Jena period, Habermas accepts, Hegel interpreted labour and interaction in terms of an identity theory: *Geist* is the absolute condition of nature. In other words, Hegel's account of the self-formation of humanity was always an idealist one. While rejecting Hegel's idealism, and although not having access to the Jena lectures, Marx nevertheless was able to appropriate the notions of labour and interaction from Hegel: these appear in Marx, Habermas says, in the shape of the dialectic of the forces and relations of production.[5] The progressive development of the forces of production, therefore, manifests the transformation of the world through human labour. The self-formative process, in Marx's writings, no longer expresses the externalisation of Spirit, but is rooted in the material conditions of human existence. However, the concept of labour in Marx, Habermas emphasises, remains an epistemological category; nature is only constituted for us through its mediation in human *Praxis*.[6] Marx presumes that 'nature-in-itself' exists, but this is a kind of counterpart in his thought to the Kantian 'thing-in-itself': we only directly encounter nature in our practical interchanges with it. This 'preserves', according to Habermas, 'nature's immovable facticity despite nature's historical embeddedness in the universal structure of mediation constituted by labouring subjects'.[7]

Marx's treatment of labour, in Habermas's view, is in some respects a decisive advance over that set out by Hegel. But at the same time it also represents something of a retrogressive step, because Marx does not provide an adequate epistemological support for sustaining the mutual irreducibility of labour and interaction. Marx's scheme of analysis gives a great deal of prominence to interaction, in the shape of the notion of the relations of production. The foundation of subjectivity and self-reflection in communicative frameworks of interaction are not, however, grasped epistemologically by Marx because of the dominant place accorded to the role of labour. This result stems from the very success of Marx's repudiation of Hegel's identity theory. Marx's works are thus fundamentally imbalanced, in a way which has major consequences for the later history of Marxism. In his empirical works, Marx always gives strong weight to the relations of production as well as to the forces of production. Concepts which properly belong to the former – to interaction in Habermas's terms – especially domination and ideology, thus have a primary role in Marx's empirical writings. But they do not have the philosophical underpinning which labour – the material transformation of the world and of human conditions of existence – enjoys. Hence Marx's concentration upon material *Praxis* became open to a misleading emphasis: it paved the way for the collapse of interaction into labour on the level of epistemology. According to Habermas, not even Marx fully grasped the implications of this, which helped to push his work in a positivistic direction. In Habermas's words:

> Although he [Marx] established the science of man in the form of critique and not as a natural science, he continually tended to classify it with the natural sciences. He considered unnecessary an epistemological justification of social theory. This shows that the idea of the self-constitution of mankind through labour sufficed to criticise Hegel but was inadequate to render comprehensive the real significance of the materialist appropriation of Hegel.[8]

It is exactly such an epistemological justification which Habermas has sought to provide in further expanding upon the distinction between labour and interaction. The collapse of interaction into labour means that instrumentally exploitable or 'technical' knowledge – the sort of knowledge we use to attempt to control the material world – becomes regarded as characteristic of the social as well as the natural sciences. All social problems then become seen as 'technical' problems. Technical reason appears to exhaust the capabilities of human reason as a whole: the defining characteristic of positivism for Habermas. The influence of Horkheimer's and Adorno's *Dialectic of Enlightenment* over Habermas's thought is evident at this point.[9] Their 'critique of instrumental reason' converges directly with the main political thrust of Habermas's writings (in which the influence of Max Weber also looms quite large): the thesis that increased human control over nature, or over the forces of production, is not at all the same as liberation from domination. The essential difference between Habermas's position and those of the earlier Frankfurt thinkers, a difference explored particularly in the debates between Habermas and Marcuse, is that Habermas rejects the theme that scientific or technical knowledge is itself ideological in its very form. The view of Habermas, which connects his discussion of labour and interaction in Hegel and Marx with his whole conception of knowledge-constitutive interests (today abandoned by Habermas?) is that it is the *universalisation* of technical or instrumental reason, as the only form of rationality, which has to be fought against. In Marx's writings, the universalisation of technical reason is traced to the epistemological dominance of labour: but the slide of Marxism towards positivism is a characteristic which Marxism shares with a great deal of modern social theory and philosophy as a whole.

II

Habermas's most systematic early attempt to elaborate the differentiation of labour from interaction appears in a critical analysis of Marcuse's views on technology.[10] Labour is equated with 'purposive-rational action' (*Zweckrationalität*), which refers, Habermas says, to 'either instrumental action or rational choice or their conjunction'. Instrumental action is action orientated to technical rules, and is founded on empirical knowledge. The technical rules involved in purposive-rational action are formulated on the basis of predictive powers which they allow. 'Rational choice' here is a matter of deciding between strategies of action, according to the most 'efficient' way of realising goals or objectives. Interaction, on the other hand, which Habermas equates with 'communicative action', 'is governed by binding *consensual norms*, which define reciprocal expectations about behaviour and which must be understood and recognised by at least two acting subjects'.[11] Communicative action is based on ordinary language communication, and depends upon the mutual understanding of social symbols. The contrast between the rules governing purposive-rational action and those governing communicative action is exemplified by the different character of the sanctions involved in each case. Habermas here echoes a distinction made by Durkheim.[12] Non-compliance with technical rules or strategies is sanctioned by the likelihood of failure in achieving goals; non-compliance with consensual norms is sanctioned by the disapproval of, or punishment by, other members of the social community. To learn rules of purposive-rational action, in Habermas's view, is to learn skills; to learn normative rules is to 'internalise' traits of personality.

The two types of action, Habermas goes on to argue, can provide a basis for distinguishing different institutional sectors of society. There are some sectors, among which he lists the economic system and the state, where purposive-rational action is most prevalent. There are others, such as the family and kinship relations, in which 'moral rules of interaction' predominate. This classification can also be applied, Habermas believes, to illuminate overall patterns in the development of societies. In traditional or pre-capitalist societies, the scope of sub-systems of purposive-rational action is kept confined by the pervading authority of morally binding frameworks of interaction. Capitalist society, by contrast, is one in which the expansion of sub-systems of purposive-rational action is privileged (first of all, as grounded in the expanded reproduction of capital), and progressively acts to erode other institutional forms. Modern science plays a major role in this process, especially as science and technological change become more closely integrated. This leads directly to the Habermasian themes of the 'scientisation of politics' and legitimation crisis:

> The quasi-autonomous progress of science and technology . . .
> appears as an independent variable on which the most important
> single system variable, namely economic growth, depends . . .
> when this semblance has taken root effectively, then propaganda
> can refer to the role of technology and science to explain and to
> legitimate why in modern societies the process of democratic
> decision-making about practical problems loses its function and
> 'must' be replaced by plebiscitary decisions about alternative sets
> of leaders of administrative personnel.[13]

The passage from abstract categories of action to a more empirical concern with processes of social development is characteristic of Habermas's style of argument, and comprehensible in the light of his conception of 'epistemology as social theory'. The labour/interaction distinction remains essential to both aspects of Habermas's work in his later writings. Although at first sight the scheme of knowledge-constitutive interests advanced in *Knowledge and Human Interests* and other writings of his earlier period seems to be threefold, it is fundamentally a dichotomous one founded upon the contrast between labour and interaction. The 'interest in emancipation' lacks content, and obtains its existence from the bringing together of nomological and hermeneutic concerns in the critique of ideology. The dichotomous character of Habermas's epistemological ventures is sustained in the format of 'universal pragmatics', in his differentiation of 'theoretical-empirical' from 'practical' discourse, a differentiation that can be superimposed, as it were, upon the labour/interaction and nomological/hermeneutic distinctions. I shall not be concerned here, however, with these ideas, but shall limit myself to following through Habermas's attempt to use the distinction between labour and interaction to analyse the evolution of societies.

Habermas's recent interpretation of social evolution recapitulates some of the elements of his earlier criticisms of Marx. Marx's theory, Habermas reaffirms, failed adequately to get to grips with communicative action in analysing the development of societies. Under the influence of Luhmann, Habermas is today prone to employ terminology associated with systems theory. Marx, he says, located the 'learning processes' associated with social evolution in the sphere of the productive forces (i.e. in labour); but learning processes are also to be discerned in 'world views, moral representations, and identity formations' (i.e. in interaction). We have therefore to complement the study of the development of the productive forces with that of 'normative structures'. Habermas believes that this can be done without essentially compromising the overall determination of social change by 'economically conditioned system problems'.[14] Habermas's account of the evolution of normative frameworks of interaction is based upon the thesis (advocated also in some form by Durkheim, Piaget and Parsons among others) of a homology between personality and social development. The forms of consciousness, and the stages of their development, of the individual member of society are the same as those characteristic of society as a whole.[15]

According to Habermas, the evolution of societal learning processes can be examined in the following terms. At certain phases of their development, societies meet with 'unresolved system problems' which present challenges to their continued reproduction, and which cannot be handled within the existing normative order. Society must then transform itself, or its continued existence is placed in question. The nature of such a transformation, and whether it occurs at all, Habermas emphasises, are not determined by the system problems, but only by the mode in which the society responds to them, by developing new modes of normative organisation. This analysis, he claims, is still worth calling 'historical materialism'. It is materialist, because problems in the realm of production and reproduction are at the origin of the tensions which provoke system reorganisation; and it remains historical because the sources of system problems have to be sought in the contingent development of particular societies. In his account of social evolution, Habermas finds archaeological justification for the integral involvement of labour and language with distinctively 'human' society. 'Labour and language,' as he puts it, 'are older than man and society.'[16]

III

Having sketched in these ideas, I want to offer a brief critical appraisal of them. I am not at all happy with Habermas's formulation of the labour/interaction distinction, or with some of the uses to which he puts it, and I shall try to express some of my reservations in what follows. I hope that the reader will understand that, in so doing, I am not seeking to downplay the significance of Habermas's contributions to contemporary social theory and philosophy. I think that I have learned more from Habermas's writings than from those of any other contemporary social thinker whose work I have encountered. At the same time, I find myself in substantial disagreement with many of Habermas's major conceptions. In respect of Habermas's views upon hermeneutics, positivism and the critique of ideology, I have expressed some of my doubts elsewhere,[17] and shall not revert to these issues in the present context. Here I shall concentrate upon what seem to me to be some of the more directly 'sociological' difficulties related to the differentiation of labour and interaction.

Let me begin, however, from a more affirmative perspective. Habermas's reappraisal of the Hegel–Marx relation (more accurately put, the Kant–Hegel–Marx relation) seems to me to contain contributions of enduring significance, even if some of his interpretations of these thinkers are questionable. I do not think that the distinction between labour and interaction is itself one of those contributions, for reasons I shall come to shortly. But there is no doubt that the making of the distinction, within the framework of Habermas's writings, helps to shed light upon some important issues. These include particularly, in my opinion, his identification of positivistic strains in Marx and the connecting of these to an analysis of the limitations of technical reason; his demonstration of the need to transcend the traditionally established division in philosophy between the 'claims to universality' of positivism and hermeneutics; and his unequivocal defence of a critical theory which insists upon the necessity of breaking with dogmatic forms of Marxism. Although some may object to the eclecticism of Habermas's work,[18] the pursuit of these themes has allowed him to bring together a diversity of erstwhile quite separate standpoints. In particular, Habermas has managed to bridge the chasm that has long separated some of the dominant Continental traditions in social theory and philosophy from those that have prevailed in the Anglo-Saxon world.

However, Habermas's formulation of the labour/interaction distinction seems to me the source of some basic ambiguities and difficulties in his writings. I shall discuss these under four headings. First, it is worth mentioning some conceptual ambiguities involved in the formulation of the distinction. Second, I shall draw attention to certain problems that arise in the case of each concept taken separately. Third, I shall review some implications for Habermas's analysis of institutions. Finally, I shall consider the application of the notions of labour and interaction to questions of social evolution or development.

1. Some of the ambiguities in Habermas's use of 'labour' and 'interaction' have been pointed out by one of his leading followers.[19] Habermas repeatedly presents the distinction as one referring to two types of action – purposive-rational action on the one hand, and communicative action on the other. One type of action is governed by technical rules, and sanctioned by the likelihood of failure to reach objectives; the other is governed by social norms, and sanctioned by convention or law. Even in his latest writings, Habermas continues to speak in this vein.[20] The same is the case for the sub-division he makes within the notion of purposive-rational action, between 'strategic' and 'instrumental' action. But none of these are actually types of action at all, as Habermas is forced to concede. They are, he says in response to this type of criticism, analytical elements of a 'complex'.[21] That is to say, they are ideal-typical features of action, like Weber's types from which they in some part draw their inspiration. All concrete processes of labour, of course, as Habermas emphasises in his discussion of Marx, and as Marx emphasised so forcibly himself, are social: or in Habermas's terms, involve interaction.

But this is wanting to have one's cake and eat it too. It is at best misleading to want to use 'labour' as equivalent to an analytical element of action and at the same time continue to use it in the sense of 'social labour'; and to use 'interaction' similarly as both an analytical element and a substantive type, opposed to 'monologic' or solitary action. I think this confusion stems from an unfortunate *mélange* of ideas drawn from sources which do not really have much in common with one another. These sources are, on the one hand, the Weberian distinction between purposive-rational action and value-rational action (*Wertrationalität*: transmuted considerably by Habermas, however); and on the other, the Marxian differentiation of the forces and relations of production. Weber's distinction is supposed to be an analytical or 'ideal-typical' one, but Marx's is not. Even within the Marxian scheme, 'labour' is not equivalent to 'forces of production', as presumably Habermas would acknowledge. But yet he continues to slur one into the other: to assimilate 'forces of production', 'labour' and 'purposive-rational action'; and to assimilate 'relations of production', 'interaction' and 'communicative action'. These ambiguities or confusions might not matter much if there were purely terminological points at issue, which could be corrected by clearer and more consistent usage. But they appear to me to lead to quite serious conceptual consequences for Habermas's work.

2. Anyone who criticises Marx as radically as Habermas has attempted to do, even (or perhaps particularly) self-professedly in the spirit of Marxism, is bound themselves to incur the wrath of more orthodox Marxists. Habermas's work has proved no exception. On the need for the reconstruction of historical materialism I am entirely on the side of Habermas, and have no sympathy with those who would assert dogmatically that no substantial revision of any of Marx's major concepts should be undertaken. When we consider Habermas's use of 'labour', and his criticisms of the Marxian notion of *Praxis*, the only question is whether or not these eventuate in a decisive advance over the original. I am bound to say that here I have to side with those critics who argue that they do not. Part of the reason is the very epistemological tone of Habermas's assessment of the Hegel–Marx transition. I do not share Habermas's overall standpoint that today epistemology is only possible as social theory, and I do not think, as Habermas does, that the concept of labour remains an epistemological one in Marx. Or at least, it only does so when assimilated to purposive-rational action, which in my opinion is not a justifiable interpretation. Habermas criticises, with some reason, the expansion of the notion of *Praxis* into a 'transcendental-

logical' one, which he thinks we find in the works of Marcuse and Sartre. But this sort of usage hardly exhausts the insights of the Marxian notion, if it is interpreted ontologically rather than epistemologically. Rather than attempting to make the idea of labour cover the whole gamut of associations made by Habermas, I would prefer to distinguish labour from *Praxis*, using the former in a more restricted sense and the latter in a more inclusive one. I should regard 'labour', in other words, as 'social labour': as the socially organised productive activities whereby human beings interact creatively with material nature. Labour then remains an intrinsically social activity, among other types of activity or forms of institution. *Praxis* can be treated as the universal basis of human social life as a whole. *Praxis*, that is to say, refers to the constitution of social life as regularised practices, produced and reproduced by social actors in the contingent contexts of social life. What can be gleaned from Marx himself on these matters is fairly sketchy, but sufficient to provide clues that can be elaborated in detail.[22]

The objections that can be raised against Habermas's use of 'interaction' are at least as important as these – perhaps more important, since a goodly amount of Habermas's writing has been concentrated upon interaction, as the 'neglected' side of the coin in historical materialism. The difficulties with Habermas's concept of interaction seem to me to derive from parallel sources to those relating to the notion of labour. Habermas identifies interaction with communicative action, this being governed by consensual norms. His emphasis upon the hermeneutic interpretation of symbols as a methodological demand of social observation, and as the medium of intersubjectivity among the members of society, is quite unobjectionable – indeed, vital to social theory. But to treat interaction as equivalent to 'communicative action' is more than simply misleading, it is mistaken. Although Habermas insists that interaction is not reducible to labour, I would say that he himself makes a triple reduction within the notion of interaction itself. First, it is wrong to treat interaction as equivalent, or reducible, to action. Second, it is wrong to treat action as equivalent, or reducible, to communicative action. And third, it is an error to suppose that communicative action can be examined solely on the level of norms. I doubt that Habermas would accept that he makes these reductions when they are thus bluntly stated. But I do not think it difficult to demonstrate that he constantly makes these elisions when he writes about interaction.

Let me develop these points somewhat. As regards the first point, perhaps the easiest way to express the matter is to say that most of Habermas's discussions of interaction do not mention *inter*action at all. To speak of interaction as a type, or even an element of action, is a misnomer. As a consequence, Habermas has little to say about – and proffers few concepts for analysing – the social relations that are constitutive of social systems. This may seem a banal enough observation, but I think it is really rather consequential: for it connects directly with Habermas's severing of the notion of *Praxis* into two. The production and reproduction of social life as *Praxis* involves identifying the mechanisms whereby patterns of interaction are sustained recursively. 'Action theory', as I have tried to show elsewhere, is not the same as 'interaction theory': an adequate account of the constitution of social systems in interaction demands a conception of what I have called the 'duality of structure' in social reproduction.[23]

It might be argued that, if Habermas barely touches upon these issues, this is simply an error of omission, and that the blank space could be filled in without compromising the rest of his ideas. But I think that consideration of the other two points I raised above indicates that this is not so. Interaction is not the same as 'communicative action', because communicative action is only one type of action. As regards this point, a lot hangs on what 'communication' is taken to mean. Again there seems some terminological ambiguity in Habermas here, in so far as he often seems to equate 'symbolic' with 'communicative'. The first does not necessarily imply, as the second normally does, some sort of intended meaning which an actor wished to transmit to others. It might plausibly be said that all action involves symbols, but it cannot be maintained that the symbolic elements of action are equivalent to communicative intent. But Habermas quite often appears to argue as though they are, perhaps in some part because of his preoccupation with speech. In so far as he does so, he tends to move back towards the sorts of intentionalist philosophical accounts of meaning which are incompatible with other of his emphases in his discussions of hermeneutics.[24]

The third point I mentioned above can be put as follows: there is more to interaction than the norms to which it is orientated. Habermas's emphasis upon the normative components of interaction follows plausibly enough from the tendency to slur interaction and communicative action. But the consequence is that his social theory is surprisingly close to the 'normative functionalism' of Parsons. Both accord primacy to norms in examining social interaction, rather than to power. It might seem surprising to make such a remark, in so far as Habermas's work is presumptively directed to the critique of domination. None the less, I think it is a valid comment.[25] I should want to make the case for arguing that power is as integral a component of all social interaction as norms are.[26] Now Habermas appears to agree with this in so far as domination or power is made one of the three fundamental aspects of social organisation linked to the knowledge-constitutive interests in *Knowledge and Human Interests*. But the knowledge-constitutive interest linked to emancipation from domination is, as I have remarked, 'content-less': the critique of domination comes to turn upon freedom of communication or dialogue, rather than upon material transformations of power relations. The implications of this, I think, appear rather prominently in Habermas's formulations of the nature of critical theory, which are focused unswervingly upon the uncovering of ideology. Provocative though his formulation of an ideal speech situation is as a counterfactual model for social critique, it operates once more on the level of communication. It gives us no indication of how other problems traditionally associated with disparities of power, such as access to scarce resources, and clashes of material interest, are to be coped with in the 'good society'.

3. The import of the critical comments I have made so far is that, in some part at least because of problems with the labour/interaction distinction, there is an 'absent core' in Habermas's writings: an adequate conceptual scheme for grasping the production and reproduction of society. This observation can be consolidated, I want to claim, if we look at those segments of his work which concern the institutional organisation of society. Here Habermas borrows in a direct fashion from Parsons's functionalism (as well as from Luhmann's systems theory, or so-called 'functional-structuralism'). Habermas has certainly not been uncritical either of Parsons or of functionalism more generally. But his disquiet with Parsons's theories, like with those of Luhmann, is mainly to do with the logical status of functionalism as an 'empirical-analytic' enquiry, rather than with the substance of those theories. The values and norms which play such a basic part in Parsons's portrayal of society cannot, Habermas argues, be accepted as 'given data' as Parsons assumes.

They presuppose hermeneutic procedures of identification, and have to be opened out to the possibilities of ideology-critique.[27]

In other respects, however, Habermas seems prepared to take on board some major elements of Parsonian sociology. Among Parsons's views, there are several which seem to me to be particularly questionable, and more than an echo of these is to be found in Habermas. The views I have in mind are Parsons's 'model of society', which accords a centrality to values and norms in social integration; the thesis that society and personality are homologous, or 'interpenetrate'; and the significance attributed to 'internalisation' in the theory of socialisation. Major objections can be brought against all of these. The thesis of the primacy of values and norms in societal integration seems to me to be connected to a point I made previously, the tendency of Habermas to reduce interaction to communication and norms. The model of society which results – if one can judge thus far from what is clearly in Habermas's writings only a tentative approach to problems of social change – seems to embody no account of *contradiction*, and to underplay the significance of *power* and *struggle* in social development. It may be that Habermas will be able to incorporate these in his scheme in a more integral way, but he has not done so thus far. Rather, his discussion moves at the level of 'functional problems' which social systems face at certain stages in their history. 'System problems', a concept which I am not very comfortable with, are not contradictions; and Habermas has not so far given much indication of just how the identification of such 'system problems' helps explain actual processes of historical change, or active social and political struggle. In lieu of a satisfactory analysis of these issues, I am more struck by the similarity of Habermas's account of social evolution to that offered by Parsons in his *Societies*[28] than I am by its closeness to Marx.

I have strong reservations about the thesis of the homology of society and personality, which has become an explicit supposition in Habermas's later writings. Although he recognises the difficulties with this conception viewed phenotypically, one cannot adopt it of course without retaining the general idea that the 'childhood of society' is like the childhood of the individual, the one a more rudimentary version of the other. But the languages of all known 'primitive societies' are as complex and sophisticated as those of the economically advanced societies, and all have rich symbolic or representational contents. The views of Lévi-Bruhl seem to me today to be less compelling than those of Lévi-Strauss.

However that may be, in the present context I am more concerned to criticise the idea of society–personality homology as an analytical postulate of social theory, in which sense it is closely connected to the notion of 'internalisation'. These have been pervasive themes of Parsonian sociology, and are again related to the assumption that the value or norm is the key defining characteristic of the social (or of 'interaction'). Parsons's account of the 'internalisation' of norms supports the idea that the mechanisms providing for the integration of the individual within society and those integrating society are the same – the moral co-ordination of action through shared values. The very same values we 'internalise' in socialisation, and which form our personalities, are those which cohere the social system. The limitations of this kind of standpoint are pronounced. It further inhibits the possibility of dealing adequately with questions of power, sectional group interest and struggle. But on the level of the society–personality relation it implies a theory of social reproduction which fails to recognise the skilful and knowledgeable character of the everyday participation of actors in social practices.[29] We are led back here, I think, to the demand for a coherent conception of *Praxis*.

4.   Let me return finally to historical materialism, and to questions of Marx's concepts of the forces and relations of production, the differentiation that provided the main source of Habermas's labour/interaction distinction. According to Marx, the development of (class) societies can be explained in terms of the progressive elaboration of the forces of production, as they diverge from an existing set of relations of production. The controversies to which this scheme has given rise, together with the associated distinction between economic 'base' and political and ideological 'superstructure', are legion. Habermas attempts to reformulate the Marxian view on a historical level in much the same way as he did earlier in a more epistemological vein. That is to say, he asserts the independent significance of interaction, as opposed to labour, as a determining influence upon social development. In some degree because of how he conceives of 'interaction', his emphasis comes to be placed largely upon moral and cognitive orders. In his discussion of these matters, Habermas admits to being influenced by the writings of 'structuralist Marxists' such as Godelier. He flirts with the idea of 'determination in the last instance',[30] and seems to want to maintain a version of the idea of social formations as exhibiting 'structures in dominance'. But I do not think this idea is a persuasive one even at source, and in Habermas's hands it seems even more elusive. Habermas claims that, for him, 'culture remains a superstructural phenomenon', but I do not think he provides convincing demonstration of this assertion. Talk of 'economically conditioned system problems' is not only vague but suggests a view closer to Weber than that of Marx.

The problem, as I see it, is that Marx underestimated the distinctiveness of industrial capitalism, as compared with previous types of social formation. The notion of *Praxis*, in my opinion, is an essential idea which applies generically to the production and reproduction of society. But the dialectic of forces and relations of production is more confined in its historical scope – at least in anything like its classical form. Only with the advent of capitalism does the accumulation process, and associated technological innovation, become the driving motor of social change. Only then does the scheme of divergence between the movement of the forces of production and the persistence of established relations of production have general application. But of course with the global spread of capitalism, this is nevertheless a phenomenon of world-historical significance.

References

1. Jürgen Habermas, 'Historical materialism and the development of normative structures', *Communication and the Evolution of Society* (Boston: Beacon, 1979) p. 95.
2. See Habermas, 'Remarks on Hegel's Jena *Philosophy of Mind*', *Theory and Practice* (London: Heinemann, 1974) p. 168; Karl Löwith, *From Hegel to Nietzsche* (New York: Anchor Books, 1967).
3. *The Philosophy of Mind* and *System of Morality*.
4. 'Remarks on Hegel's Jena *Philosophy of Mind*', p. 159.
5. Ibid, p. 168.
6. Habermas, *Knowledge and Human Interests* (London: Heinemann, 1972) pp. 28–34.
7. Ibid, p. 34.
8. Ibid, p. 45.
9. Habermas has spoken in a recent interview of the strong impression reading the *Dialectic of Enlightenment* made upon him in his early intellectual career. Interview with Habermas by Dethef Korster and Willem van Reijen, Starnberg, 23 March 1979, p. 6.

10. 'Technology and science as "ideology"', in *Toward a Rational Society* (London: Heinemann, 1971). This essay also makes plain the significance of certain ideas of Max Weber for Marcuse and Habermas.
11. Ibid, pp. 91–2.
12. Durkheim distinguished between what he called 'utilitarian', or technical, and 'moral' sanctions. In the latter, the sanction is defined socially, in the former by objects and events in nature. Emile Durkheim, 'Determination of the moral fact', in *Sociology and Philosophy* (London: Cohen & West, 1953).
13. 'Technology and science as "ideology"', p. 105.
14. Habermas, 'Historical materialism and the development of normative structures', in *Communication and the Evolution of Society* (Boston: Beacon, 1979) pp. 97–8.
15. Habermas makes various qualifications to this assertion, however. See ibid, pp. 102–3, 110–11.
16. 'Toward a reconstruction of historical materialism', in *Communication and the Evolution of Society*, p. 137.
17. See 'Habermas's critique of hermeneutics', in *Studies in Social and Political Theory* (London: Hutchinson, 1977).
18. Cf. Göran Therborn, 'Habermas: a new eclectic', *New Left Review*, no. 63, 1970.
19. Thomas McCarthy, *The Critical Theory of Jürgen Habermas* (London: Hutchinson, 1978) pp. 24–6.
20. See, for example, his portrayal of the two concepts in 'Historical materialism and the development of normative structures', pp. 117–19.
21. Habermas, 'A postscript to *Knowledge and Human Interests*', *Philosophy of the Social Sciences*, vol. 3, 1973.
22. As I have tried to do in *Central Problems in Social Theory* (London: Macmillan, 1979) pp. 53–9.
23. Ibid, *passim*.
24. Cf. my *New Rules of Sociological Method* (London: Hutchinson, 1974) pp. 68–9 and 86–91.
25. I have made the same argument previously in 'Habermas's critique of hermeneutics'.
26. *Central Problems in Social Theory*, pp. 88–94.
27. Habermas, *Zur Logik der Sozialwissenschaften* (Frankfurt: Suhrkamp, 1970) pp. 170ff.
28. Talcott Parsons, *Societies: Evolutionary and Comparative Perspectives* (Englewood Cliffs, N.J.: Prentice-Hall, 1966).
29. Cf. *Central Problems in Social Theory*, pp. 101–3 and *passim*.
30. 'Toward a reconstruction of historical materialism', pp. 143–4.

9
Durkheim, Socialism and Marxism

My aim in what follows will not be to offer a textual examination of the various discussions and comments on socialism that are to be found scattered through Durkheim's writings.[1] Rather, I want to pose the question: is there anything in Durkheim's account of socialism that remains of value today, when we inhabit a world which has changed profoundly since Durkheim's time? I do not write as a particular admirer of Durkheim's views about sociology. These views have had an enormous influence, in varying ways and contexts, upon the subsequent development of the social sciences, but in my opinion this influence has not always been a fruitful one. I do want to argue, however, that Durkheim's analysis of socialism – not an aspect of his work which has been debated as frequently as some others – contains some ideas that are a stimulus to reflection about contemporary political problems.

Let me first sketch in a few of the elements of Durkheim's discussion. Durkheim draws a distinction between 'communist' and 'socialist' doctrines. 'Communist' ideas, in Durkheim's use of the term, have existed at various different periods of history. Communist writings typically take the form of fictional utopias: examples are to be found in the diverse works of Plato, Thomas More and Campanella. Such utopian writings tend to treat private property or wealth as the main origin of social evils; the private accumulation of wealth is regarded as a moral danger that must be kept strictly in check. In 'communist' utopias, political and economic life are kept separated, so that the latter should not be corrupted by the former. Thus in the ideal form of the republic as projected by Plato, the rulers have no right to intervene in the economic activities of the producers, and the latter are not permitted to participate in administration or legislation. This is because wealth and its temptations are a source of public corruption, a phenomenon 'stimulating individual egoisms'. The guardians of the state and the artisans or labourers even live in physical separation from one another: 'All communist theories formulated later,' according to Durkheim, 'derive from Platonic communism, of which they are hardly more than variations.'[2]

As such, they all stand in decisive opposition to socialism, which is much more recent, is related to social movements rather than being the isolated creation of individual authors, and has a different basic content in terms of the ideas which it involves. The word 'socialism' dates only from the turn of the eighteenth and nineteenth centuries, as do socialist movements themselves; socialism, says Durkheim, is a product of the social changes transforming the European societies from the late eighteenth century onwards. In complete contrast to communist theories, which presuppose that polity and economy must be separated, the main thesis of socialism, as Durkheim conceives of it, is that the two should be merged. That is to say, it is not wealth as such which is the source of social evils, but the fact that it is not socialised in the hands of a centralised directive agency. Here we come to a vital element of Durkheim's argument. In socialist doctrines, production is to be centralised in the hands of the state; but the state is conceived of in a purely economic way. The Saint-Simonian theme that, in the anticipated society of the future, the 'administration of human beings' will give way to the 'administration of things' is taken by Durkheim to be a specific and defining characteristic of socialist ideas as a whole. In this respect socialism, including its Marxist version, shares certain parameters of thought with one of its principal opponents, political economy. Each regards economic reorganisation as the essential basis for coping with the problems facing the contemporary societies; each considers it both possible and desirable to reduce the activities of the state to a minimum. The classical economists propose that the scope of government be limited to the enforcement of contracts, such that the market can be given free play; the socialists wish to replace market mechanisms by centralised economic control.

Communist theories usually have an ascetic character, but socialist ideas are founded upon the proposition that modern industrial production holds out the possibility of abundant wealth for all, if the economy is rationally organised. Communism and socialism, Durkheim claims, tend to be frequently confused or mingled with one another. This is partly because both seek to combat perceived sources of social disquiet, and partly because each proposes forms of regulation (*reglèmentation*, in Durkheim's term) to do with the relation between economic and political life. However, Durkheim adds, 'one aims to moralise industry by binding it to the State, the other, to moralise the State by excluding it from industry'.[3] It seems evident, although Durkheim does not spell the idea out in detail, that the distinction between communism and socialism connects closely to the themes of *The Division of Labour in Society*. Communist ideals are those that appear sporadically in societies having a low division of labour, which are segmental in character, and where there is little co-operative dependence in production. Since there is little mutual dependence in production, the possibility of socialisation of economic life does not raise itself. Consumption, rather than production, is communal. Socialism, by contrast, could only arise in societies having a high degree of interdependence in the division of labour, i.e. in societies cohered by organic solidarity. It is a response to the pathological condition of the division of labour in societies undergoing the transition from mechanical to organic solidarity.

This explains Durkheim's guarded but undeniably positive attitude towards socialism (in his formulation of it). Parsons's comment, in his famous discussion of Durkheim in *The Structure of Social Action*, that Durkheim's sympathies were closer to communist than to socialist doctrines, seems entirely wide of the mark.[4] Socialism, according to Durkheim, is in certain degree a symptom of the strains to which contemporary societies are subject; but socialists are correct in holding that these strains call for the regulation of economic activity in the interests of the whole of the community. I don't think it would be correct to call Durkheim a 'socialist' as such, either in terms of his personal involvement in politics – which was in any case fairly limited – or in terms of the overall themes of his social analyses. His political sympathies were close to liberal republicanism, and he saw socialist ideas as limited in respect of providing a programme of social reconstruction appropriate to the demands of the day. In the context of the Anglo-Saxon reception of Durkheim, it is important to accentuate these things, because one prominent line of thought has stressed a presumed association of Durkheim's thought with conservatism. The view that Durkheim's writings, if not his political attachments, are inherently conservative in character has been stressed by various commentators, most particularly by Nisbet and by Coser.[5] It has contributed, in my opinion, to serious distortions in the interpretation of Durkheim's work – distortions that have had various ramifications for the development of social theory in recent times.[6]

Critical comments

Of course, Durkheim was not a revolutionary, and one of the main features of his definition of socialism is his attempt to argue that the notion of class conflict is not fundamental to socialist thought. As he admits, this stance seems at odds with the importance that socialists, especially Marxists, attribute to class struggle in the constitution and transformation of society. But it is possible to demonstrate, he asserts, that the workers' movement is only of secondary concern in socialism. The improvement of the lot of the worker is merely one aspect of the more all-encompassing economic reorganisation that socialist doctrines point to; and 'class war is only one of the means by which this reorganisation could result, one aspect of the historic development producing it'.[7] The main factor responsible for the degradation of the worker is that productive labour is not harnessed to the universal interests of the societal community, but instead to those of an exploitative class. The overthrow of this exploiting class is not an end in itself, but rather the mode whereby a rational and fair system of production can be set under way.

Durkheim's portrayal of the history of socialism unfortunately remained unfinished, and he did not continue through to an exhaustive discussion of Marx – although we can glean some idea of what his appraisal of Marx's writings might have involved via his review of Labriola's exposition of historical materialism.[8] In lieu of such a discussion, we perhaps should be somewhat cautious in subjecting Durkheim's analysis of socialism to critique. None the less, it is not particularly difficult to point to basic difficulties in the contrast Durkheim wanted to draw between communism and socialism, and in the manner in which he sought to characterise socialist theories. The utopian writings Durkheim isolated were certainly not the only form of 'radical Leftism' to have existed prior to the origins of modern socialism in the late eighteenth century; one can think, for example, of the Levellers or of Winstanley in seventeenth-century

England.[9] Moreover, Durkheim seems not only to write as if socialist authors were unaware of differences between their ideas and
those of 'communism', he also appears to attribute too much unity
to 'socialism'. In criticising what he sometimes called 'utopian
socialism', after all, Marx showed himself to be acutely aware of the
importance of creating a socialist movement that would have a real
part to play in furthering social change. A conception of what
Habermas would call 'self-reflection' is built into Marx's writings.
He was as aware as Durkheim was of the fact that socialist ideas
both express circumstances of social transformation and simultaneously can be drawn upon critically to promote further social change.

Particularly dubious, I think, is Durkheim's effort to remove class
conflict from occupying a central position in socialist thought. He
accomplishes this rather remarkable feat only by virtue of a specious
trick of definition. Having characterised socialism as 'in essence'
concerned with the centralised control of economic activity, with
the regulation of economic life, he is able to declare labour movements and class struggle as of secondary importance to socialist
thought. But this conception only has any plausibility at all because
Durkheim uses 'socialism' in a very broad sense, and because he
suppresses any analysis of *capitalism* in Marx's usage of that term. In
Marx's view, capitalism is a generic type of society, constituted
upon an economic foundation of the capital/wage-labour relation.
Class struggle is thus inherent in the capitalist mode of production;
and the revolution due to be brought about by the rise of the
workers' movement is the necessary medium of the realisation of a
socialist society.

Durkheim's attempt to disconnect socialist thought from class
conflict by means of terminological juggling serves in some part to
conceal some very profound divergences between Marx's conceptions and his own. Durkheim not only traces the origins of socialism
primarily to Saint-Simon, his own thought is embedded in traditions
that owe a considerable amount to Saint-Simon's specific doctrines.
Saint-Simon helped to found what I have elsewhere called the
theory of industrial society (besides coining the very term 'industrial
society').[10] According to Saint-Simon, the emergent industrial
order is already on the verge of becoming a 'classless' society, in the
sense of a 'one-class' society of *industriels*. Durkheim developed the
theory of industrial society well beyond the point at which Saint-
Simon had left it, even if he only rarely used the term itself. For

Durkheim, class conflict expresses the tensions involved in the maturation of an industrial order, in which organic solidarity in the division of labour has not yet fully matured. The conflicts deriving from the 'forced division of labour' will be overcome by the progressive removal of 'external inequalities' – barriers to equality of opportunity – and by the transcendence of anomie through the normative regulation of industrial relations. The *corporations*, or occupational associations, were to play a major role in each of these processes.

The revolution that Marx projected may not have occurred, but it seems to me quite plain that Marx's assessment of the endemic character of class conflict in capitalism is closer to contemporary industrial reality than the views which Durkheim offered. Labour unions have not ceded place to *corporations* such as Durkheim envisaged them. Class conflict appears inherent in the capitalist societies at two related 'sites'. One is class struggle at the level of day-to-day practices on the shop-floor. I have in mind here the attempts of workers to control or influence the nature of the labour process. The other is class struggle pitting the various sectors of organised labour movements against employers. These intersecting axes of class conflict, I think, can be readily explicated in terms of Marx's portrayal of the capitalist labour contract, but they are not particularly amenable to explanation within the frame of reference which Durkheim used. Marx emphasised that the capitalist labour contract contrasts radically with class relations in prior types of society. The worker sells his or her labour power in exchange for a monetary wage, but in so doing sacrifices all formal control over the labour process and over other aspects of the organisation of production. But wage-labour refuses to be treated as 'a commodity like any other'. Through modes of informal sanctioning, and through the substantive use of the threat of the collective withdrawal of labour, workers establish themselves as a force to be reckoned with at both sites of conflict.

The state: Durkheim and Marx

While Marx's analysis of capitalism as a class society remains of great importance, nobody today can be content with an unreconstructed version of Marxism. For those who would situate themselves 'on the Left' today politically, whether or not they want to call themselves 'Marxists', it seems to me to be an increasingly pressing task to re-think the legacy of Marx. Has Durkheim's account of socialism, whatever its deficiencies, any contribution to make to such a process of reconstruction? I think perhaps it has, although this does not entail accepting Durkheim's own formulations as they stand.

Durkheim criticised socialist ideas, as he understood them, by arguing that the solutions they propose remain upon a solely economic level. He allowed that various types of economic regulation envisaged by socialists are necessary as part of a programme of social reform. But they cannot be sufficient, because the difficulties facing contemporary societies are not wholly, not even primarily, economic. The contemporary *malaise* derives in an important sense from the very *predominance* of economic relationships over other aspects of social life. No amount of economic transformation will cope with the moral gap that has been left by the dissolution of traditional norms in the face of the expansion of industrial production. This leads Durkheim to an exposition of the nature of the state which contrasts considerably with that contained in Marx's writings. According to Durkheim, the state must play a moral as well as an economic role in a society dominated by organic solidarity. In conjunction with this argument, he rejects the thesis that the state can be 'abolished' in the emergent society of the future – or if the state were 'abolished', the results would be quite the opposite to those anticipated by socialists. Socialists, including Marxists, Durkheim argues, are only able plausibly to advocate the abolition of the state because they imagine that the state can be reduced to a purely economic agency. The state is supposed to restrict the scope of its operations to the 'administration of things'.

Durkheim's discussion of the state and democracy is worth taking seriously. It has to be read against the backdrop of the analysis of mechanical and organic solidarity established in *The Division of Labour*. The moral order of societies cohered by mechanical solidarity provided a binding framework of authority, in which problems of *anomie* did not arise. At the same time, however, they were repressive. The individual was subject to the 'tyranny of the group': the strength of the moral consensus involved in mechanical solidarity inhibited the development of freedom of expression or action. This emphasis is one reason why it is mistaken to see Durkheim as a conservative thinker, even in a broad sense of that term, because at no point in his writings did he evoke a nostalgia for this lost (or rapidly disappearing) moral community. On the contrary, the whole point of the arguments developed in *The Division of Labour* is to demonstrate that there can be no regression to mechanical solidarity, to traditional norms and values: for a new type of societal totality has emerged. The characteristic issue facing the modern world is that of reconciling the individual freedoms which have sprung from the dissolution of the traditional order with the sustaining of the moral authority upon which the very existence of society depends. The contemporary moral order, however, cannot be the same as that which used to exist, and it necessarily involves different institutional mechanisms.

Such mechanisms, in Durkheim's view, must both sustain the independence of the state from society, and at the same time not allow the state wholly to dominate the activities of individuals in the civil sphere. The expansion of the activities of the state, according to him, is an inevitable accompaniment of the maturation of societies having a complex division of labour. As a moral agency, the state takes the lead in fostering the sorts of changes involved in promoting the ideals of 'moral individualism' – ideals stressing the dignity of the individual, and justice and freedom among individuals. Where the state is not strong enough to assume a directive role in this way, the result is likely to be stagnation under the yoke of tradition. There has to be a two-way flow of information between the state and individuals in civil society; and there has also to be a balance of power between them, a balance of power in which the occupational associations are supposed to play an essential mediating role. In a developed 'industrial society', the state cannot be transcended as is presumed in socialist theory. If circumstances which approach this came about in fact, in a developed society, the result would precisely be a reappearance of the 'tyranny of the group' characteristic of mechanical solidarity.

By means of such an analysis, then, Durkheim sought to distinguish his political theory from those of both Right and Left. Thus in the former – in, for example, the works of Hegel and his followers – the state is the very incarnation of societal ideals, and envelops the individual. If put into practice, this type of political theory leads to despotism. The socialist conception of abolishing the state, of re-absorbing the state into civil society, on the other hand, if put into practice, produces tyranny. This is not, however, for Durkheim a tyranny of an individual ruler, rather a tyranny of blind habit or prejudice.

I have said that Durkheim's ideas on the state should be taken seriously, but this does not mean I am particularly persuaded by them. Some writers have tried to develop Durkheim's notion that there should be 'secondary groups' intervening between individuals and the state, into a theory of the origins of totalitarianism. But I do not think such attempts have proved to be illuminating.[11] I do not believe any discussion of the state and democracy can be well founded unless it takes account of the class character of the capitalist societies; and, as I have previously pointed out, Durkheim's sociology is specifically opposed to such a view. Why Durkheim's political writings are worth taking seriously is because they focus upon themes which are at best confronted only in a rudimentary way in Marx. I shall single out only two such themes for discussion here: first, the problem of the importance of the range of individual rights which Durkheim labelled generically 'moral individualism' in the modern state; and second, the question of the relevance to Marxist thought of the Saint-Simonian notion of the state as concerned only with the 'administration of things'. Durkheim's writings on these matters are thought-provoking, and I believe they address issues of major importance. In discussing them here, however, I shall abandon Durkheimian terminology because, as I have said, I do not propose to try to salvage much of Durkheim's own mode of approach to these themes.

The rights involved in moral individualism are essentially those which Marx called 'bourgeois rights'. Marx quite often wrote in a dismissive fashion about them, on the basis that they form an ideological prop to the capitalist class system. The worker is 'free' to sell his or her labour-power to any employer; but this 'freedom' is actually closely bound up with the degradation of labour resulting from the nature of the capitalist labour contract. 'Political freedom', in the nineteenth century at least, was for the working class a sham in two senses. It was a sham in a quite manifest sense, in so far as property qualifications on the vote ensured that the mass of the work-force was not enfranchised. But Marx saw a more deep-lying limitation than this. For the participation of the 'citizen' as a periodic voter in the sphere of 'politics' leaves economic life untouched. On entering the factory gates, the worker leaves behind any rights of participation; democracy in the state permits the autocracy of capital over wage-labour.

I think this analysis to be broadly correct, but it has left something of an ambiguity for subsequent Marxist thought. Are 'bourgeois freedoms' wholly ideological, nothing more than a mode in which the dominant class supports its hegemony? Many Marxists have in fact taken such a view. But it is none the less quite a mistaken standpoint, in my opinion. 'Bourgeois freedoms' in Marx's terminology – rights attaching to 'moral individualism' in that of Durkheim, or, as T. H. Marshall says, 'citizenship rights'[12] – have proved to be of great significance in explaining certain features in the development of the capitalist societies over the past century. Durkheim saw the state as the principal instrument of the furthering of citizenship rights, independently of class interests. Such a view will not do, for reasons I have mentioned. The state, in capitalism, is a state in a class society, in which political power is skewed by the nature of class domination. But the existence of citizenship rights, and the struggles of labour movements to actualise or expand them, have brought about major social changes. The nineteenth-century state was, as Macpherson has said, a 'liberal' state: one allowing the organised formation and competition of parties, but where such parties only represented certain dominant interests.[13] The transformation of the liberal state into the 'liberal-democratic' state was in most countries in substantial degree the result of struggles of labour movements to form recognised parties and to achieve the universal franchise. As Marshall has pointed out, there has occurred in most Western countries a threefold expansion of citizenship rights, leading from 'legal', to 'political', to 'social' (or welfare) rights.[14]

I do not want to argue, as Marshall does, that the development and actualisation of citizenship rights have substantially dissolved pre-existing class divisions. But I do think it very important to resist the idea, which can no doubt be supported by various textual excerpts from Marx, that such rights are merely a means of 'ensuring the reproduction of labour-power'. This view radically undervalues the struggles of labour movements that have played their part in the formation of liberal democracy; and it therefore does not provide an accurate basis for analysing past transformations. But those of us who still have sympathy for socialist thought, however, have to give some considerable thought to the question of the normative significance of citizenship rights. Liberal democracy remains a sham in the second sense of Marx's critique mentioned above. However, rights which until quite recently many Marxists have accepted quite casually as of only marginal importance to a projected socialist society of the future turn out to be very important indeed. I shall rather arbitrarily mention here only two aspects of this, one from the West, and one from Eastern Europe. The resurgence of conservatism in various Western countries, including Britain and the USA, has made manifest the fact that the 'welfare state' is no mere comfortable functional mechanism cohering capitalism. Welfare rights and services are under severe attack, and in such a context it is surely not possible to see them as mere devices of capitalist domination. Rather, it seems that citizenship rights are important bases of freedoms that those in subordinate positions are able to sustain; and that, far from being able to take them for granted, we have to emphasise that in the context of liberal democracy they are continually subject to contestation.

State power and citizenship

The development of 'Euro-communism' has served to provide a focus for some of these issues. But there is no doubt in my mind that a good deal of re-thinking is required concerning the relation of socialism and democracy. Questions of the significance of various types of citizenship rights are of course only one angle on this; and at this point I can appropriately turn to the other aspect of Durkheim's writings on socialism which I have argued continues to have a certain relevance today. Durkheim's claim that, both in socialist theory in general and in Marxism in particular, the state is reduced to a purely economic agency is perhaps exaggerated and oversimplified. But in stressing certain common threads in political economy and Marx's views, he makes an important observation. Marx's writings were undeniably influenced by the form of social thought which he devoted most of his mature work to criticising. For both the political economists and for Marx, the expansion of industrial capitalism signalled the increasing pre-eminence of relationships of economic exchange over other types of social relation. Moreover, in the anticipation of the abolition of the state in socialism, there is more than an echo of the Saint-Simonian formula that 'the administration of human beings' will be replaced by 'the administration of things'.

Now we know that for Marx the term 'abolition', in the phrase 'abolition of the state', has to be understood as *Aufhebung* – transcendence. Marx was explicitly opposed to anarchism, and rather than doing away with the state altogether envisaged its radical reorganisation with the advent of socialist society. But he gave little indication of what form this would take, and how concretely it was to be achieved. The notion of the 'abolition of the state', I consider, is not simply an archaic idea to be forgotten about in the altered circumstances of the twentieth century. But, in the context of the history thus far of the 'actually existing' socialist societies, no one can afford to be in the least complacent about the thesis that there is some clear and direct tie between socialism and the transcendence of the state. Nor can we merely wish away the claims of right-wing political theorists that socialism is linked 'at source' with totalitarian elements which actually accentuate rather than diminish the power of the state over individuals in civil society.

But Durkheim's own conception of the state does not advance much beyond that of Marx. Durkheim's writings provide very little conceptual grasp of two features of the state that have proved to be of fundamental significance in our era. One of these refers to 'internal', the other to 'external', characteristics of the state. So far as the latter are concerned, we have at this point to stop talking of 'the state' in the abstract. For at least since the origins of industrial capitalism, 'the state' has been the *nation-state*; and nation-states have existed in interrelation with one another. Industrial capitalism, as a form of economic production, emerged in conjunction with a pre-existing European state-system. The recent writings of Tilly and Skocpol, among others, have done much to help explicate the nature of this relationship.[15] The nation-state system today, of course, has become a world-wide one, a common denominator among political systems of otherwise widely variant complexions. Of the various elements of the modern nation-state by far the most important for us to seek to understand and analyse is its monopoly of the means of violence. Marxism specifically lacks a tradition that can provide the source for such an analysis. I have argued elsewhere[16] that it *is* possible, however, to forge connections between Marx's discussion of capitalism and the concentration of the means of violence in the hands of the state. I have earlier drawn attention to the importance of the capitalist labour contract in Marx's explication of the nature of capitalist production. A singular feature of capitalistic enterprise, as involving formally 'free' wage-labour, is that the main form of constraint ensuring the compliance of the labour force is the need of workers to have paid employment in order to survive. The worker loses any rights of participation in the organisation of the labour process; but the employer also forgoes the capacity to achieve compliance through threat of the use of violence. In contrast to virtually all prior class systems, the dominant class does not have direct access to the means of violence in order to secure its appropriation of surplus production. Control of the means of violence becomes 'extruded' from the exploitative class relation itself, and monopolised in the hands of the state.

The historical conditions that gave rise to this 'extrusion' were complicated, and I have no space to offer an analysis of them here. But they involved concomitant processes of the 'internal pacification' of nation-states. The recent writings of Foucault and others, in my view, have helped considerably to illuminate the mechanisms contributing to these processes. For a distinctive trait of states from the late eighteenth century onwards has been a vast expansion in the range and intensity of their activities of *surveillance* over their subject populations. 'Surveillance' refers to two sets of related phenomena (although these are not distinguished as such by Foucault).

The first concerns the collation of information used to 'keep tabs' on those subject to the authority of the state. As archaeologists have frequently stressed, the close association between the formation of early agrarian states and the origins of writing is not accidental. Writing seems to have been invented first of all as a recording device whereby states could 'store' information used in their governance. Surveillance in this sense has always been closely bound up with states of all kinds. But there is no doubt that the eighteenth and nineteenth centuries in Western Europe witnessed a vast extension and intensification of the activities of the state in this respect. The mushrooming of 'official statistics' is perhaps the best single exemplification of this.

Surveillance in its second sense refers to the direct or indirect *supervision* of the conduct of subject populations on the part of the state. The development of internal police forces is a major element here. But 'policing', as Donzelot has recently argued,[17] has to be understood in a broader sense than it has come to assume in language today. When he talks of, and seeks to examine, the 'policing' of the family in the nineteenth century, he is concerned to study how the supervisory activities of states penetrate to the interior of family life. The very period at which the differentiation of 'state' from 'civil society' was most taken for granted in the political literature was the period at which states began to spread their tentacles into numerous spheres of everyday life. We should not ignore this when we acknowledge the importance of Marx's discussion of the severance of the 'economic' from the 'political'. One of the major errors of social theory from the eighteenth century to the present day has been to presume that the 'economic' can be equated with the sphere of 'civil society'.

The relation between citizenship rights and the nation-state is an interesting and in some part an asymmetrical one. Marx might have believed that 'the workers have no country', but this has hardly turned out to have been one of his most trenchant observations. Struggles to achieve citizenship rights have almost wholly been carried on within the bounds of nation-states, and the very notion of 'citizenship' (in contrast to its earlier association with towns in the context of post-feudal society) has come to be defined in nationalist terms. One consequence of this is that there is not necessarily a direct connection between the nature and prevalence of citizenship rights within particular states, and the external conduct of those states. In this sense, it could perhaps be argued, there is a basic asymmetry between the USA and the Soviet Union in the world today. One would be hard put to it to argue that the Soviet Union is a 'freer' society internally, as regards the rights of its citizenry *vis-à-vis* the state, than the USA. But the role of the Soviet Union in the world at large, Poland and Afghanistan notwithstanding, tends to be less reactionary than that of its capitalist adversary.

The relation between citizenship rights and the surveillance activities of states is also not an unambiguous one. Collation of information and the supervision of at least certain sectors of the behaviour of subject populations is part and parcel of, for instance, the operation of any universal franchise that is not corrupt. At the same time, surveillance activities of various kinds can be directly inimical to the freedoms of individuals in civil society. Brutal forms of police repression are probably not the most disturbing instance of such a phenomenon. More insidious and difficult to combat are the rapid development of centralised modes of information storage and processing made possible by modern computer technology. Surveillance in the first sense of the term I distinguished threatens in the modern age to become a more potent threat to freedom than surveillance in its second sense. But in so far as Left political theory has tried to come to terms with surveillance at all as a mode of state domination, it is mainly in respect of its second aspect.

I cannot attempt in the compass of this discussion to work out the implications of all this for contemporary socialist thought. Anyone interested in, or sympathetic to, socialism today is quite clearly in a very different position from either Marx or Durkheim, writing in the nineteenth and early twentieth centuries. Socialism has to be theorised today on two intersecting levels, and it will not do to work on either without reference to the other. For both Marx and Durkheim, socialism was a project, a set of possible developments for the future. For us, however, socialism is an 'actually existing' reality, and yet at the same time remains a set of ideals capable of generating potentialities as yet unrealised anywhere. Herein reside some of the most urgent problems of political theory. The contemporary world is the world of the Gulag, of warlike confrontations between socialist nation-states, and of something close to genocide in Kampuchea. Socialism no longer walks innocently in this world. One possible response to this is to follow the direction taken by the 'new philosophers' in France. They are the protagonists of the 'May events' of 1968 who find themselves, not in a world of liberated humanity, but in an age of a 'barbarism with a human face'. In consequence, they have moved from Marx to Nietzsche, declaring power and the state to be intransigent barriers to the realisation of any sort of socialist ideals. In a certain respect they are correct: the state is an altogether more formidable and pervasive phenomenon than was ever conceived of in the dominant traditions of thought in the nineteenth century. We should not tread their path and acquiesce helplessly in the triumph of state power. But if we do not wish to follow them, if we do not wish to move from Marx to Nietzsche – if we want to keep socialist political thought alive – we may have to be prepared to place radically in question some of the most cherished concepts of classical Marxism.

References

1. See my article 'Durkheim's political sociology', in *Studies in Social and Political Theory* (London: Hutchinson, 1977).

2. Emile Durkheim, *Socialism* (New York: Collier, 1962) p. 68.
3. Ibid, p. 70.
4. Talcott Parsons, *The Structure of Social Action* (New York: Free Press, 1949) pp. 340–1.
5. Robert A. Nisbet, *The Sociological Tradition* (London: Heinemann, 1967); Lewis A. Coser, 'Durkheim's conservatism and its implications for his sociological theory', in Kurt H. Wolff (ed.), *Emile Durkheim* (New York: Harper & Row, 1960).
6. Cf. my 'Four myths in the history of social thought', in *Studies in Social and Political Theory*.
7. Durkheim, *Socialism*, p. 58.
8. Review of Labriola, *Revue philosophique*, 1897.
9. Cf. Christopher Hill, *The World Turned Upside Down* (London: Temple Smith, 1972).
10. See 'Classical social theory and the origins of modern sociology', *American Journal of Sociology*, vol. 81, 1976.
11. Cf. William Kornhauser, *The Politics of Mass Society* (London: Routledge & Kegan Paul, 1960).
12. T. H. Marshall, *Citizenship and Social Class* (Cambridge: Cambridge University Press, 1949).
13. C. B. Macpherson, *The Real World of Democracy* (Oxford: Clarendon Press, 1966).
14. Marshall, *Citizenship and Social Class*.
15. Charles Tilly, *The Formation of National States in Europe* (Princeton University Press, 1975); Theda Skocpol, *States and Social Revolutions* (Cambridge: Cambridge University Press, 1979).
16. *A Contemporary Critique of Historical Materialism* (London: Macmillan, 1981).
17. Jacques Donzelot, *The Policing of Families* (London: Routledge & Kegan Paul, 1979).

10

Literature and Society: Raymond Williams

The past few years have seen a remarkable merging of issues in a number of erstwhile largely separate areas of intellectual endeavour. C. P. Snow some while ago provoked a storm of controversy by arguing that a chasm had opened up between the natural sciences and the humanities. But one could perhaps claim (as some did at the time) that this in fact understated the case.

In so far as academic disciplines are concerned, there were actually three broad areas largely sealed off from one another: for to these two separate constituencies of knowledge one could add the social sciences. Although the dominant tradition in the social sciences was one that set out to ape natural science, few sociologists either knew much about natural science or were well read in the literature of the philosophy of science. Fewer still paid any attention to aesthetics or literary criticism: the suggestion that these might have some bearing on problems of sociology, or vice versa, would have been received with scorn or incomprehension. All this has now changed. Social theory is today the meeting-ground of the philosophy of science and poetics; at the same time, these influences have transformed, and have themselves been changed, by new conceptions of the character and goals of social analysis.

Marxist writings have been at the centre of these transformations, although the discussions involved have by no means been dominated by Marxist authors. 'Marxism' is no longer a single body of doctrines, if it ever was, but includes a variety of differing epistemological, theoretical and practical viewpoints. Some of these viewpoints, such as those associated with the input of phenomenology or structuralism into Marxist thought, have emanated from intellectual schools that used to be virtually unknown in Britain.

Britain has in any case classically lacked a strong tradition of Marxist thought. One of the main contributions of the *New Left Review*, since Perry Anderson assumed the editorship, has been to promote a sophisticated forum for the development of Marxist debate in Britain. Under Anderson's leadership, the *New Left Review* has followed a definite 'house line': the presence of Althusser and of those substantially influenced by him has brooked large. None the less there is no doubt that the journal has played a part in furthering the goal of integrating Britain more directly into the diversity of what Anderson calls 'Western Marxism'. By the same token, it has tended to operate in a rather rarefied and arcane intellectual atmosphere, and some have not welcomed initiation into the 'mysteries of Paris'. The influence of Althusser and his students, not only as promoted by the *New Left Review*, but also as expressed in a different form in the writings of Hindess, Hirst and others, has recently been violently attacked by E. P. Thompson in a book called *The Poverty of Theory*.

The perspectives and style of the contemporary *New Left Review* are not at all to the taste of some of the 'older generation' of socialists who were connected with the earlier years of the evolution of the journal, originally formed from a merger of the *Universities and Left Review* and *New Reasoner*. All, however, is not sectarian bitterness. Raymond Williams is one of the most distinguished of those in the 'older generation' associated with the initial founding of the *New Left Review*, and he has continued to publish in its pages.

Politics and Letters takes the form of a dialogue between Williams and three members of the editorial board of the *New Left Review*, Perry Anderson, Anthony Barnett and Francis Mulhern.[1] Williams was interviewed by these three – presumably collectively, although this is not indicated and the separate questioners are not identified – over a period of some months in 1977–8. The result is a bulky volume, in which the questions are often longer and more complicated than the answers. How Williams managed to understand them immediately and fully, as he appears to have done, I do not know. The foreword does not explain how the book has been edited, if at all. At any rate, there are no ums and ers, or any places at which the subject of the grilling says, 'I didn't quite follow' or 'Would you mind repeating that?' However the book was actually put together, it contains a great deal of interesting material and the questioning is frequently acute.

The road Raymond Williams has travelled in his career runs not from Eton to Wigan Pier, but from a working-class background in Pandy, on the Welsh borders, to Jesus College, Cambridge. This was his personal long revolution, and in the course of the interviews it becomes apparent how closely his writings have been bound to his own experiences. In being forced to confront his own biography, and his own bibliography, Williams does not – or so it seems to the reader, anyway – attempt to force his intellectual career into a framework that is of recent construction. Rather, with the candour and modesty of a man slightly surprised about his own success, he admits to major limitations in various sectors of his work, and talks freely of the chance factors that have affected the direction of his life.

Williams came from a family with strong Labour Party affiliations, and moved in socialist circles from the early years of his life through to his studies as an undergraduate in Cambridge – which were interrupted by the Second World War, and resumed afterwards. Rather than creating a source of tension or dissonance for the working-class boy 'making it' to Cambridge, Williams's socialist connections and interests provided a cushion against the potentially disruptive experience of moving between two very different milieux. His parents strongly believed in the desirability of education and were a source of consistent support; the Socialist Club in Cambridge offered a network of friends within the university.

As an undergraduate prior to the war, Williams joined the Communist Party but not, as he says, with the consciousness that he was abandoning reformist politics in favour of an actively militant stance. He speaks of the atmosphere of the Socialist Club as a 'confident culture', and this was obviously in both a personal and political sense very important to him. It left untouched the formal pattern of university work, since political activities were mostly kept separate from the university as an organisation. It was very different, he remarks, from the climate of the late 1960s: not only because of the direct clashes with the university administration in which radical students were involved in the second period, but because of the 'intense divisiveness' among different groups on the Left at the later time.

Williams did not stay in the Communist Party after being called up to serve in the war. His leaving was not brought about in a calculated fashion, he says; he merely allowed his membership of the party to lapse. By the time he returned to Cambridge after the war, in which he served in an anti-tank unit and participated in the Normandy landings, he was no longer a part of this 'confident culture'. A period of disillusion and self-doubt was combined with a drive to take up academic work 'quite fanatically'.

The influence of Leavis was by that time beginning to make itself felt, and certain of his ideas attracted Williams strongly. From that time to this, Williams has been preoccupied with 'culture' in its various senses. Three elements of Leavis's views seemed to Williams to lend themselves to the formulation of a 'cultural politics' very distant in other respects from Leavis's position. One was the radical nature of Leavis's attacks upon academic literary criticism and contemporary standards of journalism. Another was the discovery of practical criticism: a discovery Williams found 'intoxicating' at the time, but towards which he today maintains a more reserved attitude. Just as important as these was Leavis's emphasis upon the significance of education, which Williams of course interpreted in his own fashion, but which accorded with his own experience.

He shortly afterwards acquired a job teaching literature for the WEA in Oxford – a job which he found discouraging in some ways, but which also influenced his academic work in a direct fashion. He remained teaching in adult education until moving to a lectureship in Cambridge in 1961. Cambridge, one is tempted to say, always reclaims its own.

Culture and Society and *The Long Revolution* were the books that made Williams famous, but the second was very much an extension of certain basic ideas established in the earlier book. Each has actively contributed to the long revolution which they diagnosed, in the sense that they have reached a very broad audience.

In *Culture and Society*, Williams suggested that it was both possible and necessary to move towards what he called 'a new general theory of culture'. The main theme of the book was that both the notion of culture and the term itself, in recognisably modern usage, came into currency in England during the period of the Industrial Revolution. The connection, Williams tried to demonstrate, was not a fortuitous one, and he attempted to chart the progress of the idea through the works of a variety of authors from the opening of the nineteenth century through to the mid-twentieth century. The book introduced a number of other 'key words' which he showed came into use, or were substantially modified, in the period of the Industrial Revolution: 'industry', 'democracy', 'class' and 'art'. He had intended to include an appendix which would detail no less than sixty such key terms; by the dictate of the publisher this was removed from the published version, and only appeared some twenty years later, in 1976, as a separate book, *Keywords*. But the keyest of Williams's key words remained that of 'culture', which, he argued, in *Culture and Society* and *The Long Revolution*, expressed two related sets of processes. The emergence of the term marked an acknowledgement of the separation of a particular sphere of moral and intellectual concerns from the driving-force of the new society, industrialism.

But the development of the concept of culture also provided what he called 'a court of human appeal . . . a mitigating and rallying alternative' to the experience of industrial production. As he made clear in *The Long Revolution*, the idea of culture was a response to political change as well as to economic change, more specifically to development of democratic ideals. There is no easy and obvious correlation, he pointed out, between industrialisation and democracy. But economic growth and political transformation, he thought, had been fairly well documented by previous writers. Such documentation had, however, to be related to a 'third revolution', the expansion of culture in its interrelation with economic and political development: this was the analysis he set out to provide in *The Long Revolution*.

The book, like its predecessor, provoked some considerable controversy, as their author had meant them to do. Many critics objected especially to the strongly defined 'sociological' components of Williams's analyses, as expressed in the relating of intellectual or literary culture to the 'structures of sentiment' of the culture of the common people. Williams's interviewers press him quite hard on what they see as the shortcomings of the two works. He does not concede everything, but evidently himself feels at some distance from them today, and he is particularly critical of *Culture and Society*.

He shows himself to be as penetrating a reviewer of his earlier work as his interrogators, and in the discussion some of its principal limitations emerge rather clearly. The books counterpose 'industry', rather than 'capitalism', to culture, and do not adequately explore either the dislocations between different sectors of cultural life, or situate them within the context of class struggles. Cultural development appears as something of a separate and abstracted process – an emphasis which derived in some part, but certainly not completely, from the presumption that economic and political transformations had already been relatively well chronicled and the problem was to 'add on' the third dimension of culture.

Williams's subsequent writing career has been a very productive one, and although in one sense he has ranged over a considerable span of subjects, his work can none the less be readily seen as comprising a single overall project. He has not deviated from the goal of analysing and furthering the long revolution towards a 'participatory socialism', and of concentrating upon developing methods of cultural diagnosis and critique relevant to that goal. This continuity is evident enough in *Communications* and his book on *Television*. But both his novels and his more specialised discussions of drama and literary criticism relate closely to his other writings. The connections between the various aspects of Williams's work are covered in an illuminating way in the interchanges between him and his questioners.

There are of course again strong biographical elements in Williams's novels, but their theme is not simply the description of personal experience: it is the relating of such experience to broad-based movements of social change. Just as in *The Long Revolution* he protested against the equation of working-class culture with a few 'proletarian novels', so in *Border Country* he wanted to avoid an account of an encapsulated working-class community separated from the rest of the world. The novel differs from the characteristic tone of much British fiction of the 1950s, the individual escaping, for better or worse, from the grip of a working-class upbringing; there is a greater emphasis upon the changes that the community itself undergoes. The transition between the personal and the public, the intersection between private experience or feeling and 'structures of sentiment', come through as predominant features of Williams's concerns and ones with which he has continually struggled.

It is prominent also in his works on drama. As an undergraduate he wrote a long essay on Ibsen, later partially incorporated in *Drama from Ibsen to Eliot*. Ibsen early on crystallised certain of Williams's own feelings at a time when he had lost some of the certitude he had previously enjoyed. But in Ibsen the combating of despair is treated as a subjective project, and it took some while before Williams managed to recognise in full the need to amend this view of 'individual liberation' in the light of a conception of 'social liberation'.

The position expressed in the book, he later came to realise more clearly, was an 'inherently unstable' one for this among other reasons. His discovery of Brecht, and the highly original discussion of that author which appears in *Drama from Ibsen to Brecht*, enabled him to modify his earlier view. Williams did not see Brecht merely as a 'political dramatist'. Brecht transcended one of the main confines of naturalistic drama by refusing to treat events 'off-stage' as unexplicated determinants of the on-stage drama; not, however, by substituting politics for naturalism, but by making the actual dramatic actions embody the presence of erstwhile 'outside' history.

There seem to me to be many unresolved difficulties in Williams's work prior to the present decade, in which the publication of *Marxism and Literature* marks something of a break with the general continuity in his earlier writings. I do not think that some of the most basic of these difficulties are explored fully enough by the *New Left Review* group. Among these I would mention particularly Williams's long-standing emphasis upon the concept of culture as the key word that opens more latches than any other; the pronounced concentration of his writings upon British sources and British history; and a series of latent 'hermeneutic problems', or problems of language, meaning and epistemology, that are especially manifest in *Keywords*. The first two of these points can be bracketed with one another. In fastening upon the notion of culture, Williams was able to open up new horizons for social history. Whatever he may feel about them now, there is no doubt that *Culture and Society* and *The Long Revolution* were outstanding contributions, works whose contemporary relevance is far from exhausted.

At the same time, there is equally no doubt in my mind that the centrality Williams accorded to 'culture' as an organising concept has proved to be a double-edged sword. It created dilemmas that I do not think he has been able to resolve satisfactorily in his subsequent writings. These dilemmas are various, but they stem in some degree from promoting the idea of 'culture' and demoting the idea of 'society'; and from the essentially conservative context from which he took the notion, although he tried to turn it to radical advantage. Even in *Keywords*, written relatively recently, when discussing the origins of modern uses of 'culture', Williams seems to me to underplay the significance of its derivation from *Kultur* and from German Romanticism. He agrees with his *New Left Review* critics that it was a mistake to have written *Culture and Society* as if British thought developed in isolation from the Continent, and makes it apparent that of his earlier works this is the one he feels least affinity with today. None the less, he continued to centre his writings on the concept of culture.

Both the German Romantics and their English admirers or counterparts on the conservative side – up to and including Eliot – juxtaposed culture and industry or technology. In seeking to radicalise their thought, Williams continued the same juxtaposition. But it is just this polarity which obscures the grounding of modern technology in the capitalist accumulation process, and which in my opinion opposes 'idealism' to 'materialism' in an unacceptable manner. It is very much connected to the assertion of the primacy of 'culture' over 'society'. As used by many sociologists to imply some sort of harmonious societal unity, the term 'society' may justly be regarded with suspicion. But if understood as social relations of both dependence and struggle, it supplies an essential mediation between the polarity of 'culture' and 'industry' as these appear in Williams's writings.

Partly for these reasons, I think, what I have previously mentioned as one of Williams's most persistent preoccupations, the relations between 'structures of sentiment or feeling' and the nature of day-to-day personal experience, remains elusive. Throughout his writing he has argued that, as he put it in *The Long Revolution*, 'What we are looking for, always, is the actual life that the whole organisation is there to express.'

Day-to-day experience involves both continuity and change, change which in the modern era is expressed in linguistic mutations such as are analysed in *Keywords*. Two overlapping traditions of philosophy seem to be particularly relevant to conceptualising these matters, but neither, so far as I know, is drawn upon by Williams: hermeneutic phenomenology, and the philosophy of the later Wittgenstein. One of the most important developments marked by each of these forms of contemporary philosophy is that they insist that personal experience is known to the self as a 'self' only via the public categories of language. They specifically reject the dualism of private experience and socially formed culture which, it seems to me, Williams's analyses still presuppose, however much he might insist they are to be related to one another. It is a mistake to associate these philosophies with the 'linguistic turn' that is so frequently regarded as a major feature of contemporary social thought. For both stress the interweaving of language and practice, the 'other face' of language in 'Being' or 'what cannot be spoken'. Hermeneutic philosophy has also for a long while raised an issue that is posed rather acutely by *Keywords*, and the mode of cultural analysis it expresses: the issue of the historical character of human knowledge.

If the changes in terminology Williams describes are more than just changes in terminology – if they are, as he holds, changes in overall frames of experience or meaning – there is no obvious reason why his own analyses of such changes should themselves be exempt from the historical process. Problems of the relativity of human knowledge, which crop up not only in hermeneutics but in the post-Kuhnian philosophy of science, seem integral to Williams's enterprise. *Keywords* does not confront such problems at all.

These comments, as I have said, refer to Williams's work before the appearance of *Marxism and Literature*. This is a much more abstract or 'theoretical' book than anything he attempted previously, and among other things delves into problems of relativism in a fairly direct way. So much so, in fact, that his interviewers are slightly scandalised; could Williams himself be tumbling into a relativist position? Williams's response to this, and the reasons he states in the opening part of *Marxism and Literature* as to why he wrote the book, bring us back to the themes I mentioned at the beginning.

Marxism today is embroiled in a series of debates which are transforming contemporary intellectual life. As Williams says in *Marxism and Literature*, two decades ago, in the English-speaking world, it seemed as though Marxism was 'a settled body of theory or doctrine' and that literature was also 'a settled body of work, or kinds of work, with known general qualities and properties'. The relation between the two could be examined, and Marxism 'applied' to literature. Williams has never been a 'Marxist' in this sense, and his earlier books were written from the point of view of what he now calls a 'radical populism'.

Marxism, however, he argues, has become an open and flexible tradition of thought, rather than a dogmatic set of doctrines. At the same time, what 'literature' is has become problematic. In response to these changes, Williams has become considerably more sensitive to what he describes as the 'danger of relativism', but denies that he has succumbed to it.

He identifies his standpoint as one of 'cultural materialism', and although the book expresses a major transition in his thought, the new Williams retains a great deal of continuity with the old. The book again begins with the concept of culture, and the notion of structures of feeling plays a pivotal role. But this time language is seen to be involved in a complex way with these ideas, and Williams tries to integrate a discussion of meaning with an analysis of the base/superstructure problem in Marxism. He begins to formulate a viewpoint which sees 'language and signification as indissoluble elements of the material social process itself involved all the time both in production and reproduction'. I think this conception to be essentially correct. I am not at all convinced, however, that Williams manages in the book either to elaborate upon it successfully, or that it is rendered compatible with some of his earlier ideas which he claims to sustain.

We have recently been passing through a phase of 'rabid idealism', Williams says at one point. He then adds that while on the one hand 'there is no natural seeing and therefore there cannot be a direct and unmediated contact with reality', on the other 'it is necessary to recall an absolutely founding presumption of materialism: namely that the natural world exists whether anyone signifies it or not'. This sounds more like some sort of version of Kantianism than anything else. I imagine that Williams would not wish to advocate a Kantian position. However that may be, it seems to me that some of the main dilemmas raised by Williams's earlier work remain unresolved after *Marxism and Literature*, and indeed have become to a certain degree compounded.

If I have sounded a negative note in the above paragraphs, it is in the same spirit, if not wholly along the same lines, as the attitude adopted by Williams's questioners. However, it is quite plain that the work of Raymond Williams – still in progress – represents an extraordinary achievement. Like its author, it stands up robustly to critical battering and there is indeed justification for the assessment given in the blurb on the book jacket: 'Raymond Williams is the most productive and most influential socialist writer in England today.' I have as strong reservations about some aspects of the political content of his writings as I have about the elements I have mentioned just previously. But Williams's sustained commitment to the long revolution towards a participatory socialism, a commitment that is both reasoned and deeply felt, offers a source of inspiration to everyone interested in radical social change.

Reference

1. Raymond Williams, *Politics and Letters: Interviews with New Left Review* (London: New Left Books, 1979).

11

The Improbable Guru: Re-Reading Marcuse

'The improbable Guru of surrealistic politics': a phrase used in *Fortune* magazine in the late 1960s to describe Herbert Marcuse.[1] Why improbable? Because Marcuse, already at that time 70 years old, had for many years laboured in relative obscurity, a writer less than limpid in style, whose works were known only to certain sectors of the academic community. One book above all others propelled Marcuse to a fame – or brought to him a notoriety – which stretched far beyond the bounds of the academy. First published in 1964, *One-Dimensional Man* coincided with the initial rise of the student movement in the USA, and became something of a manifesto for student activists associated with the New Left in many countries. Today the New Left already appears positively ancient, in a climate of opinion and political activity which has seen the rise of a New Right. Marcuse himself, of course, was far from wholly content with the ways in which his work was invoked by New Left radicals. Indeed, while lending his support to various of the radical activities of the period, Marcuse foresaw that the impact of the student movements might be limited; and he anticipated their dissolution. In 1969 he wrote that neither the students, nor the New Left more generally, could be seen as the progenitors of a new society; when their activities reached their limits, he feared, 'the Establishment may initiate a new order of totalitarian suppression'.[2]

It is not my object in this discussion to attempt an assessment of the influence of the New Left, or Marcuse's involvement with it. Neither shall I make any endeavour to examine the development of Marcuse's work as a whole. I shall concentrate my attention mainly upon *One-Dimensional Man*. What can a reading, a re-reading, of the book offer today? Was the book expressive of a transient phase in Western political life, or does it contain an analysis of contemporary society of enduring importance?

Marcuse's analysis: its leading themes

Naturally it would be misleading to sever *One-Dimensional Man* completely from Marcuse's other writings, for in some ways it represents a synthesis of them. It was written in English, and takes the USA as the prime focus of discussion. But the book continues and amplifies notions first worked out some thirty years previously, in Marcuse's early writings, formed through the combined influences of Marx, Hegel and Heidegger.[3] Although Marcuse later repudiated certain of the views adopted from Heidegger, he remained more strongly influenced by that thinker than did either of the other two principals of the 'Frankfurt School', Horkheimer and Adorno.[4] Prepared to revise Marx in a thoroughgoing fashion where necessary, Marcuse retained a life-long affiliation to a philosophical anthropology drawing in a significant fashion upon the early Marxian texts – most notably the 'Paris Manuscripts' of 1844. From Hegel he took over a conception of the 'driving power of the dialectic' as 'the power of negative thinking', employed in order to disclose the 'internal inadequacies' of the given, empirical world.[5] The inadequacies of the given world are revealed by showing how the actual inhibits the development of immanent possibilities of change that would negate the existing state of affairs. Marcuse never took this view to imply negative dialectics shorn of any transcendental basis, in the manner of Adorno. Such a conception would be inconsistent precisely with Marcuse's philosophical anthropology in which, in the later phases of his work, of course, he conjoined Freud to Marx.

All these emphases are displayed in *One-Dimensional Man*, and constitute an essential background to understanding it. The book is explicitly introduced as a work of critical theory, an analysis of society which tries to assess the range of unrealised possibilities in circumstances of apparent industrial affluence. 'Negative thinking' and the positive goals of a philosophical anthropology are here shown by Marcuse to be connected elements of a single critical enterprise. He seeks to formulate

a critical theory of contemporary society, a theory which ana-
lyzes society in the light of its used and unused or abused capabilities for improving the human condition. [Such an analysis]
implies value judgments . . . the judgment that human life is
worth living, or rather can be and ought to be made worth living
. . . [and] the judgment that, in a given society, specific possibilities exist for the amelioration of human life and specific ways of
realizing these possibilities. Critical analysis has to demonstrate
the objective validity of these judgments, and the demonstration
has to proceed on empirical grounds.[6]

One-Dimensional Man is organised into three main sections. In the
opening chapters of the book, Marcuse portrays what he calls the
'one-dimensional society', or what he often also refers to as
'advanced industrial society'. The second part is concerned with
'one-dimensional thought' – what Marcuse terms 'the defeat of the
logic of protest' which results from the specific mode of development of the advanced industrial order. In conclusion, the author
poses the question 'What alternatives are there?' What possibilities
offer themselves for transcending a form of society which Marcuse
sees as fundamentally repressive, but in which potential forms of
protest have seemingly been undermined?
    Basic to Marcuse's discussion of the first of these themes is his
interpretation of social changes that have occurred since the nineteenth century. Marx's critique of political economy was con-
structed at a period in the development of capitalism when the two
classes, bourgeoisie and proletariat, faced each other as contending
antagonists. In its classical form, in Marx's texts, critical theory was
anchored in the anticipation that the working class would bring
about the demise of capitalism, and usher in a socialist society of a
radically different character. Although these remain the basic
classes, Marcuse says, in the Western societies today, the working
class can no longer be understood as the medium of historical transformation. The working class has ceased to be the 'material negation' of the advanced industrial order, but instead has become an
integral part of that order. Advanced industrial society, according
to Marcuse, is formed of a conjunction of the welfare state and the
'warfare state'. Internally, nineteenth-century competitive capitalism has ceded place to an organised industrial economy, in which
the state, large corporations and unions co-ordinate their activities

to further economic growth. But this is also an economy geared up to the threat of war, in which vast sums are spent on armaments, and where the threat of 'international communism' is used to bolster a political unity between supposedly divergent political party programmes. 'Mobilized against this threat,' in Marcuse's words, 'capitalist society shows an internal union and cohesion unknown at previous stages of industrial civilization. It is a cohesion on very material grounds; mobilization against the enemy works as a mighty stimulus of production and employment, thus sustaining a high level of living.'[7]

Collaboration of unions with business leadership and the state is not by any means the most fundamental characteristic of advanced industrial society influencing the incorporation of the working class. More deep-rooted are changes in technology and the production process. The mechanisation of production, in which labour-power is increasingly part of the overall design of technology,[8] remains the focus of alienation. But the enslavement of the human being to the machine is concealed by the gradual disappearance of the more openly harsh, brutalising work environments. Moreover, the machine itself becomes absorbed into much more encompassing systems of technical organisation which cut across divisions between manual and non-manual labour. Class domination now appears as merely neutral 'administration'. Capitalists and managers, Marcuse says, tend to lose their separate identity as a manifestly exploiting class, just as workers lose theirs as an exploited one. Class division and alienated labour are not eliminated, but become swamped by the expansion of organisational hierarchies. Political power, for Marcuse, also becomes merged with the technical apparatus of production. However much they may regard themselves as liberal democracies, contemporary societies are totalitarian. 'For "totalitarian",' in Marcuse's view, 'is not only a terroristic political coordination of society, but also a non-terroristic economic-technical coordination which operates through the manipulation of needs by vested interests.'[9]

The social and political cohesion of advanced industrial society gives rise to a corresponding cohesion, Marcuse continues, on the level of culture. In earlier times, 'high culture', or 'intellectual culture', as he often says, celebrated ideals distant from, and was thus explicitly or implicitly antagonistic towards, existing social realities. This was never, he admits, a major stimulus to social change in and of itself; for high culture was the preserve of a minority, and operated at a distance from the mundane activities of day-to-day life. Nevertheless, it kept alive a range of alternative conceptions of the world that are today in the process of being swallowed up. The liquidation of 'two-dimensional culture' does not occur simply via the destruction of high culture, but rather through its appropriation within the established order. The values embodied in high culture are disseminated through the mass media and reduced to comfortable banalities stripped of their negating force. This is described as a process of 'repressive desublimation', a notion that connects directly with the views sketched by Marcuse in *Eros and Civilization*. Literature and art, as previously practised, rested upon the sublimation of instinctual impulses, mediated instinctual gratification. But the easy diffusion and trivialising of values and ideals permits their immediate gratification. Such desublimation is repressive because it serves only to reinforce the totalitarianism of the one-dimensional society. Sexuality is expressed within confines that repress exactly that diffusion of the erotic which Marcuse sees as the precondition for the liberated society. The erotic has become reduced to permissive sexuality. This is a civilisation whose discontents have been rendered palatable by a happy consciousness deriving from an absorption of the reality principle by the pleasure principle. Repressive desublimation 'manifests itself in all the manifold ways of fun, relaxation, and togetherness which practise the destruction of privacy, the contempt of form, the inability to tolerate silence, the proud exhibition of crudeness and brutality'.[10]

In advanced industrial society, technical reason becomes the only form of reason admitted as valid. Technical reason, the rationality of technology, defines reason purely instrumentally, in terms of the relation of means to ends. In seeing this conception as the foundation of positivism in intellectual discourse, and of contemporary ideology more generally, Marcuse's analysis at this point converges closely with that of the other members of the Frankfurt School. Reason, Marcuse says, rests upon the potentially subversive character of negation, as objectively linked to the revealing of 'internal inadequacies' of the existing world. But this subversive power of reason has itself become subverted in the 'one-dimensional thought' of technological rationality. In Classical philosophy, as in a good deal of Western metaphysics until recent times, philosophy connnected truth with the good life, with possible modes of living a free and rewarding existence. The quest for truth operated dialectically, exposing contradictions between thought and reality, and connecting such contradictions to the promise of the good life. But in instrumental reason truth concerns correspondence not contradiction, and truth (or 'fact') is separated from values.[11] Thus values cannot be rationally justified in relation to the objective world, but become matters of subjective assessment. Instrumental reason is supposedly wholly neutral in respect of values, but actually preserves as an overriding value the one-dimensional world of technical progress.

The primacy of science, conceived of as a means of controlling nature, brings the actuality of technology into direct relation with philosophy, which is more and more dominated by positivism:

> The principles of modern science [Marcuse avers] were *a priori* structured in such a way that they could serve as conceptual instruments for a universe of self-propelling, productive control; theoretical operationalism came to correspond to practical operationalism. The scientific method which led to the ever-more-effective domination of nature thus came to provide the pure concepts as well as the instrumentalities for the ever-more-effective domination of man by man *through* the domination of nature. Theoretical reason, remaining pure and neutral, entered into the service of practical reason. The merger proved beneficial to both. Today, domination perpetuates and extends itself not only through technology but *as* technology, and the latter provides the great legitimation of the expanding political power, which absorbs all spheres of culture.[12]

The ordinary language philosophy of Austin and others, and the philosophy of the later Wittgenstein, fall prey to such tendencies, however much they may superficially differ from positivism. For their aim is the freeing of philosophy from metaphysics, a cleansing operation which shows metaphysics to rest upon the misuse of language. The task of philosophy is again a 'technological' one, that of controlling its own past metaphysical excesses through the correction of language. As a therapeutic endeavour, Marcuse suggests, linguistic philosophy shares a common orientation with modern psychiatry. The unreason of madness is thus held to have an underlying affinity with the reason of metaphysics. For madness is a form of negation of the real, the concern of psychiatry being to 'adjust' the individual to the existing world, however insane that world may be. Like psychiatry, linguistic philosophy 'abhors transgression'.

A striking feature of *One-Dimensional Man* is the relative brevity of its third, concluding section: 'the chance of the alternatives' to the one-dimensional society and to one-dimensional thought. Much of what Marcuse has to say in this section is highly abstract, in a book which as a whole does not impress the reader with the detail of the discussions which it offers. The 'transcendent project' of the alternative society is spelled out in terms of its particular rationality, contrasting with the rationality of technique. The transcendent project, Marcuse claims, must retain its connection with Marx's materialism in the sense that it must be concerned with real possibilities of change at the current level of material and intellectual culture. It must demonstrate its 'higher rationality', as contrasted to technological rationality, by showing that its negation of the present (compared, for example, with nihilism) affirms values of human freedom and self-realisation. Since technology, and technological rationality, are the underlying foundation of advanced industrial society, the transformative project must focus upon the development of a 'qualitatively new technics'. Technical reason has already become the basis of politics, and its reversal would necessarily imply a political reversal. The possibility of the transcendence of technological rationality, Marcuse argues, is built into its own progression, for it is approaching its limits within the repressive order of advanced industrialism. The furthering of the mechanisation, and automation, of labour reaches a phase at which it can no longer be contained within the one-dimensional society, but threatens its disintegration. It heralds a revolutionary rupture, a movement from quantity into quality:

> It would open the possibility of an essentially new human reality – namely existence in free time on the basis of fulfilled vital needs. Under such conditions, the scientific project itself would be free for trans-utilitarian ends, and free for the 'art of living' beyond the necessities and luxuries of domination. In other words, the completion of the technological reality would be not only the prerequisite, but also the rationale for *transcending* the technological reality.[13]

On its appearance, *One-Dimensional Man* was regarded by many of its critics as a profoundly pessimistic book, since its author appeared to hold out little concrete opportunities for social change, such was the seeming success of the one-dimensional society in closing off opposition. When, in *An Essay on Liberation* and other later writings, Marcuse made overtures towards student and other militants, this was widely seen as marking a change in posture towards a more optimistic outlook. But this was only partly the case, and rested upon a double misinterpretation. Marcuse did not regard the student movement and other militant tendencies of the time as the vanguard of a coming revolution, but rather as expressive of immanent tensions within the system. The chief basis of revolutionary transformation is not to be found in the activities of those not yet wholly incorporated within the one-dimensional society. It is to be found in the very centre of the one-dimensional society itself, in the potentially explosive consequences of that very force that is the origin of its coherence: the rationality of technique. In its own terms at least, *One-Dimensional Man* is a strongly revolutionary tract, and remains faithful to what Marcuse saw as an essential thread of Marxist thought, the tension between the relations of production (of the one-dimensional society) and emergent changes in the forces of production presaging a new society. The strands of pessimism that are to be found in the earlier works of Horkheimer and Adorno, and which eventually became strongly defined in their appraisal of the age of 'the end of the individual', are largely absent from Marcuse's writings from beginning to end. Moreover, the common assertion made against Marcuse that his works are merely 'utopian' ignores his reassessment of the meaning of 'utopia' in the contemporary age. What is utopian, he argues, has changed its character in virtue of the very level of development of technology in advanced industrial society. The utopian is no longer that which is specifically implausible, or has 'no place' in history; utopian possibilities are contained in the very technical organisation of the advanced industrial order.[14]

Some substantive comments

Re-reading Marcuse today does not lead me to alter the critical perspective from which I approached his texts some years ago.[15] In some respects Marcuse is an easy target for critical attack, although he hardly deserved the short shrift he received from some adversaries on both Right and Left.[16] However, it now seems to me worth while recognising two levels upon which *One-Dimensional Man* can be read. The book can be read, as it were, as a 'substantive' text, which advances certain theses about the nature of contemporary societies. On this level much of what Marcuse has to say seemed to me a decade ago, and seems to me now, to be almost naively inadequate. But the work can also be taken, as one has to presume Marcuse really intended it to be taken, as a 'symptomatic' study: that is to say, as a probing of the possibilities of defending a critical theory of society in an era in which orthodox Marxism appears seriously deficient. Reading the work in this second aspect, one may still want to differ from some of Marcuse's views, but they remain of considerable interest and importance.

As a substantive analysis, Marcuse's work shares a good deal in common with writers with whom his ideas in other respects diverge dramatically. Bell, Lipset and many others had written of the successful incorporation of the working class in what they called 'industrial society' rather than 'capitalism'. The shift in terminology, for these writers, was not a fortuitous one. According to their view, 'capitalism', as a form of society resembling that described by Marx, was at most a transitory social order, confined to the late nineteenth and early twentieth centuries. 'Capitalism' is a subcategory of the more generic type of 'industrial society' which has come to fruition in the twentieth century. In such a society, it was argued, a general consensus upon goals of economic advance and political liberalisation replaces the old ideological disputes which polarised the social classes. The 'end of ideology' meant the end of radicalism, 'the defeat of the logic of protest' of which Marcuse also spoke.

In disputing the 'end of ideology' thesis, Marcuse confronted such views, in considerable degree, on their own terms. The one-dimensional society is a society in which the revolutionary subject of Marxist theory no longer carries the promise of radical change. The task Marcuse set himself was to demonstrate the validity, in some depth, of the remark by which C. Wright Mills almost casually dismissed the claims of the end of ideology thesis: that it itself is an ideology. *One-Dimensional Man* sought to show exactly how this could be so. The absorption of clashing opinions, of the driving power of negation, into technological rationality actually means that 'advanced industrial culture is *more* ideological than its predecessor'.[17] It is more ideological than early capitalism, according to Marcuse, because ideology has become part of the very process of production. False consciousness is integral to the 'truth' of the logic of technical reason.

The very real interest of his discussion of this point should not lead us to forget the equally significant shortcomings of the social analysis which informs it. Marcuse's adoption of the terms 'industrial society' or 'advanced industrial society' is ambiguous and confusing. He continues occasionally to use the term 'capitalism', and recognises differences between Western industrialism and that of the East European societies.[18] Moreover, in 'advanced industrial society' class relations remain constitutive of the relations of production, however much this may be concealed by the technical administration of the one-dimensional order. But by making the term 'industrial society' the preferred centre-point of his analysis, Marcuse undoubtedly moves too readily into the discourse of his opponents. This terminological preference is not merely fortuitous in his case either. Marcuse portrays a society in which capitalist mechanisms of production no longer supply the key to explaining its major institutions.

The shift in terminology must be resisted, as must Marcuse's embrace of some of the tenets of the 'theory of industrial society'.[19] In emphasising this, Marcuse's Marxist critics were surely justified.[20] If Western capitalism in the 1950s and 1960s appeared to have overcome its tendencies to crisis and depression, and to be able to generate sustained rates of economic growth, this hardly reflected fundamental alterations in the social and economic system. The expansion of the activities of the state, the increasing centralisation of national economies, and the development of regularised modes of economic bargaining, were all prominent features of the post-1945 period. But the relevance of established Marxist notions to the understanding of 'neo-capitalism' remained much more considerable than Marcuse seemed to acknowledge. In some large part this was surely due to the ambiguous and inconsistent character of his use of the concepts of 'organised capitalism' and 'advanced industrial society'. In shifting between the two, Marcuse moves between a Marxist standpoint and one instead more indebted to Max Weber: 'organised capitalism' is dominated by technical reason, or what to Weber is 'formal rationality'.[21] The changes which Marcuse holds to have stabilised capitalism, needing now to be analysed as 'advanced industrial society', conceal a shift in theoretical stance concerning the nature of capitalism itself. This unresolved tension – crudely put, a tension between Marx's conception of capitalism as a class society and the Weberian association of capitalism with the rationality of technique – is a main factor introducing inconsistencies in Marcuse's position.

In any case, the term 'one-dimensional society' surely was, and is, a misleading one. I have emphasised that Marcuse saw an immanent contradiction at the heart of the seemingly consensual order he portrayed. But his identification of that contradiction is sharply delimited by its association with the progression of technical reason as the unifying focus of the one-dimensional order. Both 'internally', and in the context of international economic and political relations, the USA and the other capitalist societies were much more divided and conflictful than Marcuse's analysis suggests. Marcuse sought to stand pluralism on its head. The pluralist political theorists, and the many advocates of the theory of industrial society, portrayed a picture of the capitalist countries seemingly quite contrary to that of Marcuse. For him, the picture was one of increasing, 'totalitarian' conformity; the others argued that the Western societies were becoming more internally differentiated, although they also supposed that a balance of 'cross-cutting conflicts' dissolved the likelihood of radical social change. But the opposition between the two viewpoints is less dramatic than one might imagine. For in agreeing that transformative conflict had been successfully contained, each underestimated the divided and fragmentary character of the 'advanced industrial societies'; and failed to connect internal sources of tension or antagonism with strains in the world system.

Moreover, the two viewpoints converged in tending to dismiss the significance of class analysis to the study of contemporary societies.[22] According to the pluralists, and some proponents of the theory of industrial society, class relations lose their significance precisely as a result of the increasing diversification of the social order. Differentiated social and economic relationships, according to such a standpoint, are incompatible with the continued importance of overall class formations. In Marcuse's view, capitalism remains a class society – although, as I have pointed out, this emphasis does not appear wholly consistent with his adoption of the conception of the primacy of technical reason in the structuring of the system. But class divisions and class conflict are no longer major sources of schism, under the impact of the harmonising effects of the one-dimensional order. Marcuse states this quite unequivocally: 'The integration of the largest part of the working class into the capitalist society is not a surface phenomenon; it has its roots in the infrastructure itself, in the political economy of monopoly capitalism.'[23] Each version of the growing irrelevance of class analysis to current struggles in the advanced societies, I think, must be strongly disputed. We cannot be satisfied today with orthodox Marxist modes of class analysis; but the conception of the 'institutionalisation of class conflict', accepted both by Marcuse and his pluralist antagonists, has also to be subject to criticism. I have set out the basis of such criticism elsewhere, and shall not detail it here.[24]

Marcuse's discussion in *One-Dimensional Man* is explicitly based upon the USA. As a diagnosis of trends of development in that society, for the reasons I have indicated, it is at best only of limited plausibility. But the presumption that the USA, as the technologically most advanced capitalist society, blazes a trail that others are destined to follow – such a prevalent conception among liberal thinkers of the period, and still not uncommon today – should be treated with some scepticism. There are two important considerations of social theory involved here. One is that we should not imagine that there is only a single model of 'advanced capitalism', other societies simply lagging behind in respect of moving towards that model. The second is equally important, however. It is that the relations between societies must be regarded as integral to studying their 'internal features'. Marcuse discusses this only from one aspect, and then in rather a crude way. The one-dimensional character of American society, he says, is stabilised by the 'controlled hostility' between the USA and the Soviet Union. How valid this is – as contrasted to an interpretation that would focus upon the extreme instabilities associated with the activities of the superpowers in a world potentially threatened by nuclear war – might be questioned. But the point in any case holds in a more general way. The political and economic involvements of American capitalism with the Western European countries, for example, help produce *differences*, as well as similarities, between them.

Technology, freedom, politics

A symptomatic reading of Marcuse reveals a much more subtle and significant set of ideas than is suggested by the remarks I have made in the above paragraphs. *One-Dimensional Man* is a radical book in a true sense. Marcuse is above all concerned to sustain a commitment to profound social transformation, and refuses to have any truck with palliatives. That a supposedly 'pessimistic' book should have served to contribute to political activism is easy to understand when it is seen in such a light. Not only does Marcuse attack all forms of compromise, he seeks to demonstrate how these in fact take on an opposite guise to their apparent one. 'Repressive tolerance', 'repressive desublimation', these terms convey Marcuse's diagnosis of the 'internal inadequacies' of one-dimensional culture. The opening sentence of the first chapter of *One-Dimensional Man* sets the tone for the whole of the book. In the West, Marcuse proposes, 'a comfortable, smooth, reasonable, democratic unfreedom prevails'.[25]

It is really not very difficult, in my opinion, to see where the continuing importance of Marcuse's work lies. Marcuse is not, as I have commented previously, a utopian thinker – at least, in the pejorative sense which that term has acquired since Marx treated 'utopian socialism' so dismissively in the nineteenth century. Whatever reservations one might have of the interpretation of Freud which Marcuse adopts, in the context of his philosophical anthropology Marcuse develops a radicalism concerned in a fundamental way with issues that are only weakly dealt with in more orthodox forms of Marxism. These are in some part, but only in some part, shared by the others in the Frankfurt School. I shall emphasise here only the following issues, among various other important problems which could be discussed: that of sexuality; and that of technology.

The time has long since passed when Marcuse could be identified, as he was by some who had only a casual acquaintance with his writings, as a protagonist of the 'permissive society'. He emerges rather as one of its strongest critics, as is made perfectly clear both in *Eros and Civilization* and in *One-Dimensional Man*. 'Sexual liberation', as understood by a good number of Marcuse's self-proposed followers ten or so years ago, and by many others today who may have barely even heard of Marcuse, is explicitly one of his main objects of attack. In this context it is perhaps worth remarking that Marcuse's discussion of sexuality is not as distant, or opposed, to that of Foucault as might appear.[26] Foucault's view of Freud and Marcuse's 'critical Freudianism' might seem quite irreconcilable, and no doubt in some respects this is the case. But when Foucault argues that, in contemporary Western civilisation, rather than liberating ourselves through sexuality we need to liberate ourselves from sexuality, there is more than an echo of Marcuse's thought in what he has to say. The discourse of 'sexuality', and a preoccupation with 'sex' is for both writers a concomitant of, rather than a mode of dissolving, the 'internalised' discipline characteristic of contemporary forms of social organisation. In Marcuse's argument, the liberation of the erotic is predicated upon the transcendence of 'sexuality', seen as a compartmentalised mode of activity distinctly separated from the rest of life. The specifically interesting feature of Marcuse's argument is the idea that the liberation of the erotic does not derive from the release from repression as such – as Reich proposed. It can only be achieved by a transformation in the very character of sublimation itself.

On the face of things, Marcuse's attempt to combine a rather orthodox version of Freud with a distinctly unorthodox version of Marx would seem to be doomed to failure. Marcuse forcibly rejects the 'revisionism' of authors such as Fromm and Horney. According to Marcuse, Freud's theory 'is in its very substance "sociological"'; it follows that 'no new cultural or sociological orientation is needed to reveal this substance'. Marcuse regards Freud's theory as already pointing to the possibility of the achievement of a non-repressive society. The most troublesome, and most frequently discarded, element of Freud's views by the psychoanalytic revisionists – the death instinct – is accorded an essential role by Marcuse in demonstrating the emancipatory potential of Freudian theory. The merging of Eros and Thanatos, in Marcuse's interpretation of Freud, is inherent in the formation of human self-determination, and closely involved with the active promotion of historical change emphasised by the early Marx. Pleasure is distinct from the 'blind satisfaction of instinct', characteristic of the behaviour of animals. In pleasure, which is generalised, instinct is not exhausted in immediate gratification, but contributes to the self-formation of the individual. This is what Marcuse calls a 'sensuous rationality'.[28] Pleasure would not be '*released*' in the society Marcuse anticipates for the future, but would have *form*. Erotic energy 'would surge up in new forms of cultural creation'. The result, he accentuates:

> would not be pansexualism, which rather belongs to the image of
> the repressive society . . . To the extent that erotic energy were
> really freed, it would cease to be mere sexuality and would
> become a force that determines the organism in all its modes of
> behaviour, dimensions and goals.[29]

Placed against the drabness, and the superficiality, of 'main-stream Marxism', these ideas retain their provocative character. They place at the fore issues that do not brook large even in the most interesting current attempt to 'reconstruct historical materialism', that of Habermas. Habermas draws extensively upon Freud in formulating his version of critical theory. But his use of Freud appears to be almost wholly 'methodological': psychoanalytic therapy demonstrates how increased autonomy of action can be achieved via the individual's own self-understanding. Habermas's conception of critical theory has been amplified in recent years through his introduction of the notion of an 'ideal speech situation' as a counterfactual condition of language-use.[30] In his earlier writings, where the psychoanalytic model of critical theory appears prominently, Habermas gives very little indication of how much he accepts of the *content* of Freud's writings. In this respect his appropriation of Freud stands in distinct contrast to that of Marcuse – and this has ramifications for Habermas's later work. For the conception of an ideal speech situation, interesting as it may be in its own right, remains on a peculiarly cognitive level. What of affect, of sexuality, love, hate and death? Whereas Marcuse's formulation of critical theory is founded upon an abiding concern with these phenomena, Habermas's account provides little way of coping with them conceptually.[31]

From his earliest works, under the influence of Heidegger, Marcuse set himself against the view – which seems to be that of the later Marx, and certainly became strongly established in orthodox Marxism – that nature is merely a means of realising human purposes. Marcuse's connection with Heidegger – one which, I have suggested earlier, was of more abiding importance for him than some critics have argued – gives his critique of instrumental reason a rather different character from the views of either Horkheimer or Adorno. For all three writers, the succumbing of orthodox Marxism to the sway of instrumental reason is inherently related to the degeneration of socialism into nothing more than an alternative mode of promoting industrialisation to that offered by capitalism. However, Marcuse's disavowal of an 'ungrounded' negative dialectics led him to emphasise that critical theory must incorporate a theory of Being. His juxtaposition of 'technics' with aesthetics' owes a lot to Adorno; and his preoccupation with technology as a medium of domination in some respects has close affinities with similar concerns of conservative authors such as Freyer, Schelsky and Gehlen. But the synthesis he worked out differs significantly from all of them. The most obvious element differentiating Marcuse's views from those of these other writers is his emphasis upon the liberating potential of technology itself. He agrees that technical progress and the progress of humanity are certainly not one and the same. But technical advance, and increasing productivity, generate the increasing possibility (even probability) of their own negation: 'increasing productivity in freedom and happiness becomes increasingly strong and increasingly rational'.[32]

As follows from Marcuse's account of the generalisable character of the erotic, this transformation cannot merely take the form of the lifting of repression. Certainly in stressing the significance of automation, Marcuse emphasises the importance of altering the character of technology itself, and of overcoming human subordination to the machine. He is fond of alluding to the passages in the *Grundrisse* in which Marx speaks of automation freeing the human being from bondage to production, and instead allowing the individual to become master of the production process. But in what he has to say about the consequences of this process, Marcuse proposes an ontology according to which humanity would again live 'in' nature and not merely 'from' it. Contemporary capitalism preys upon nature, protecting only certain areas from this destructive attitude: recreation areas, parks, etc. Nature survives here only as repressive desublimation. A drive out to the country at weekends may allow a person to recover from the pressure of work and urban life, but is a poor substitute indeed for the rich, aesthetically rewarding, relation between human beings and nature which Marcuse envisages. Here again, if it is in some part nourished from conservative sources, Marcuse's radicalism surfaces in full force. A recovery and extension of the erotic cathexis of nature, Marcuse argues, would allow human beings to 'find themselves in nature'; nature is to be found as 'a subject with which to live in a common universe'. This would in turn demand breaking through the dominant understanding of the world as commodified time–space:

> Existence [he affirms] would be experienced not as a continually expanding and unfulfilled becoming but as existence or being with what is and can be. Time would not seem linear, as a perpetual line or rising curve, but cyclical, as the return contained in Nietzsche's idea of the 'perpetuity of pleasure'.[33]

These ideas retain their relevance to current social theory. To say this, however, is not to endorse them as they stand. It would be surprising if an analysis so open to criticism on a 'substantive' level should prove unobjectionable when read 'symptomatically'. And indeed there are basic shortcomings in Marcuse's thought which cannot be overcome simply by trimming away some of the difficulties or ambiguities in his appraisal of the one-dimensional society.

Marcuse calls the contemporary Western liberal democracies 'totalitarian'. In using this term he is well aware of the differences between such societies and those more directly based on terror. 'Bourgeois democracy,' he accepts, 'is still infinitely better than fascism.'[34] Such comments, however, are no substitute for an adequate analysis of the political conditions of liberty; and such an analysis, in my opinion, is absent in Marcuse's writings. This has consequences both for his interpretation of existing societies, and for his envisaged society of the future. Marcuse's basic attitude towards liberalism was established in some of his early writings, and I do not think it changed a great deal thereafter. Liberalism, according to Marcuse, and the 'bourgeois rights' associated with it, were products of the entrepreneurial capitalism of the nineteenth century. Bourgeois freedoms, always class-biased in any case, decline with the replacement of competitive by organised capitalism. 'Liberalism,' Marcuse wrote in 1934, '"produces" the total-authoritarian state out of itself, as its own consummation at a more advanced stage of development.'[35] Liberalism and fascism, Marcuse continues, are closely affiliated: the real enemy of both is radical Marxian socialism.

This standpoint, in my assessment, is fundamentally defective. Rather than providing a basis for political analysis, it avoids it. Political power – as Marcuse makes plain in *One-Dimensional Man* – is no more than an extension of the dominance of technological rationality, of the 'power over the machine process'.[36] In the one-dimensional society, bourgeois rights and liberties become of only marginal importance, eroded by the pervasive influence of technical reason. Such a conception ignores the fact that 'bourgeois freedoms' have from the early years of capitalist development provided a stimulus to change for those excluded from them: the subordinate classes in society. Marcuse underestimates the significance of struggles to universalise rights and liberties previously effectively the privilege of the few – a forgivable view, perhaps, in Germany in the early 1930s, but not when generalised to 'advanced industrial societies' as a whole. The contemporary capitalist societies are of course in some very basic respects quite different today from those of the nineteenth century. But they have changed in some substantial part as a result of class struggle. In this respect, T. H. Marshall's account of the importance of citizenship rights, when adopted in a modified version, is highly significant.[37] By seeing the limitations of the 'democratic' in 'liberal democracy', we have some hope of constructing a political theory demonstrating how the scope of democratic participation might be expanded in a prospective socialist order.

No one today, however committed a socialist he or she might be, should complacently accept the idea that socialism (in whatever form it is conceived of) inevitably extends the range of human freedoms. But in Marcuse's writings, this idea does not appear in the least problematic. Why not? The answer is to be found in the most central of Marcuse's themes, the relation between technology and emancipation. The transformations in technology which Marcuse anticipates and advocates are *themselves*, in his analysis, the guarantee of freedom. Freedom and servitude are not, in Marcuse's theory, phenomena of politics, or even of power more broadly understood. Freedom, Marcuse repeatedly argues, is to be interpreted in relation to the satisfaction of need. In a society in which the erotic energy of the personality will be freed, the emancipation of the single individual is simultaneously the emancipation of all. Here there lurks an old-established but entirely unsatisfactory doctrine: the domination of persons will cede place to the administration of things, as the foundation of free society. Marcuse, the improbable Guru of a novel radicalism, is revealed as a latter-day adherent of an archaic political philosophy, that of Saint-Simon.

References

1. Cf. Paul Breines, *Critical Interruptions* (New York: Herder & Herder, 1972).
2. Herbert Marcuse, *An Essay on Liberation* (Boston: Beacon, 1969) p. viii.
3. Some of these appeared in translation much later, in Marcuse, *Negations* (Boston: Beacon, 1968) and in other sources. Certain early essays remain untranslated, but are readily available in the reprinted edition of the *Zeitschrift für Sozialforschung* (Munich: Deutscher Taschenbuch Verlag, 1980).
4. For an analysis which makes this particularly clear, see David Held, *Introduction to Critical Theory: Horkheimer to Habermas* (London: Hutchinson, 1980). Held remarks that, 'Of all the members of the Frankfurt School, Marcuse's life-long relation to his early work and political ambitions is perhaps the most consistent' (p. 73). For Marcuse's 'Heideggerian version' of Marx, see 'Contributions to a phenomenology of historical materialism', *Telos*, vol. 4, 1969 (originally published in 1928).
5. Marcuse, *Reason and Revolution* (New York: Oxford University Press, 1960) p. viii.
6. Marcuse, *One-Dimensional Man* (Boston: Beacon, 1966) pp. x–xi.
7. Ibid, p. 21.
8. Cf. on this point Marcuse's essay, first published in 1941, on 'Some social implications of modern technology', reprinted in Andrew Arato and Eike Gebhardt (eds), *The Essential Frankfurt School Reader* (Oxford, Blackwell, 1978).
9. *One-Dimensional Man*, p. 3.
10. Marcuse, *Eros and Civilization* (Boston: Vintage, 1961) p.x.
11. *One-Dimensional Man*, pp. 131ff.
12. Ibid, p. 158.
13. Ibid, p. 231.
14. *An Essay on Liberation*, p. 4.
15. See *The Class Structure of the Advanced Societies* (London: Hutchinson, 1973) ch. 14 and *passim*.
16. See, for instance, Alasdair MacIntyre, *Marcuse* (London: Fontana, 1970), who bluntly announced in the opening pages of his book that 'almost all of Marcuse's key positions are false' (p. 7).
17. *One-Dimensional Man*, p. 11.
18. Cf. Marcuse, *Soviet Marxism* (London: Routledge & Kegan Paul, 1958) p. xi and *passim*.
19. Cf. 'Classical social theory and the origins of modern sociology', in this volume.
20. See Paul Mattick, *Critique of Marcuse* (London: Merlin, 1972); also Claus Offe, 'Technik und Eindimensionalität. Eine Version der Technokratiethese?', in Jürgen Habermas *et al.*, *Antworten auf Herbert Marcuse* (Frankfurt: Suhrkamp, 1968).

21. Marcuse's critical assessment of Weber, it should be noted, turns more than anything else upon the assertion that what Weber saw as the formal reason of bureaucracy, and as the inevitable concomitant of contemporary society, is actually capable of radical transformation. He accepts the general thrust of Weber's analysis of 'rationalisation', while disputing its inescapable character. See 'Industrialisation and capitalism in the work of Max Weber', in *Negations*.
22. Cf. my 'Postscript' to the second edition of *The Class Structure of the Advanced Societies* (1981).
23. Marcuse, *Counterrevolution and Revolt* (Boston: Beacon, 1972) p. 6.
24. 'Postscript', pp. 312–19. See also 'Power, the dialectic of control and class structuration', in this volume.
25. *One-Dimensional Man*, p. 1.
26. Michel Foucault, *The History of Sexuality*, vol. 1 (London: Allen Lane, 1978).
27. *Eros and Civilization*, p. 4.
28. Ibid, p. 208.
29. Marcuse, *Five Lectures: Psychoanalysis, Politics and Utopia* (London: Allen Lane, 1970) p. 40.
30. See 'Habermas's social and political theory', in this volume.
31. Habermas, of course, has his own criticisms of Marcuse, whom Habermas none the less claims as one of the main influences upon his own work. See *Antworten auf Herbert Marcuse*; see also Marcuse, Habermas, *et al.*, 'Theory and politics', *Telos*, no. 38, 1978–9.
32. *Five Lectures: Psychoanalysis, Politics and Utopia*, p. 17.
33. Quotations from *Counterrevolution and Revolt*, p. 60; and *Five Lectures: Psychoanalysis, Politics and Utopia*, p. 41.
34. Marcuse, Habermas, *et al.*, 'Theory and politics', p. 148.
35. 'The struggle against liberalism in the totalitarian view of the state', in *Negations*, p. 19.
36. See especially pp. 3ff in that work.
37. See 'Class division, class conflict and citizenship rights', in this volume.

12

Class Division, Class Conflict and Citizenship Rights

I

In this essay I propose to discuss some aspects of the class structure of the 'advanced societies' in the contemporary era. But I want to preface what I have to say about 'society in the 1980s' with a brief discussion of 'sociology in the 1960s'. In the West we have passed from a period, in the 1950s and early 1960s, of apparently expanding prosperity and economic growth, to one fraught with economic ills and political perils. Some of the most influential ideas in sociology, and in the social sciences more generally, were penned during a time of seemingly stable economic development and political consensus. I do not want to say that all these ideas now have to be thrown into the dustbin, but I do think it important to learn some lessons from the shortcomings of sociological analysis at that period. For some of these shortcomings remain with us.

At the risk of sounding overly didactic, here is a short list of sociological 'don'ts' which anyone seeking to analyse the structure of societies today should observe. These strictures form the background to the substantive part of this essay. They can be summarised as follows.

1. *Don't overgeneralise from a short period of time.* Looking back at the sociology of the 1960s – prior to the student movement, and the 1968 events in France and elsewhere – it seems quite extraordinary how confidently existing trends were projected into the indefinite future. The expansion of higher education, to take just one example, was presumed by many to be an inherent and ever more prominent feature of the industrialised countries. Who could possibly be so sanguine today, as universities in many countries face severe retrenchment?

2. *Don't generalise on the basis of one society.* Nothing was more common in the 1960s than the invention of sweeping theories about the industrialised societies as a whole, for which the evidence came largely from a single society. Most commonly, the USA was seen as showing the rest of the industrialised, or at least the capitalist-industrial, world its probable future. This standpoint often rested upon a more or less direct form of technological determinism: if technology is most advanced in the USA, we see there forms of life other societies are destined to copy. But the tendency to generalise on the basis of events in one society was not limited to those who took the USA as their model, or to a perspective of technological determinism. Some who proposed, for example, mainly on the basis of material in France, that a 'new working class' was to form a potential revolutionary vanguard in capitalism were just as prone to this failing. The 'new working class', whatever its fate in France, proved to be rather less than revolutionary in countries such as the USA and Britain.

3. *Don't suppose that social change is controlled solely by immanent developments in a society.* One of the most prevalent tendencies of much sociological writing in the 1960s was to suppose that the main forces of change in a society – or even in a generic type of society – were 'built in' to that society. This I would call an 'unfolding' conception of social change; it imagines that there is something like a natural evolutionary tendency contained within societies which propels them along predicted paths of development. What the stance ignores, among other things, is something Max Weber drew attention to rather forcibly many years ago: the *contingent* character of major processes of change. It is surely an unfortunate approach which allocates the study of necessity to the sociologist, while the historian is left to dabble with contingency!

4. *Don't ignore the international context of social organisation and social change.* Surveying today much of the sociology of the 1960s it is very striking how common it was to write as though societies were isolated entities. These accounts were produced by people sitting, for example, in Britain, writing with pens made in France, wearing clothes made in Hong Kong, and whose books were printed on machines made in Japan. World system theory has now entirely correctly become a central part of sociology.

By mentioning these four points I don't want to say 'don't generalise'. I have a great fondness for generalisation, and certainly would not suggest abandoning something without which there would not be much point in doing sociology anyway. Rather, these four injunctions should serve as a cautionary reminder of the tentative character of sociological analysis. Sociology in the 1980s should not recapitulate the mistakes of those writing twenty years ago. None the less one could hardly claim that sociological writing today has at all become fully liberated from the tendencies I have just mentioned. Instead of seeing a more or less permanent political and economic consensus in the West, as many did twenty years ago, a newer generation sees endemic disarray or disintegration. Others diagnose momentous social transformations – from an 'industrial' to a 'post-industrial' society, for example – within parameters of thought which ignore all four of the points I have made. In what follows I shall at least try to follow the precepts suggested by my list of 'don'ts'. I shall endeavour to analyse some facets of class structure and class relations relevant to 'Europe in the 1980s' via a critical appraisal of certain ideas produced by the earlier generation I have been referring to, in the light of the points I have made. My analysis will not be a purely descriptive one, but I hope it will avoid the excesses of overgeneralisation.

II

I want to discuss the relation between class and citizenship rights in the contemporary European societies, a topic that is well established in the literature of social and political theory, but which at the same time allows fresh insights into some very fundamental current problems. My discussion will be founded upon a critique of views that achieved prominence in the 'sociology of the 1960s'; but in revising these ideas I want to develop a standpoint that has direct relevance to issues in the decade which we have now entered, towards the close of the twentieth century. The best way to approach the subject, I think, is via a famous analysis, by a British social thinker, which helped to set the ground for contemporary debates. This is the work of T. H. Marshall, published some thirty years ago under the title *Citizenship and Social Class.*[1] *Citizenship and Social Class* is composed of two lectures delivered at Cambridge in 1947 – in the very early years of the development of the welfare state in Britain. It is a very short book, but its influence has deservedly been quite disproportionate to its size. Its themes became taken up by some of the writers who dominated sociological thought in the 1950s and 1960s, at least in the English-speaking world – writers such as Seymour Martin Lipset, Reinhard Bendix, Ralf Dahrendorf and many others. Rather than looking at the ways in which they incorporated Marshall's ideas into their own perspectives, however, I shall discuss them at source, in Marshall's own writing.

In the list of 'don'ts' which I have given, Marshall was not as culpable as some of those who made use of his ideas. He cannot be found guilty of the first two shortcomings. His analysis of citizenship and social class was based upon a long-term historical survey, and, being concerned mainly with Britain, Marshall refrained from suggesting that it could be applied *en bloc* to other countries in Europe, or to the USA. He did, I think, contravene my 'don'ts' 3 and 4, as I shall indicate in criticising his account.

Marshall argues that, over the past 200 years or so, two sets of influences have been in opposition in capitalist society: class divisions on the one hand, and rights of citizenship on the other. Class is a source – *the* source – of fundamental inequalities in society. 'Citizenship' is a contrary influence – one towards equalisation – because to be a citizen in a national community is to have universal rights, shared by every member of that community. The notion and reality of citizenship, Marshall argues, are among the great driving-forces of our time, something unique to the modern era.

According to Marshall, we can distinguish three forms of citizenship in the modern state: these he calls the civil, the political and the social. The civil element refers essentially to legal rights – freedom of the individual to live where and how he or she might choose; freedom of speech and religion; the right to own property; and to justice before the law. As this list indicates, the main institutional focus of the administration of civil rights is the *court of law*. The political aspect of citizenship, the second form, refers to the rights of every member of the society to participate in the exercise of political power, as a voter, or in a more direct way in the practice of politics. Its corresponding institutions are those of *parliament* and *local government*. The third dimension of citizenship, the social, concerns the rights of everyone to enjoy a certain minimum standard of life, economic welfare and security.

Citizenship rights, Marshall says, have taken a considerable period to develop, and of course he has in mind the stark contrast to how things used to be under the old feudal order. Rights were not universal – not applicable to every person in a national community. Neither were they separated out in the threefold way just mentioned. Aristocracy and commoners had different rights and duties in relation to one another: they effectively belonged to separate communities. Moreover, these rights and obligations tended to form single clusters; only in fact since the eighteenth century have the institutions on which the three aspects of citizenship depend become distinguished from one another. If I might quote from Marshall:

> when the institutions on which the three elements of citizenship depended parted company, it became possible for each to go its separate way, travelling at its own speed under the direction of its own peculiar principles. Before long they were spread far out along the course, and it is only in the present century . . . that the three runners have come abreast of one another.[2]

Marshall's thesis, expressed concisely, is this. The three aspects of citizenship have developed at different rates, such that each has served as a sort of platform for the expansion of the others. Only with the creation of the welfare state, a product of the post-1945 period in Britain and the other West European societies, have the three fully come together.

The main formative period of the development of civil or legal rights – in Britain at least – was the eighteenth century, when rights of liberty of the individual, and full and equal justice before the law, became firmly established. Marshall gives some considerable attention to the right to work and to live where one pleases, something in earlier centuries prohibited by custom and also by statute. The traditional view, Marshall says, only gradually ceded place to the new principle that restrictions on the movement of the population are 'an offence against the liberty of the subject and a menace to the prosperity of the nation'. The courts of law played a decisive role in advancing this new idea, delivering a series of judgements that progressively freed individuals from their bondage to the places in which they were born and the occupations they were born into.

Civil freedoms were essentially an end-process in the dissolution of the remnants of feudal society. They were the necessary foundation for the emergence of political rights; for only if the individual is recognised as a capable, autonomous agent does it become either possible or sensible to recognise that individual as politically responsible. Whereas civil freedoms were largely secured in the eighteenth century, the establishment of universal political rights belonged to the nineteenth and early twentieth centuries. This process was not so much one of the formation of new rights, as the extension of old rights, previously the monopoly of the privileged few, to the whole of the national community. Early in the nineteenth century, in Britain, those having the right to vote in elections made up no more than one-fifth of the adult male population. As in most West European countries political rights of citizenship, in the shape of the universal franchise, were not fully realised until the twentieth century.

Social rights, the third dimension of citizenship, according to Marshall's analysis, belong almost wholly to the present century. The nineteenth century was the period of the triumph of competitive capitalism, in which those who were unable to survive in the free market had few sources of support or welfare to fall back upon. Poverty became treated as an indication of social inferiority; in Britain, paupers placed in the workhouse forfeited the rights possessed by other citizens – to virtually the same extent as criminals in prison. Why has this become reversed in the twentieth century? Marshall answers this mainly in terms of the second type of citizenship right, the political. With the establishment of the universal franchise, the organised working class was able to secure the political strength to consolidate welfare rights *as* rights.

And thus, in Marshall's view, it is only in the twentieth century that the development of citizenship rights has seriously challenged or undermined the inequalities of the capitalist class system. The development of social rights has been accompanied by a general impetus to the blunting of inequalities through progressive income taxes, death duties, and so on. As Marshall puts it:

In the twentieth century, citizenship and the capitalist class system have been at war . . . The expansion of social rights is no longer merely an attempt to abate the obvious nuisance of destitution in the lowest ranks of society . . . It is no longer content to raise the floor-level in the basement of the social edifice, leaving the superstructure as it was. It has begun to remodel the whole building, and it might even end by converting the skyscraper into a bungalow.[3]

Marshall here injects a note of scepticism into his analysis. Social rights do not wholly dissolve inequalities of class, neither are they likely to do so in the future. Marshall's proposal is that social rights form a vital element in a society which is still hierarchical, but which has mellowed the tensions deriving from class conflict. The war between citizenship rights and the capitalist class system results in a negotiated truce, not an unqualified victory for either side.

In taking this view, Marshall differed significantly from some of his followers. Rather than analysing what Marshall saw as a balance between the equalising influence of citizenship and the divisive effects of class, they saw society as having moved beyond class divisions altogether. Citizenship rights do not, for them, simply mollify class inequalities and class conflict, they open the way to overcoming them altogether – at any rate, in anything like the form they assumed in the nineteenth or early twentieth centuries. Such views, developed from Marshall's account, belong to the 'sociology of the 1960s'. Those responsible for their formulation tended to do all of the things I have mentioned as 'don'ts'. They built a simplified version of Marshall's ideas into an unfolding model of the trend of development of Western societies as a whole – a model of progressive industrial maturity, social liberalisation and overall political consensus, such as I have alluded to previously.

In this form, the 'sociology of the 1960s' became obsolescent almost overnight, in the face of resurgent conflicts in the Western societies, and the subsequent erosion of stable economic growth by a period of 'stagflation'. In spite of this, I want to propose that Marshall's conception of citizenship rights is of immediate relevance to European society in the 1980s. However, from the vantage-point of the 1980s, there are clear deficiencies in the scenario which Marshall sketched in; and today we must substantially rethink the relations between class, class conflict and citizenship rights which he originally set out. In so doing, I think, we can make some sense of some otherwise puzzling trends in contemporary Western Europe: the marked contrast, for example, between contemporary Britain and the future form of British society, as a consolidated welfare state, that Marshall anticipated three decades ago; or the equally striking contrast between Thatcher's Britain and Mitterrand's France.

My interest is not just that of making some sense of events in the 1980s, but of generating an analysis that will place these events in a deeper sociological context. First of all, then, I shall criticise Marshall's standpoint, and develop an alternative one. Subsequently I shall identify some of the questions of significance that this raises for analysing current social issues.

III

I think Marshall is entirely right to point to the significance of citizenship rights, and their relation to class inequalities, for understanding the societies in which we live today; and I think his division of three types of citizenship right is also useful. But I want to use his contributions in a different framework from that which he adopts, as well of course as from that formulated by his followers. There are three main critical observations to be made of Marshall's account.

First, he does not avoid the third of my 'don'ts'. He writes as though the development of citizenship rights came about as something like a natural process of evolution, helped along where necessary by the beneficent hand of the state. There is an odd similarity here between his interpretation of the development of contemporary capitalism and that of some Marxist authors who, in other respects, have very different views from those of Marshall. Such authors see citizenship rights as ways in which the working class is kept in line by those in positions of power: that is, by the dominant class. Both types of account, in my opinion, fail to emphasise that citizenship rights have been achieved in substantial degree only through *struggle*. The extension of citizenship rights, in Britain as in other societies, was in substantial degree the result of the efforts of the underprivileged to improve their lot. Each of the three sets of citizenship rights referred to by Marshall had to be fought for, over a long span of historical time. The right of everyone to vote, for example, was a principle stubbornly resisted by those in ruling circles – both as regards the male working class, and as regards women in general. It is surely not accidental that, in various European countries, the universal franchise was only achieved in the shadow of the First World War. Here Marshall tends to contravene the fourth of my 'don'ts'. The war helped to break down some traditional sources of resistance to social change. But governments also needed the commitment of the population to national objectives;

the new citizens became cannon fodder on the battlefields of Europe.

My *second* point concerns Marshall's discussion of the original type of citizenship rights, civil or legal rights. Marshall treats what he calls 'economic civil rights' – the rights to form labour unions, to engage in industrial bargaining, and to strike – as an extension of civil rights in general. But this interpretation is not convincing when examined more closely. The civil rights of individual freedom and equality before the law were fought for and won by the rising bourgeois or capitalist class in pursuit of their quest to destroy feudal obligations and restrictions on trade. As Marx pointed out, and Marshall agrees, the freedoms thus gained served in some considerable degree to strengthen the power of employers over workers, helping to consolidate the early formation of capitalist enterprise. For the formation of modern capitalism was dependent upon 'formally free' wage-labour, allowing employers to hire and discard workers according to the economic vicissitudes of their companies.

'Economic civil rights' – or what Marshall sometimes alternatively calls 'industrial citizenship' – are in some respects quite *different* from legal rights of individual freedom. For the most part, 'economic rights' had to be won by the working class in the face of opposition both from employers and from the state. The right to form trade unions at all was certainly generally not gracefully conceded, but was achieved and sustained only through bitter struggles. The same applies to the extension of the activities of unions in their attempts to secure regularised bargaining procedures, and to defend their claims by strike action. All this implies rather strongly that there is something awry in lumping together such phenomena with civil rights in general.

My *third* objection in some part derives from the first two. It is that Marshall tends to treat the expansion of citizenship rights, culminating in the creation of the welfare state, as a one-way phenomenon, as so many steps in an irreversible trend of development. Such a conception tends to follow, of course, from treating citizenship as an evolutionary process, rather than as the outcome of the active endeavours of concrete groups of people. The resurgence of deep economic crisis, the prevalence of recession rather than growth, and the cutting-back on welfare services carried out by various Western governments, do not accord with this vision of the progressive development of the welfare state. In Marshall's analysis, citizenship rights are represented as considerably less fragile and contested than they really are.

IV

Meeting these objectives means diverging from Marshall's standpoint. Here I want to establish the outlines of a portrayal of the class structure of Western societies which I consider to be of enduring importance – the foundation upon which one should seek to interpret current developments and potentialities in the 1980s. This involves using Marx against Marshall; but later on I shall then tip the scales the other way a bit, using Marshall against Marx. In my view a basic concept involved in analysing the class structure of capitalism, over the whole period discussed by Marshall – i.e. from the eighteenth century to the present day – is that of the *capitalist labour contract*. The capitalist labour contract is a purely economic relation. An employer hires a worker, or more accurately the labour-power of the worker, in return for a monetary wage. The early establishment of the capitalist labour contract in the emergence of capitalist-industrial production involved two conditions of particular importance.

First, the sphere of the 'economic' – work life – became separated from that of the 'political': participation in the state. The creation of a distinctive sphere of the 'political' was established by the overthrowing of feudal, courtly power, and its replacement by parliamentary government. The consolidation of the separation of the 'economic' from the 'political' was in some part achieved *by the very legal freedoms Marshall refers to as civil rights*. Civil and political citizenship rights developed *together*. They were not, as Marshall describes them, successive steps in the expansion of 'citizenship' in general.

Second, the separation of the 'economic' from the 'political' served to undercut the very freedoms upon which the state depended. What Marshall calls civil and political citizenship, Marx, as we know, more scathingly regarded as mere 'bourgeois freedoms': that is to say, freedoms that are universal in principle but favour the dominant class in practice. In substantial degree, Marx was surely right. The capitalist labour contract excluded the worker from participation in, or control over, the organisation of the work-place. This exclusion was, and is, sanctioned by the inherent form of the capitalist state. The sphere of industry is specifically defined as being 'outside politics'. The right to vote periodically to elect members of parliamentary and local governing bodies does not extend to the sphere of production, to work.

Given this starting-point, we can explain why 'industrial citizen-ship', or 'economic citizenship rights', in Marshall's terms, are not simply an extension of civil rights in general. The separation of the economic and the political has tended to canalise the conflicts in which workers' organisations have been involved in two, related, ways. In each of these, citizenship rights have been, and continue to be, a *focus* of class conflict, rather than standing opposed to it, as Marshall suggests.

In the political sphere, the formation of labour or socialist parties – actively resisted by pre-existing governments in many countries – has been geared to winning the universal franchise, and then to implementing what Marshall calls social or welfare rights. Here labour movements certainly have been able to build upon a combi-nation of civil and political rights, which have been broadened in the process. But in the sphere of industry itself, the situation was – and continues to be – different. For the separation of the 'economic' from the 'political' meant that, in the early years of capitalist development, the worker who walked through the factory gates sacrificed all control over the work process. What was in prior types of society a taken-for-granted phenomenon, a significant degree of control by the worker over the process of labour, had to be won all over again. In all the Western countries unionisation, backed by the threat or actuality of strikes, has formed the principal source of power that workers can turn to in the (ideologically) 'non-political' sphere of labour. This power has turned out, in some circumstances and contexts at least, to be quite formidable. But as sheerly negative power it almost inevitably tends to appear as obstructive – and often is obstructive – to those who actually form policies either in industry or government.

My argument can be summarised as follows. In my view it is more valid to say that class conflict has been a *medium of the extension of citizenship rights* than to say that the extension of citizenship rights has blunted class divisions. All three forms of citizenship distin-guished by Marshall are double-edged. They *do* serve, as levers of struggle, to extend the range of human freedoms possible within Western societies; but at the same time they continue to be the sparking-points of conflict. Marshall's account has by no means lost its contemporary relevance to the critique of Marx, and of some contemporary forms of Marxism. Marx, and many subsequent Marxists too, have been altogether too dismissive of the so-called 'bourgeois freedoms' associated with Western capitalism. Marx strongly emphasised their empty character, as sanctioning the rule of the capitalist class. He did not fully anticipate the developments I have sketched in – an actualisation of citizenship rights within the framework of liberal democracy, rather than in the wake of a social-ist revolution.

V

Let me now return to the theme of 'society in the 1980s'. So far I have been concerned to situate my analysis in a long-term historical and structural setting, refusing those exercises in futurology which are so easy to make, and which so many social commentators find quite irresistible. I want to claim none the less that my discussion does raise questions of basic significance in current times, in which the scenario of the 'sociology of the 1960s' seems so inappropriate.

There are four basic questions, or sets of questions, which I want to raise and briefly discuss. The first concerns the fate of the welfare state, particularly in relation to the renewal of conservatism witnessed in a range of countries today. The second is to do with the significance of *civil rights*, which Marshall almost takes for granted in his analysis, but to my mind are subject to continuing struggle. The third, which derives partly from the first two, concerns theoris-ing socialism: what can we learn from analysing the connections between class and citizenship rights for rethinking socialist pro-grammes today? Finally, I want to refer briefly to issues raised by the fourth on my list of 'don'ts'. In this case this means: don't forget the relation between citizenship and the world of *nation-states* in which we now live.

First, then, the welfare state. In Marshall's analysis, the founda-tion and expansion of the welfare state appeared as something like the natural accompaniment of the development of citizenship rights. The establishing of civil rights leads in turn to political rights, which then in their turn produce a concentration upon welfare rights. The welfare state is the outcome of this process. There are several flaws in this analysis. The sequence of development of rights, even in Britain – and certainly in other societies – does not flow as evenly as Marshall suggests; Marshall sets out this sequence in just the sort of evolutionary fashion which contravenes the third of my 'don'ts'; and class alignments tend to dominate the effectiveness of citizenship rights to a considerably greater degree than Marshall presumes.

The analysis I have developed suggests that welfare rights, and the welfare state, are much more fragile and contested than Marshall's discussion proposes – and also than is suggested in functionalist Marxism, where such rights appear as the means whereby the bourgeoisie keeps the working class quiet.[4] If we see welfare rights as a pivot of class conflict, rather than as simply acting to dilute or dissolve it, we are able to understand both the limited success of the welfare state in creating greater equalisation, and the conservative reaction to it now under way in various societies. The welfare state is neither the result of the liberal proclivities of government (Marshall) nor the instrument of bourgeois class domination (functionalist Marxism). It is a contradictory formation, entangled in the asymmetrical relations between class division and social or welfare rights. There is, of course, strictly speaking, no 'welfare state' as such: welfare provisions, and their relation to state institutions and class relationships, vary quite sharply between different societies. The contradictory character of state welfare institutions, however, helps us grasp these differences as well as whatever similarities might be observed. In Britain, the welfare state has been made the object of a strong attack by Mrs Thatcher's government; something similar is happening in the USA. Such phenomena are to be understood, I think, as a middle-class backlash, in straightened economic circumstances, against institutions that predominantly connect with the interests of the working class, or the less privileged sections of the community. A class analysis that would contribute to explaining a contrary outcome in France would emphasise substantive differences in class alignments, but would be located in the same framework of the contradictory character of the welfare state. In Claus Offe's terms, this implies variations in the constant push and pull between the commodification and de-commodification of relationships characteristic of contemporary Western states.[5]

I offer these observations for discussion; they could, of course, be expressed in considerably greater detail. Let me move on now, however, to my second theme, that of civil rights. As I have said, Marshall tends to treat civil rights as having been *achieved* by the mid-nineteenth century, then becoming a base upon which other rights were built. Even if this were true for Britain, it hardly makes much sense in other countries. My view, as I have stated, is that civil, political and social rights are much more entangled than they appear in Marshall's account. We cannot suppose, as he tends to do, that the battle for civil and political rights has been won, and the main problem is to extend the range of welfare measures for the rest of the population. The courts of law are certainly not as uninfluenced by what happens in other spheres of society as Marshall's discussion seems to imply. The entanglement of civil rights with political struggles is demonstrated in stark fashion within Britain by the events in Northern Ireland. The IRA hunger-strikers in the Maze prison were denied various civil rights, but at the same time the British government insisted that they were 'ordinary criminals', without special claims to the status of 'political' prisoners. The attempts of the hunger-strikers to gain this status demonstrates that what counts as 'political' is a matter of continuing contestation. What is political and what is not is also an issue that frequently arises in strikes – in the very nature of the case. Strikes are rarely especially popular with anyone in industrial management or government. But the activities of strikers become a matter of particular opprobrium when they are overtly seen as 'political', as being directed towards other ends than 'economic' ones.

There is a danger that contemporary discussion of the significance of civil rights can degenerate into the vague, and largely empty, concern with 'human rights' of which President Carter made much – or at least about which he talked a good deal. Marshall's specification of civil rights allows for more precision, if detached in some part, as I have been suggesting, from the themes of his own work. There is good reason to suppose that civil rights are going to come under increasing pressure in Western societies in the years to come. We live in societies in which the extension of what Foucault calls the 'surveillance' activities of the state is becoming more and more pronounced. The storage and control of information about subject populations, via the use of computer and micro-chip technology, becomes a major medium of state power. In my opinion, these developments are as yet only poorly understood in social and political theory – lumped together with other phenomena as part of a 'post-industrial society', and so forth. But they demand our specific attention in respect of the defence of civil rights, most of which have been developed in times when the surveillance operations of the state (and other organisations) were considerably more restricted.

This brings me to my third theme, that of socialism. In my opinion neither in liberal political theory (to which Marshall is affiliated) nor in Marxism has the storage and control of information as a medium of domination been adequately theorised. Both traditions of thought have tended to associate power with property, and its differential distribution. But while the surveillance capabilities of the state are today greatly expanded, state power has nevertheless always involved surveillance. Surveillance participates in just those contradictions of the welfare state which I have discussed. The formation of welfare measures has from the outset been closely intertwined with the surveillance and control of the conduct of the underprivileged. Marxist thought lacks a sufficient awareness of this issue, but in the light of the experience of the existing socialist societies, in Eastern Europe and elsewhere, it is one that demands urgent scrutiny.[6]

Marx tended to take civil rights for granted, criticising them because they helped to sanction bourgeois rule. I have accepted that Marx was right in the latter respect; but we cannot today be content to leave their positive features unanalysed. The protection, and further development, of civil rights has to be a major part of a pro-gramme of democratic socialism in current times. But it is no use pretending that this can be achieved directly and solely through the traditional avenue of Marxist critique of the liberal democratic state. I think this critique is right to claim that the severance of the 'economic' from the 'political' is the foundation of capitalist class domination. Schemes of workers' self-management therefore retain a basic importance to socialist theory today. But a democratically run industrial order is unlikely ever to be achieved if civil rights are presumed to be automatically guaranteed by the establishment of workers' councils.

Political theory today, including Marxist political theory in its various contemporary forms, is in something of a crisis. For if the 'welfare socialism' or social democracy described and advocated by Marshall has not so far lived up to the hopes of its proponents, few in the West are likely today to regard the socialist societies of Eastern Europe as a desirable example for others to follow. There are ironies here for those on both the Right and the Left of the political spectrum. The very same people, for example, who are the first to condemn strikes, especially 'political strikes' in Britain, enthusiastically welcome the strike activities of the Polish workers. Those on the Left, on the other hand, have been prone to regard strikes as specifically a protest against capitalist modes of production. They might still see the activities of Solidarity in Poland as relevant only to turning a deformed socialist state into a more authentic form of socialism. The power to strike, as I have remarked before, in the setting of the liberal democratic state, is almost wholly of a negative sort – the power to impede. Where the lot of underprivileged groups in society is substantially founded upon such power, I think it correct to say that social democracy falls a long way short of what I would conceive to be democratic socialism. But perhaps the right to strike, whether or not we regard it as a principle of citizenship, should be part of any programme of socialism that might be drawn up for the future?

In conclusion I want to return to my fourth 'don't' in criticism of the 'sociology of the 1960s'. This was: don't write as though societies can be treated as self-contained entities. The other face of citizenship rights is nationalism and the nation-state. There is no necessary correspondence between the extension of democracy, or the achievement of socialism, and the power-politics of nation-states. Liberal thinkers, including Marshall, but more particularly Reinhard Bendix, have written on nationalism and the nation-state, but in their thinking it occupies a strictly subordinate role to citizenship. As we see in Bendix's recent and most important work, *Kings or People*, the nation-state appears as the 'political community' within which citizenship rights may be realised, not part of a global nation-state system.[7] Marx anticipated the transcendence of the state in the future society he envisaged. But he did not adequately analyse the sources of state power, or offer an interpretation of the rise of nation-states. We cannot just ignore the fact that, to date at least, the nation-state has proved as significant an aspect of socialist as of capitalist societies. Socialist states are nation-states, and have shown themselves to be as jealously territorial and aggressive as others.

Neither liberal nor Left political theory has a tradition of theorising the 'world violence' of the contemporary system of nation-states and power blocs. What Marx called the 'anarchy of the market' appears in our times as an international phenomenon. We live in a 'world capitalist economy', in which capitalist economic relations pertain on a world scale. But even more important, we live in a world nation-state system that simply has no precedent in prior history: in which a fragile equality in weaponry by the two major superpowers is the only brake upon the *political anarchy* of the international order. Marx thought he discerned a real movement of change – the labour movement – that would provide history's solution to the anarchy of the capitalist market and the degradation of work. But where is the dialectical process that will transcend the political anarchy that threatens us with universal destruction? So far as I can see, there is none in view. The cunning of reason here seems to have deserted us.

References

1. Since republished in T. H. Marshall, *Class, Citizenship and Social Development* (Westport, Conn.: Greenwood Press, 1973). (Marshall's later work shifts some of his emphases. See, for instance, 'The welfare state – a comparative study', in the same volume.)
2. Ibid, p. 73.
3. Ibid, pp. 84 and 96–7.
4. See some of the contributions to John Holloway and Sol Picciotto (eds), *State and Capital, a Marxist Debate* (London: Arnold, 1978).
5. See the 'Postscript' to the second edition of *The Class Structure of the Advanced Societies* (London: Hutchinson, 1980).
6. Ibid.
7. Reinhard Bendix, *Kings or People* (Berkeley: University of California Press, 1978).

13

Classes, Capitalism and the State[1]

Ten years is a long time in sociology. Less than a decade ago, Frank Parkin published *Class Inequality and Political Order,* a work which deservedly became well known.[2] The book made some important contributions to the then existing literature on class analysis. At that time, the sociological literature was dominated by a particular viewpoint about the nature of classes and class conflict. The entrenched liberal establishment of orthodox sociology in the USA and Europe had elaborated a version of class theory associated with the then dominant notion of 'industrial society'. 'Class' for these writers had become either replaced by 'stratification', or regarded as one aspect of stratification among others, and not necessarily the most important. Class conflict, for the various proponents of the theory of industrial society,[3] had been drained of any threatening qualities by the progressive incorporation of the working class within the social and political order. The future appeared to be set by the progressive expansion of liberal freedoms within a rapidly maturing industrial system. Many of those who took such a view were influenced by the ideas of Max Weber, understood in an appropriately bowdlerised form. The elements of Weber appearing in their works were not those of the sombre prophet of a numbing all-encompassing world of bureaucratic domination. In so far as they were concerned with 'stratification', these authors saw Weber as the originator of a 'multidimensional' approach to inequalities and divisions in society. This conception fitted well with the theory of industrial society, which emphasised that the monolithic class formations of nineteenth-century Europe, founded upon private property, had long since ceded place to much more differentiated or diversified forms of social organisation.

In his book, Parkin set out to provide 'a critique of currently fashionable neo-Weberian approaches to stratification'.[4] The views he himself went on to develop owed much to Weber; but he rejected the 'multidimensional' approach, suggesting that Weber's conceptions of class and status 'have been somewhat trivialised by his present-day followers'.[5] One of the most noteworthy features of his analysis was his insistence that power is not an additional 'dimension of stratification' to class and status. Weber's triad was not, as it has been frequently rendered, a contrast between 'class, status and power', but between 'class, status and party'. All three, for both Weber and Parkin, have to be grasped as phenomena of the distribution of power. The Weberian insistence upon the independent significance of party played an important role in Parkin's book. Parkin asserted that Weber was correct to argue that political power can be mobilised separately from class power, through the agency of party formation in the modern Western state.

Parkin was also concerned to confront the problem of classes in the East European societies – one of the distinctive features of his book compared with most general accounts of class theory, then and now. In these societies, according to Parkin, the mobilisation of power in the hands of the Communist Party becomes of decisive importance. Although Parkin spoke of the East European societies as 'socialist' societies (contrasting them with social democracy in the West), he made it clear that these were *state* socialist societies: the Party monopolises control of the state apparatus, and replaces class as the major focus for the organisation of power. Parkin's discussion of the state socialist societies was contrasted with Western 'capitalism'. He wrote about capitalism and socialism rather than about 'industrial society', and perceived much more striking and fundamental differences between the two than most of the theorists of industrial society were prepared to admit. Some of the threads of his argument on this point echoed Goldthorpe's earlier rejection of the 'convergence thesis', which had characteristically been adopted in one form or another by many of those favouring the conception of industrial society.[6] In his book, Parkin accepted that capitalism is split into dominant and subordinate classes, locked into endemic conflict, and he pointed to the achievements of the labour movement as informed by what he called a 'radical value system'. While labour movements in Western societies have not brought about revolutions, they have played a major role in softening the excesses of capitalist class domination through the emergence of social democracy or the welfare state. There has long been a tendency, Parkin believed, for Western labour movements to become less radical, to move from revolutionary rhetoric to reformist practice. But he did not find this particularly difficult to understand. It could be attributed in large part to the considerable success of labour parties in achieving political power, and to what seemed to him to be their much more limited, but none the less far from negligible, success in actually influencing the pre-existing nature of capitalist societies.

Re-reading *Class Inequality and Political Order* today, it is quite striking how little attention is given in the book either to Marx's writings, or to those of prominent Marxist luminaries of the time – whether belonging to what for a while became known as the 'Old Left', or affiliated with the 'New Left'. Marx is mentioned fairly often, but his theories about classes and class conflict are barely analysed. Virtually all the sections of the book dealing with the more theoretical aspects of class are devoted to considering Weber's views. The strongly conveyed implication is that what was significant in Marx's works was picked up and elaborated upon in a superior fashion by Weber: 'Weber's approach thus resulted in a refinement of Marx's model.'[7] Hence, while Marxism is important as implicated in the 'radical value system', and as the ideological vehicle of the domination of the Communist Party apparatus in Eastern Europe, little can be drawn from the work of Marxist authors that might shed light upon the actual tasks of class analysis confronting the sociologist. Parkin's disinclination to confront Marx's writings in a systematic way was connected, in my opinion, with some of the chief shortcomings of his book. Although he presented a picture of modern capitalism as involving two opposed classes in an interest conflict, the dominant and subordinate classes were defined almost exclusively in terms of the occupational division of labour. The differential between blue-collar or manual, and white-collar or non-manual occupations, was identified as the major line of class polarisation. Parkin's whole attention was upon 'market forces', defined almost exclusively as formed in the labour market. He provided little in the way of showing how the labour market connects with the broader institutional setting of Western societies – with the mechanisms of capitalistic enterprise and private property. Private property is briefly mentioned in the book, but only as a marginal adjunct to 'the market'; 'the market', Parkin claimed, 'plays a key part in determining occupational rewards in our type of society'.[8]

Parkin abandons the notion that the division between manual and non-manual occupations is the basis of the capitalist class system in his new work. Although sustaining a strong adherence to some of Weber's ideas, *Marxism and Class Theory: A Bourgeois Critique* contrasts interestingly with the earlier book in several respects. The climate of intellectual opinion in sociology has changed, and the chief targets of Parkin's polemical energies are no longer Weberians but Marxists. With the advancing years, or perhaps with the alteration in the objects of Parkin's criticisms, there has also arisen a vivid change in his writing style. The first book was written neutrally and dispassionately; the current one, as the partly tongue-in-cheek subtitle suggests, adopts a deliberately provocative tone. Parkin's discussion of contemporary Marxist accounts of class is heavily ironic and often openly sarcastic. 'Contemporary Western Marxism,' he announces on the first page of the Preface, 'unlike its classical predecessor, is wholly the creation of academic social theorists.' 'The natural constituency of this Marxism,' he continues, 'is not of course the working class, but the massed ranks of undergraduates and postgraduate students in the social sciences.' And he concludes:

> This is not necessarily to suggest that the new breed of Marxists are less dedicated than the old to the revolutionary transformation of society; their presence at the gates of the Winter Palace is perfectly conceivable, provided that satisfactory arrangements could be made for sabbatical leave (pp. ix–x).

Having armed himself with a sense of the absurdity of contemporary Marxism, Parkin sets off on a short critical journey across this wasted terrain. The reader is warned in advance not to expect a comprehensive analysis of recent Marxist literature on class theory. Little apology is needed for this, Parkin feels, because much of that literature is 'intrinsically forgettable'; even a selective account has to 'run the risk of being charged with paying undue respect to certain arguments to which the only appropriate response is incredulous laughter' (p.xi).

Although he acknowledges that today one can no longer readily talk about 'the' Marxist theory of class – because of the variety of views and interpretations differing authors claiming affiliation to Marxism have put forward – Parkin proceeds to do just that. By the Marxist theory of class, Parkin means principally the ideas developed by writers broadly influenced by Althusser – Poulantzas, Hindess and Hirst, Carchedi, Wright, and others. Parkin has two main criticisms of the standpoint he attributes to these authors. One is that, in stressing the significance of class relations as 'objective components' of social formations – or, in other words, stressing that the 'places' actors occupy in a structured totality are vastly more important than the agents themselves – these writers are unable to grasp 'the role of conscious agency and volition' (p.4). Here Parkin has gone into reverse gear compared with his earlier book, in which he sought to show that the 'neo-Weberians' had exaggeratedly emphasised subjective factors in their analyses. And whereas in the previous book he seemed to argue that the 'multidimensional approach' spread its net too wide, treating sexual, ethnic and religious differences in conjunction with class differentials, he now wants to attempt to conceptualise just this conjunction. The standpoint represented by Althusser & Co. cannot account for the intersection of these factors with class relations.

The plausibility of the Marxist theory of class, Parkin argues, is closely dependent upon the claims characteristically made for the explanatory qualities of the concept of 'mode of production'. When examined, however, this concept is found to have serious shortcomings. Sometimes it is used to refer to a particular element or part of a society; on other occasions it is applied as a shorthand label characterising a society as a whole. When employed in the former sense, production is treated as in some way determining other institutional features of society: 'On the second reading, productive relations are defined in a far more catholic sense to encompass most of the key institutions of a society, so rendering any distinction between a set of independent and dependent variables largely inappropriate' (p.6). The first view, Parkin says, is discredited today and associated only with 'vulgar Marxism'. But the perspective replacing it substitutes such a vague sense of casual determinism – Althusser's metonymic causality – that the concept of mode of production loses all utility whatsoever. The conclusion one must draw, Parkin asserts, is that production has no kind of primacy over distribution at all. 'Distributive arrangements', by which he means sexual, ethnic and religious factors, cannot be explicated in terms of the production relations of capitalism, or indeed of any type of production system. These other factors have become especially important in the modern era, Parkin emphasises, again apparently departing from the main thrust of his earlier book, and adopting a position closer to that advocated by Glazer and others (while stopping short of fully endorsing their position). 'Racial, ethnic and religious conflicts,' Parkin reasons, 'have moved towards the centre of the political stage in many industrial societies' (p.9). But Parkin does not think, like Glazer, that these conflicts have almost completely submerged those associated with class.

Why has Marxist class theory attracted so much attention in sociology if it is so fundamentally inadequate? One reason, Parkin suggests, is that alternative versions of class analysis have thus far been even less inspiring. He now places his own earlier standpoint among this dull company. According to Parkin, if there has been any generally agreed-upon notion of class accepted by non-Marxists in recent years, it is similar to his original model. That is to say, most sociologists have seen the basic dividing-line between classes in capitalist society to be the distinction between manual and non-manual labour. But this could only be regarded as the main form of class schism in capitalist society, Parkin says in his present work, if the society were an industrial firm writ large. The manual/non-manual division is only an important source of conflict in the context of the factory or work-place. He now accords a much more important place to property than he did in *Class Inequality and Political Order*.[9] Property, in the shape of capital, has of course always been an intrinsic component of every sort of Marxist analysis of the class system of capitalism. But the Marxist theory of class, Parkin points out, has encountered major difficulties in translating the abstract notions of capital and wage-labour into the substantive classes of bourgeoisie and proletariat. This poses particular problems in the context of the advanced capitalist countries, marked by the expansion of the state's administrative apparatus, its increasing intrusion into the centre of productive processes themselves, and the growing relative numbers of propertyless administrative workers within large corporations. Various interpretations of where the boundary lies between bourgeoisie and proletariat have been offered by Poulantzas, Carchedi and Wright. Each of these authors, Parkin comments, has been forced tacitly to admit the significance of a phenomenon to which Weber drew particular attention, but which has not traditionally brooked very large within Marxism: authority. The term 'authority' itself is usually avoided by various cumbersome circumlocutions – 'global function of capital', and the like – but the objective of these authors is to be able to place higher managers along with owners of capital as compromising the bourgeoisie or dominant class. In effectively making authority rather than property the hub of their concern, Marxists have tended to forfeit one of the principal emphases of classical Marxian theory which needs to be defended and elaborated: the role of private property in the class system.

The 'boundary problem' – the problem of where to draw the lines between the classes in a society – is inevitably part and parcel, Parkin suggests, of the question of the internal differentiation of classes. Both Marxist and non-Marxist class theorists have usually tried to interpret divisions and fragmentations within classes in terms different from those employed to explain the overall class system. Such divisions and fragmentations have normally been explained by referring to historical/cultural features of particular societies that 'cut across' generalised class categories. Hence forms of schism arising on the basis of non-economic divisions are only accorded a secondary role as mere 'complications' of the general model. But if we are to deal adequately with 'the renaissance of ethnic identity and conflict in the very heartlands of Western capitalism' (p.32), we cannot rest content with such a standpoint. The issue of how to relate the analysis of ethnic and other divisions to class theory has in turn to be connected to the 'boundary problem' if we are to make any headway. We can make this connection, Parkin wants to claim, by using Weber's concept of social closure. 'Social closure' refers to the process whereby groups of individuals seek to use a group attribute (e.g. ethnic characteristics) as a basis for monopolising opportunities or capabilities denied to 'outsiders'. Weber focused mainly upon how the positively privileged sustain closure, but we can also apply the concept to the strategies of the 'outsiders' or the subordinated groups themselves. 'Exclusionary closure' involves the use of power on the part of the privileged as the mode of defending or maintaining such privilege; reaction on the part of those who suffer exclusion through such a process represents an attempt to break down the exclusion, or otherwise gain a greater share of the resources monopolised by the dominant group or

groups. The objective of the underprivileged is to usurp the prerog-
atives of those to whom they are subordinated. Thus we can refer to
two generic types or strategies of social closure: exclusion and
usurpation.

We can reformulate class concepts according to this distinction,
Parkin argues, as well as use it to derive a more general conception
of exploitation than that available in the theory of surplus value.

> The familiar distinction between bourgeoisie and proletariat, in
> its classic as well as in its modern guise, may be conceived of as an
> expression of conflict between classes defined not specifically in
> relation to the place in the productive process but in relation to
> their prevalent modes of closure, exclusion and usurpation,
> respectively (p.46).

Exploitation is to be understood as using exclusionary tactics
to sustain privilege, of whatever kind. Relations between the sexes,
between ethnic and religious groups, and between both classes and
sectors of classes can be seen as potentially exploitative in this sense:
one group of workers can exploit another, just as they themselves
are exploited by a dominant class. In a capitalist society, the
dominant class achieves and protects its situation of dominance
by two primary methods of exclusionary closure. Private property
can be regarded as a mode of closure, bolstered and sanctioned by
the legal system, which allows the bourgeoisie to monopolise access
to control of the means of production. Parkin emphasises the need
to distinguish property as possessions, and property as capital.
Many sociologists have seen property as a set of exclusionary rights
of possession, but only property as capital is immediately relevant to
class analysis, since it confers the capacity to organise and subordinate those who are without it.

The other form of exclusionary closure relates to the occupational
division of labour, and concerns closure achieved through possession of 'credentials' or 'qualifications'. 'Credentialism' operates
primarily through control of the inflow of personnel to the occupation, providing a leverage for power in the labour market. The
bourgeoisie maintains its dominance by combining material and
cultural capital to its advantage. Control of access through the
labour market is not, of course, limited to professional and managerial occupations: skilled workers have typically employed the same

strategy. Whereas the exclusionary closure of the dominant class is protected by the legal framework, and therefore institutionalised, the 'usurpationary' activities of subordinate classes normally occur much more on the margins of the law. Although there is in most capitalist societies a 'right to strike', it had to be won; demonstrations and sit-ins frequently involve activities that are semi-legal or illegal. Fragmentation of the working class can be explained in terms of what Parkin calls 'dual closure'. A union controlled by white workers, for example, may engage both in usurpationary activities against employers and exclusionary activities directed against black workers. For definitional purposes, then, Parkin says:

> the dominant class in a society can be said to consist of those social groups whose share of resources is attained *primarily* by exclusionary means; whereas the subordinate class consists of social groups whose *primary* strategy is one of usurpation, notwithstanding the occasional resort to exclusion as a supplementary strategy (p. 93).

In the concluding sections of *Marxism and Class Theory,* Parkin discusses the nature of the modern state in capitalist society and the origins of state socialism. Contemporary Marxist approaches to the state, particularly that associated with Poulantzas, are subjected to a critical appraisal. While Marx's renowned analysis of Bonapartism in nineteenth-century France provides a major reference-point for the writings of Poulantzas and others on the capitalist state today, the connection is at best tenuous, in Parkin's view. The contemporary notion of the 'relative autonomy' of the state does not presume a 'balance of class powers', a temporary empty space into which the state enters, as Marx's account did. It presumes a more chronic independence of the state from the immediate control of the dominant class, in which the state secures the long-term interests of that class. This is in fact, according to Parkin, an overgeneralisation of the independence of the state from class interests, and makes the notion of relative autonomy fairly vacuous. Rather than assuming the relative autonomy of the state as an invariant feature of contemporary capitalism, we should attempt to analyse various ways in which political elites and dominant classes can combine. In absolutist or fascist regimes, a corporate state elite is conjoined with a dominant class; in liberal democratic orders, the state has a relative autonomy, not being directly under the sway of the dominant class;

in state socialism, a definite political elite holds power in the absence of a dominant class. Such a typology, Parkin says, again shows up deficiencies of the Marxist conception of the state, as the protector of the long-term interests of the bourgeoisie in a class society. The state can be organised to protect the interests of a dominant ethnic group or party. The fusion of state and party in state socialism is a phenomenon that eludes the grasp of Marxist analyses of socialism.

This brings Parkin back to one of his leading concerns in *Class Inequality and Political Order,* the comparative achievements of state socialism compared with Western social democracy. Marxism is again found wanting in several key respects, although here Lenin is given much more attention than the 'Marxist professoriat' who appear in the previous chapters. Parkin seems to have revised his original views about social democracy and state socialism less than he has his formulation of class theory as such; the general thrust of his interpretation is the same as before. The split in the European labour movement between West and East, expressed ideologically in the antagonism of Kautsky and Lenin, has put socialists in an unenviable position. The choice is between the slow and only moderately effective changes brought about by social democracy, in a form of society still dominated by property rights, and the imposition of autocratic Party rule. Parkin still definitely inclines towards the former, and will have no truck with those Marxist authors who suggest that further alternatives are realistically possible. Parkin's Weberianism here is full-blown, and his tone of prodding sarcasm, largely suspended while his account of social closure was presented, returns with some gusto. For Parkin, in the contemporary world we face 'a stark choice . . . between the twin evils of property and bureaucratic domination' (p.193). Marxists who think otherwise are lambasted as utopians with their heads firmly buried in the sand.

Parkin apparently wrote *Marxism and Class Theory* partially as a provocative gesture against what he sees as some sort of 'Marxist establishment' in Western university social science departments. If there is such a phenomenon, I have yet to encounter it; one of the most striking features of the social sciences today, contrasted with the situation ten years ago, is the variety of viewpoints, especially in social theory, which coexist somewhat uncomfortably with one another. This variety in substantial degree – although not of course completely, by any means – cross-cuts the divisions existing between

'Marxism' and 'sociology'. The contrasts between 'phenomenological Marxisms', 'structuralist Marxisms' and 'critical theory' express
dilemmas in social theory that are certainly not peculiar to Marxist
authors. The views Parkin attributes to 'the Marxist theory of class',
as I have mentioned earlier, are almost wholly those of Althusser's
followers. I have no particular sympathy with many of these views,
but at the same time they seem to me considerably more important
and fruitful than Parkin's almost wholly dismissive account would
imply. If they depart from the original texts of Marx, or if they seek
to criticise other forms of Marxism, Parkin finds them as culpable as
when they faithfully adhere to traditional Marxian ideas. When he
discusses Bonapartism, Parkin accuses these writers of a failure to
follow the doctrines of the master; when they adhere to these doctrines, they stand accused of dogmatism. I would have no quarrel
with the assertion that there are strongly dogmatic elements in the
writings of Althusser and many influenced by him, a dogmatism that
manages to be both ponderous and arcane. Nor are these writings
generally linked to political views I admire. These things having
been said, we must not neglect the fruitful aspects of Althusser's
'intervention' within Marxism. Althusser's rejection of 'vulgar' or
'economistic' Marxism, and the concomitant emphasis upon the
different combinations of the economic, political and ideological
that are possible in varying social formations, may not in the end be
satisfactory. But this was by no means a futile exercise, and has
helped to generate a succession of works in different areas – works
of varying quality and importance, it is true, but none of them insig-
nificant. However much Parkin may dislike Poulantzas's writings,
they are to my mind a considerably more important contribution to
contemporary social science than the works of many earlier
Marxists of the 'vulgar' sort. They demand a much more sustained
critique than the cavalier and offhand survey Parkin offers. One can
place together with Poulantzas the works of Castells and those who
had led the revival of 'Marxist anthropology', such as Meillassoux,
Godelier and Terray. Whatever quarrels one might have with the
ideas of these writers, all of whom have been more or less strongly
influenced by Althusser, they have each produced interesting and
worthwhile writings.

Parkin admits that there are a diversity of current Marxist
approaches to class theory. In spite of this, he carries on speaking of
'the Marxist theory of class', while referring to only a limited sector

of contemporary Marxist writings. If his book is not especially adequate as a critique of Althusserian-style works, its shortcomings as a critique of current Marxist class theories as a whole are more pronounced, for some of the more significant of these are barely mentioned. There are only passing references to British 'empirical Marxism', as furthered by such writers as Bottomore, Westergaard and Miliband. The work of those associated with the *Journal of Radical Political Economy,* which has proved so important in revitalising radical American labour history, is nowhere mentioned. Finally, although O'Connor's *Fiscal Crisis of the State* is briefly alluded to, the contributions of Habermas, Offe and their colleagues are not discussed anywhere. But their work, it could be argued, is at least as relevant to the themes which Parkin pursues as that of Althusser and Poulantzas – the more so since this work has in effect been elaborated in the context of a 'dialogue with the ghost of Max Weber'.

Parkin bases his critical analysis of 'the Marxist theory of class' on two general points: the 'objectivism' that has no mode of explaining human agency or purposive conduct; and the reliance upon the concept of 'mode of production' as explanatory. I entirely agree with his emphasis that a theory which reduces human actors to the passive occupants of 'places' in social systems will not do. The problem of agency in social theory, however, is extremely complicated and difficult. It is not enough simply to stress that human actors are reasoning, purposive agents: put more crudely, to accentuate the 'subjective' side of human social conduct. Such a stress has to be related conceptually to a theory of institutions, and to the large areas of social life that not only escape human intent but in some sense condition it. Some elements of the hostility which 'structuralist Marxist' writers have displayed towards 'voluntaristic' or 'action' theories are justified. I do not think that in *Marxism and Class Theory* Parkin overcomes the dualism of structure and action[10] any more effectively than Althusser and his followers have been able to. As he employs the notion of social closure, Parkin uses a strongly voluntaristic vocabulary, the consequence of which is that his analyses are, in my opinion, as one-sided as those of Althusser & Co., but from the opposite direction. The constraints experienced by Parkin's groups in struggles for exclusionary closure and usurpation are the constraints of the limits of the power wielded by each conflicting group. Social life is presented as the interplay of struggles for inclusion and exclusion. What this account lacks is what 'actionist' interpretations in the social sciences traditionally have lacked: a satisfactory analysis of the nature of structural constraint directly integrated with the terminology of human agency.

The implications of this can be traced out more concretely and related to what Parkin has to say about the usefulness of 'mode of production'. The opposition between capital and wage-labour, or bourgeoisie and proletariat, Parkin says, can be redefined as concerned with two modes of group closure, exclusion and usurpation; this rescues us from the Marxist error of locating class relations above all in the productive process. He seems to think that his redefinition overcomes a major source of difficulty, which in my view he quite rightly diagnoses in Marxist theories of class: how to relate the capital/wage-labour distinction on the one hand to the bourgeoisie/proletariat distinction on the other. But it does not do so at all; it simply redefines the second of these two differentiations as groupings involved in various strategic activities in a struggle for power. This simply moves class analysis away from processes of production by fiat, and is no less arbitrary or dogmatic than the views Parkin sets out to criticise. The capital/wage-labour distinction is in effect quietly dropped, although Parkin does occasionally continue to employ the terms themselves. The capital/wage-labour relation is not, as Parkin says, merely a more abstract version of the differentiation of working class from dominant class, nor can it be assimilated into struggles for social closure. If there is anything in Marx's analysis of capitalism at all, it depends upon his insistence that the capital/wage-labour relation is built into the very mechanics of capitalist production. The accumulation process involves the extraction of surplus value – not a surplus product as in previous types of class society – built into the centre of the labour process. The capitalistic labour contract, as I have argued elsewhere,[11] is hence a fundamental intersection between the mechanics of commodity production through the exploitation of labour and struggles in the labour market. Parkin is right to emphasise the importance of the latter, and to say that Weber provided more clues for analysing such struggles than Marx; he is wrong in supposing that this excludes the foundation of class conflict in production.

To say this is not to endorse the idea of the mode of production as a 'master concept' in analysing all forms of human society. It is reasonable enough to inveigh against the frequent tendency of

Marxist authors to apply the notion as a sort of magical formula that protects against the menace of idealism or of bourgeois interpretations of history. But such targets are easy game, and Parkin does not mention that Marxists of various persuasions, in the 'post-Althusserian' period, have subjected the concept to detailed critical analysis; some have even abandoned it altogether. In my opinion, although it is important to defend the notion of *Praxis* as a universal feature of human interaction with nature, the concept of mode of production is more limited in its application, in so far as it is tied to some kind of thesis about the primacy of 'economic factors' in social change. But far from severing capitalist production from the class system, one can argue that the two are integrally connected, in an unprecedented way, with the emergence of modern capitalism. Only with the advent of capitalism does the profit and investment cycle, associated with an impetus to constant technological innovation, become the major driving-force of social transformation. Only in capitalism are class relations established as intrinsic to the process of labour. The fact that 'capitalism' can serve to indicate both a set of economic mechanisms and a type of society as a whole is expressive of this. Such a view involves being both for and against Marx. Capitalism, one might say, is the only society in which the dialectic of forces and relations of production has a broad explanatory power: the only society, in fact, which both has and is a mode of production.

These points already imply the conclusion that the reformulation of class formation as social closure, the main thrust of Parkin's argument, should be rejected. It does not, of course, follow that the notion of social closure is of no interest to class theory; it seems to me to be a necessary idea to what I have elsewhere called 'class structuration'. However, it also appears to me that in his discussion of social closure Parkin tends to assimilate two phenomena that ought to be conceptually separated, and hence deals with them inadequately. One of these is control of resources, or the attempts of groups to monopolise resources to the exclusion of others; the second is the 'closure' of groups against 'outsiders'. Control of resources is the primary axis of power relations, but struggles to hold on to or acquire resources represent only one aspect of the 'power structure' of a society. The issues involved here have been much debated in respect to theories of power. The most pronounced conflicts in society, including class conflicts, are not necessarily struggles over power, or struggles to achieve more power, on the part of those involved. Power is involved everywhere in social life, not only in circumstances of conflict or struggle; although all struggle therefore involves the use or attempted use of power, it is not by any means always struggle *for* power. Parkin's book appears to more than flirt with the idea that all human history is the history of struggles for power; if that is indeed his view, I think it no better or worse than the thesis that all human history is the history of class struggles.

At any rate, control of resources, which are often monopolised 'silently' by a dominant class, because it is structured into the institutions of a society, should not be conflated with group closure, when this means 'exclusiveness' of group membership. Social 'exclusiveness', the differentiation of 'insiders' and 'outsiders', seems to me (as, at least on my reading of Weber, it was for him) only one mode among others of attempting to monopolise various types of resources. Partly for this reason, I think Parkin falls far short of the goal he sets himself in the opening pages of the book: to construct a theoretical statement which will allow class analysis to be coherently and plausibly related to sexual, ethnic and religious divisions in society. I found this one of the most disappointing aspects of the book, because I agree with Parkin that Marxist theories, whether classical or contemporary, have not generated credible accounts of the intersection of these schisms with class conflict. Parkin offers the concept of social closure as a means of improving upon this situation. Marxists are criticised for making class a systematic and constitutive feature of society, while treating the other sources of group schism and solidarity as merely contingent features of the development of particular societies. But it is difficult to see his own exposition as any different. Although he asserts that Marxists cannot accept 'the possibility that some line of cleavage other than that between capital and labour could constitute the *primary* source of political and social antagonism' (p.5), I found no place in the book where such instances are discussed systematically and at length. The surprising feature of *Marxism and Class Theory,* when judged in the light of this opening credo, is how closely it adheres to the same kind of questions with which Parkin was preoccupied in his first book. In other words, it is almost wholly concerned with classes, class society and problems of socialist transformation. Sexual, ethnic and religious divisions barely get a look in; they certainly do not form the central focus of the book the way class and party do. The considerable literature that now exists on gender, for example, and the 'feminism and Marxism debates, is not mentioned at all.

Most of *Marxism and Class Theory* is devoted to criticising and replacing 'the Marxist theory of class' with a self-professedly Weberian class theory. In my view, this is an inversion of what is demanded at the current juncture in social thought. Much of the strength of Marxist theories, and their continuing importance, derives not from the sort of appeal Parkin suggests they hold for gullible student audiences, but from their direct relevance to the critical analysis of capitalist society in Marx's sense – a society in which the capital/wage-labour relation is fundamental. One can accept this while at the same time holding that Marx's texts, and many subsequent writings claiming provenance from them, need a thoroughgoing critique, and that such a critique must involve reference to the 'empty spaces' in Marxist thought. Such a critique can be friendly without sacrificing its rigour, and I think it requires dispensing with the viewpoint that pits 'sociology' *en gros* against 'Marxism'.

References

1. A discussion of Frank Parkin, *Marxism and Class Theory: A Bourgeois Critique* (London: Tavistock, 1979).
2. Frank Parkin, *Class Inequality and Political Order* (London: MacGibbon & Kee, 1971).
3. For a fuller discussion and characterisation of the theory of industrial society, see my 'Classical social theory and the origins of modern sociology' in this volume; cf. also John Scott, *Corporations, Classes and Capitalism* (London: Hutchinson, 1979).
4. Parkin, *Class Inequality,* p.9.
5. Ibid.
6. J. H. Goldthorpe, 'Social stratification in industrial society', *Sociological Review,* Monograph No. 8, 1964.
7. Parkin, *Class Inequality,* p.18.
8. Ibid, p. 27.
9. See also Parkin, 'Social stratification', in Tom Bottomore and Robert Nisbet (eds), *A History of Sociological Analysis* (New York: Basic Books, 1978) pp. 608ff.
10. Cf. my *Central Problems in Social Theory* (London: Macmillan, 1979) ch. 2 and *passim*.
11. 'Postscript' to *The Class Structure of the Advanced Societies* (London: Hutchinson, 1980).

14

Power, the Dialectic of Control and Class Structuration

In this discussion I shall seek to draw some connections between certain aspects of the theory of structuration and the analysis of class structure in capitalist societies. The theory of structuration is based upon the following claims: that social theory (which I take to be relevant equally to each of the social scientific disciplines: sociology, anthropology, psychology and economics, as well as history) should incorporate an understanding of human behaviour as *action;* that such an understanding has to be made compatible with a focus upon the *structural components* of social institutions or societies; and that notions of *power* and *domination* are logically, not just contingently, associated with the concepts of action and structure as I conceptualise them.[1] I shall not be concerned to substantiate these claims, but shall attempt rather to trace out a few of their implications for issues that I take to be important to class analysis.

Let me pursue here the theme of the relation between action and power. I wish to distinguish two aspects of this issue:

1. The general implications of the logical relation between agency and power.
2. The mode in which power relations may be analysed as a chronically reproduced feature of social systems.

Of (1) we can say the following: to be a human agent is to have power, to be able to 'make a difference' in the world. This has direct consequences for (2), because it follows that, in any relationship which may be involved in a social system, the most seemingly 'powerless' individuals are able to mobilise resources whereby they carve out 'spaces of control' in respect of their day-to-day lives and in respect of the activities of the more powerful. One way of examining (1) is to consider instances which lie on the margins of action. These both help to explicate what it means to be an agent, and show how intimately this is related to power. But such examples also serve to demonstrate how closely (1) connects to (2), a connection which, I shall suggest, can best be handled by the concept of the 'dialectic of control'.

Consider first an instance where *A* is injected with a drug by *B*, rendering *A* unconscious and immobile. Such a case clearly lies outside the scope of the agency/power relation: *A* ceases to be an agent, and while *B* potentially has power over *A*'s fate, *A* has been rendered powerless. This apparently banal example is not without interest, however. If *B* can do more or less what he or she desires with *A*'s body, including ending *A*'s life altogether, it may appear that *B*'s power over *A* is absolute or unconditional. And so in a sense it is, for *A* is incapable of resisting. Complete though it may be in one aspect, it is very limited in others. For by killing or immobilising *A, B* is necessarily deprived of whatever goods or services *A* might render within a continuing social relationship. The threat to do violence to another may be very often a major sanction helping to enforce modes of domination, but the actual destruction of one agent by another can hardly be regarded as the type case of the use of social power.

Consider a second example that one might suppose to be near the margins of whether or not a person remains an agent: someone in solitary confinement in a prison. Now it is clear that in such an instance the person does retain the capability of 'making a difference'. Such a capability includes not just the chance to invent modes of occupying the mind in circumstances of extreme tedium; the solitary prisoner normally possesses at least some resources that can be brought to bear against his or her captors. 'Dirty protests' or hunger strikes in Northern Ireland are familiar illustrations. There are many ways in which the seemingly powerless, in particular contexts, may be able to influence the activities of those who appear to hold complete power over them; or in which the weak are able to mobilise resources against the strong. There are few social relations, of course, which are as markedly imbalanced in respect of power as that between prisoners in solitary confinement and their jailors. But such examples serve to highlight the points I have in mind. These can be stated as follows. Anyone who participates in a social relationship, forming part of a social system produced and reproduced by its constituent actors over time, necessarily sustains some control over the character of that relationship or system. Power relations in social systems can be regarded as relations of autonomy and dependence; but no matter how imbalanced they may be in terms of power, actors in subordinate positions are never wholly dependent, and are often very adept at converting whatever resources they possess into some degree of control over the conditions of reproduction of the system. In all social systems there is a dialectic of control, such that there are normally continually shifting balances of resources, altering the overall distribution of power. While it is always an empirical question just what power relations pertain within a social system, the agency/power connection, as a connection of logical entailment, means that an agent who does not participate in the dialectic of control *ipso facto* ceases to *be* an agent.[2]

I believe it true to say that in large areas of the social sciences – particularly (but not exclusively) in those dominated either by a general 'objectivist' position or more specifically by functionalism or by structuralism – human beings are not treated as knowledgeable, capable agents. This is perhaps most notoriously the case with Althusser's 'structuralist Marxism' and in the writings of those influenced by it: human agents are mere 'bearers of modes of production'. But, as I have argued elsewhere, a theory of action is also lacking in the functionalist sociology of Talcott Parsons, in spite of Parsons's labelling of his theoretical scheme as 'the action frame of reference'. Although Parsons may have moved towards a more objectivist stance in his later writings, as is often asserted, this was not a movement away from the concept of action as I have proposed it should be understood: for such a concept was not there in the first place. Garfinkel is quite right to say that in Parsons's theory human beings appear as 'cultural dopes', as impelled by 'internalised cultural values' that govern their activity.[3]

In the subsequent sections of this discussion, I want to try to show that, however abstract they may appear, these general considerations have direct consequences for quite fundamental issues of class analysis. I shall not concern myself with either Althusser or Parsons, but rather with two authors, one 'classic' and one more recent, whose works have made a strong imprint upon the study of classes. First, Weber's discussion of the nature of bureaucratic organisation, and its association with the expansion of capitalism. The second is Braverman's investigation of the division of labour in his *Labour and Monopoly Capital.*[4] Although Weber's views are in certain key respects explicitly anti-Marxist, while Braverman claims to defend a Marxist standpoint, there are some major similarities between the conclusions which each author tends to reach. These similarities – or so I shall claim – derive in some substantial part from deficiencies which can be analysed in terms of the concept of the dialectic of control.

Weber: bureaucracy and capitalism

Marx and Weber are widely regarded as the two most pre-eminent contributors to general problems of class analysis. It is sometimes supposed that Weber's main divergence from Marx consists in expanding upon, and modifying, Marx's views by adding the concept of 'status group' or *Stand,* and that of 'party' to that of 'class'. Others point out that, by apparently identifying the notion of class with market relations, Weber fails to pursue the Marxian theme that class divisions are founded in the relations of production. But each of these comparisons is relatively superficial. Much more significant are the differences between Weber's conception of capitalism and that of Marx; the former's interpretation of bureaucratisation, of course, plays a pivotal role in these differences. When Marx wrote about 'bureaucracy' (in, for example, his early critical discussions of Hegel), he used the term in its traditional sense, to refer to the administrative apparatus of government. One of Weber's major theoretical innovations was to provide a compelling rationale for extending the notions of 'bureaucracy' and 'bureaucratisation' to a whole variety of social organisations.

Lying behind this terminological difference, of course, is Weber's conviction that the 'steel-hard cage' of rational-legal organisation is a necessary feature of the expansion of capitalism – and that the bars of the cage would become even more confining were capitalism to be replaced by socialism. Marxists have quite rightly seen Weber's sombre projection of an increasingly bureaucratised social world – in which the alienation that Marx saw as involved for the wage-worker in the capitalist labour process would become the ineluctable lot of everyone – as constituting a direct challenge to Marx's ideas. Marxist writers have attacked Weber's conceptions of capitalism and bureaucracy from various different angles. But most such attacks have converged upon a single standpoint: the traits that Weber attributed to an overall process of 'bureaucratisation' are in fact the specific outcome of capitalist class domination, and hence will be transcended with the advent of socialism.

I do not want to say that these critical views are without foundation, and shall later argue that Braverman's work contributes in an important fashion to them; but I do think they are seriously limited because they characteristically accept *too much* of what Weber has to say about the nature and consequences of bureaucratisation. That is to say, the common tendency among Weber's Marxist critics is to accept the essential elements of Weber's characterisation of bureaucracy, while declaring bureaucratic domination to be a specific outcome of the class system of capitalism. But Weber's conception of bureaucracy has to be confronted in a more direct way than this, Below, I distinguish four respects (among others which I shall not discuss here) in which the overall interpretation of bureaucracy that Weber offered has major weaknesses.

Weber's portrayal of bureaucracy and bureaucratisation is so well known that it is necessary to give no more than the briefest representation of it here. Weber sometimes uses the term 'bureaucracy' as a general descriptive type (when talking of the traditional 'Chinese bureaucracy', etc.). But his most important formulation is as an 'ideal type': the more an organisation conforms to the features of the ideal type, the more 'bureaucratised' it can be said to be. The ideal type of bureaucratic organisation involves the following principal features: a formally delimited hierarchy, with the duties of distinct 'offices' being specified by written rules; staffing by means of full-time, salaried officials; and selection and allocation of officials by impersonal criteria on the basis of 'qualifications'. Weber avers that:

> Experience tends universally to show [that] the purely bureaucratic type of administrative organisation . . . is, from a purely technical point of view, capable of attaining the highest degree of efficiency and is in this sense formally the most rational known means of exercising authority over human beings. It is superior to any other form in precision, in stability, in the stringency of its discipline, and in its reliability.[5]

But the 'technical effectiveness' of bureaucracy exacts a heavy price. It is the source of the alienated character of bureaucratic tasks.

Weber's talk of 'precision', 'stability' and 'reliability' points to the direct connection between bureaucracy and mechanisation that he sometimes makes quite explicit. Bureaucracy, he says, is a 'human machine': the formal rationality of technique applies with equal relevance to human social organisation as to the control of the material world. A vital corollary to this is the theme that the more an organisation approaches the ideal type, the more power becomes centralised in the hands of those at the apex of the organisation. The expropriation of the worker from control of the means of production (or 'the means of administration') is a process that inevitably and irreversibly accompanies the expansion of bureaucratisation. Although Weber did not coin the phrase 'the iron law of oligarchy', his ideas strongly influenced Michels and there is no doubt that the theorem 'bureaucracy means oligarchy' is there in his writings.

Weber's specification of bureaucracy as an ideal type creates difficulties in assessing his views, since it seems to offer a mode of deflecting criticism. For if it is proposed that his conception of bureaucracy does not in fact provide a wholly valid or useful interpretation of the phenomenon with which it is concerned, the response can be made that, as it is an ideal type, one should feel no particular qualms if it does not conform to social reality. Weber adds fuel to such a rejoinder when he comments that ideal types 'do not contain hypotheses', that they are no more than a 'one-sided accentuation' of reality.[6] I do not have the space here to discuss the notion of ideal types; but however it may be most aptly described, Weber's conception of bureaucracy certainly does contain hypotheses (concerning technical effectiveness, etc.) that can be adjudged in terms of how well they cope with the subject-matter they relate to. And I want to argue that they can be placed seriously in question.

My objections each relate to the idea of the dialectic of control which I have introduced previously; they are as follows.

1.   Weber seeks to draw a generalised contrast (in an 'ideal-typical' manner) between traditional and bureaucratic organisations, in which the 'steel-hard cage' of the latter denies to individuals the autonomy and spontaneity of behaviour possible in a non-bureaucratised social world. But this 'philosophy of history'[7] is surely not particularly convincing. Some forms of traditional organisation have scarcely allowed much autonomy of conduct to their members: not in spite of, but because of their nature as small, localised community forms. One can detect in Weber's writing here the influence of a Romanticism that also resonates through Tönnies's opposition between *Gemeinschaft and Gesellschaft.*[8] In this regard, Weber's approach can usefully be balanced by a chord struck by Durkheim in the latter's discussion of so-called 'mechanical solidarity'.[9] Although communities dominated by mechanical solidarity offer the person a secure moral haven, the individual is none the less subject to what Durkheim refers to as the 'tyranny of the group'. The range of possible activities of the individual is severely curtailed by the norms of the collectivity, backed by 'repressive' sanctions. I am no more persuaded by Durkheim's account of the consequences of the expansion of the division of labour than I am by Weber's interpretation of bureaucratisation. But I think that the former author is correct in claiming that the movement away from *gemeinschaftlich* forms of organisation towards more large-scale, diversified ones is frequently in some part a liberating phenomenon.

2.   The 'iron law of oligarchy' is not a law at all; or rather it is a spurious one. The 'law' states that the increasing centralisation or co-ordination of activities which accompanies bureaucratisation necessarily means that power becomes more and more consolidated in the hands of a minority in an organisation. Stated as a universal tendency, however, such is simply not the case. It is easy enough to demonstrate this. The British economy today is considerably more highly centralised than was the case fifty years ago. But the very fact of such increased centralisation entails that certain nominally subordinate groupings of workers actually have more power now than they were able to wield previously. This is true, for example, of workers in public utilities, in the oil industry, etc. It is precisely *because* of the increased interdependence of everyone in a strongly centralised economic order that strategically placed categories of workers are able, through the threat of withdrawal of their labour power, to increase their power. What applies within the economy or the state as a whole applies in more specific organisations also. An excellent illustration of this is work on a production line. What could be a better example of a highly 'formally rational' system, in which human beings and machines are strictly co-ordinated with one another? But again the strongly co-ordinated nature of such a

production process, while it undeniably reduces labour to dull, repetitive tasks, in some respects increases rather than limits the power of workers involved in it. For a highly centralised production process tends to be much more vulnerable to disruption by small groups of workers than one in which labour tasks are less interdependent.

I don't mean to suggest by these illustrations that the centralisation involved in bureaucracy leads to the opposite situation to that suggested by the 'iron law of oligarchy': that is, that more centralisation entails the greater dependence of those in formal positions of authority upon their subordinates, and hence that the result is the diffusion of power downwards. Such a conclusion would of course be more fatuous than the famous 'iron law' itself. What I do mean to say is that there is no simple movement of power 'upwards' or 'downwards' with increasing bureaucratisation; normally there are various kinds of possible 'trade-offs' in the resources which can be actualised by groupings at different levels of an organisation.

3.   The implications of point (2) are that bureaucratic organisations do not in fact look very much like Weber presents them in his 'ideal type'. It is useless to respond to this by replying that ideal types by definition only approximate more or less closely to reality; the point at issue is how far Weber's formulation provides an apposite model for analysing contemporary forms of social organisation. And in fact there is good reason to suppose that, in modern bureaucratic systems, those in nominally subordinate positions usually have considerably greater control over the nature of their labour task than Weber allows. Although some of the work by Blau and others on the significance of 'informal relations' within bureaucratic hierarchies is worth mentioning here,[10] more directly relevant is that of Crozier.[11] As Crozier shows, the social (and often physical) distance between offices allows spaces of potential control for subordinates that are not available in smaller, more traditional communities. A formal authority system of an organisation that approaches the characteristics of Weber's 'ideal-type', in fact, can often be more successfully circumvented or manipulated by subordinates than one in which those traits are less developed.[12] No doubt Weber was right to underscore the importance of written rules as a feature of bureaucracy. But the formal codification of procedures rarely conforms to actual practice; the 'rule book' may be subject to divergent interpretations, and hence can focalise

conflicts which subordinates may turn to their own advantage. The irony of the idea of 'working to rule' is certainly not lost upon those who invoke the practice as a strategy in the dialectic of control.

4. The above considerations place seriously in question Weber's theorem that the 'purely bureaucratic' type of organisation is the most 'formally rational' mode of exercising authority over human beings. This theorem is so important to Weber's association of bureaucracy with capitalism, and to his critique of socialism, that it is worth while emphasising the point rather strongly. For it is the basis of Weber's cultural pessimism, and of his diagnosis of an antithesis between bureaucracy and democracy. Bureaucratic domination, in which the mass of the population are largely powerless to influence the decisions that govern the course of their day-to-day lives, is for Weber quite literally an irresistible force that sweeps us all along. Attempts to stem the tide merely succeed in giving it a greater force. But such pessimism is misplaced if Weber's characterisation of the main elements of bureaucracy is a misleading one. This should not in any way be taken to imply that the sorts of problems Weber connected to bureaucratic domination can be ignored. Quite the contrary. They remain of great significance; but when we attempt to tackle them, on either a sociological or a political level, we have to disentangle ourselves from a good deal of what has become received Weberian wisdom.

How does such a critique of Weber's conception of bureaucracy connect with the methodological arguments I made in the opening section of the paper? For Weber was not by any streak of the imagination an 'objectivist'; rather, he stressed the 'subjective meaning' of human conduct as integral to social analysis. Without pursuing this issue in any detail, it can be said that, in respect of bureaucratic organisation, Weber associated 'meaning' with *legitimacy*. Consequently his account of bureaucracy is very much written 'from the top'; the ideal type of bureaucratic organisation is heavily weighted towards how the 'legitimate order of a rational-legal form' is sustained.

Braverman: class domination and capitalism

Braverman writes as a Marxist, and the starting-point of his analysis of capitalistic organisations is the sale of labour power as a commodity. In the sale of their labour power to the capitalist, workers cede control of the labour process; capitalists, for their part, seek to consolidate this control through 'management'. Workers have to be 'managed' without employers being able to rely either upon the moral ties of fealty involved in feudal class relations, or upon the use of physical force to make workers obey; their only real sanction is the economic constraint of the need of workers to find paid employment in order to make a living. The crux of Braverman's thesis is that managerial control is obtained above all via the effects of the division of labour. It is mistaken, Braverman argues, to talk about the division of labour in general. The 'social division of labour', which is found in all societies, has to be clearly distinguished from the 'technical division of labour', which is specific to capitalism. While the social division of labour involves the separation of tasks devoted to the making of whole products, the technical division of labour fragments the labour task into repetitive operations carried out by different individuals. The expansion of the technical division of labour, in Braverman's view, is the most basic element extending managerial control over labour, because knowledge of and command over the labour process are thereby progressively 'expropriated' from workers.

Braverman lays a great deal of stress upon the contribution of Taylorism, or 'scientific management', to this process. In Taylorism the operations carried out by the worker are integrated into the technical design of production as a whole. 'Scientific management' may seem in most countries to have made only limited inroads into industry, and to have been generally superseded by the 'human-relations' approach of Elton Mayo and his associates in the USA.[13] But Braverman claims that the impact of the 'human-relations' view has been of relatively marginal significance. Taylorism serves as the chief set of organising principles of capitalist production.

Braverman's analysis, in my opinion, stands as a major corrective to some of the elements of Weber's account of bureaucratisation. Braverman shows that the rationality of technique in modern industrial enterprise is not neutral in respect of class domination. It would be difficult to exaggerate the significance of this. For if Braverman's argument is correct, industrial technique embodies the capital/wage-labour relation in its very form. Class domination appears as the absent centre of the linkage Weber drew between the rationality of technique and the rationality of the (formally) most 'technically effective' type of organisation, bureaucracy. It would follow that bureaucratic domination, and the concomitant powerlessness of workers, are not inevitable features of contemporary organisations; the transformation of the class relations incorporated within the 'technical division of labour' could in principle furnish the basis for the democratic reorganisation of the labour process. Braverman's work should therefore provide for a more optimistic assessment of the possibilities of unlocking Weber's 'steel-hard cage' than Weber's own gloomy vision of the future allows for. In fact, however, the process of the sieving off of control of the labour process that Braverman describes appears to have just the same inevitable, irreversible character about it as the processes of bureaucratisation portrayed by Weber. The factors responsible for this, I want to argue, do in some respects have similarities to the shortcomings I have pointed to in Weber's treatment of bureaucracy; but this time they are very closely connected to an 'objectivist' methodological position that Braverman declaredly embraces towards the beginning of his book.

Labour and Monopoly Capital, he claims, is only concerned with the ' "objective" content of class', and not with the ' "subjective will" '.[14] The result is a work which, notwithstanding its self-professed Marxist standpoint, certainly drastically underestimates the knowledgeability and the capability of workers faced with a range of management imperatives. Braverman is mistaken to say that his work is unconcerned with 'subjective will': the 'subjective will' of *management,* as expressed in Taylorist strategies of control, is more than adequately represented in the book. What is lacking is a parallel discussion of the reactions of workers, as themselves knowledgeable and capable agents, to the technical division of labour and to Taylorism. Braverman bases his severance of the 'objective' from the 'subjective' components of class upon Marx's famous distinction between a class 'in itself' and a class 'for itself'. But it is important to see that this distinction conceals a possible ambiguity. For the differentiation could be taken to imply that 'class consciousness' can be equated with class 'for itself', and therefore that the 'objective' features of class can be examined without reference to consciousness (discursive or practical). This is evidently mistaken. All class relations obviously involve the conscious activity of human agents. But this is different from groups of individuals being conscious of being members of the same class, of having common class interests, and so on.[15] It is quite possible to conceive of circumstances in which individuals are not only not cognisant of being in a common class situation, but where they may actively deny the existence of classes – and where their attitudes and ideas can nevertheless be explained in terms of class relationships. Such is characteristically the case, as I have argued elsewhere,[16] with certain categories of white-collar workers.

Braverman's surprising disinclination to treat workers as capable and knowledgeable agents seriously compromises the validity of some of his conclusions. The implications of Braverman's analysis, which in emphasising the class character of managerial control begins from different premises to those of Weber, appear every bit as pessimistic as those of that author. For although Braverman's study is an explicitly Marxist one, there is no indication at all that the working class is likely to rise against its oppressors, or even that workers are able in some part to stem the advance of the processes that rob them of control over their labour. On the contrary, the spread of de-skilling, and the sieving off of control over the labour task from the worker, appear to have much the same implacable force about them as the advance of bureaucracy depicted by Weber.

The revolution may be as far off as ever; but one can certainly doubt that the processes described by Braverman are either as clear cut or categorical as his discussion suggests. One reason for this is that the technological changes constantly taking place in capitalist economies seem more complicated, in their effects upon the labour process, than Braverman allows. Certainly old craft skills are for the most part eliminated, but new types of skilled activity, albeit different in character, are continually created. Of course, what counts as 'skill' is a complicated matter, as Braverman and a host of subsequent commentators have recognised. But the factor of human knowledgeability again enters in here. For what counts as 'skilled work', or a 'skilled trade', depends in some substantial degree upon what can be *made* to count as such. There are many examples where workers have proved able to sustain the definition of themselves as 'skilled' in spite of changes in the nature of the labour task. A classic mode in which this has been achieved is via the 'balkanisation' of the labour market: where access to the occupation has been kept strictly limited by the union or the workers' association.

Equally important are the various forms of worker resistance whereby workers have succeeded in maintaining a significant amount of control over the labour process itself. Historical studies of the American working class indicate not only that Taylorism had consistently less impact than Braverman claims, in large degree because of worker resistance, but that the expansion of 'human-relations' ideology was partly due to working-class opposition to Taylorism.[17] It is perhaps worth adding that opposition to Taylorism was not confined to those most directly affected by it, the working class. Many employers and managers, in the USA and elsewhere (in contrast to the attitude of Lenin!), were either sceptical of scientific management or openly hostile to it, on a mixture of pragmatic and humanitarian grounds. In adopting such attitudes, even on purely practical grounds, managers were in fact being quite realistic. For those who attempt to control a labour force are by no means impervious to understanding the Marxist adage that 'labour power is a commodity that refuses to be treated like any other commodity'.

This is where the point that, in capitalist economies, workers have to be 'managed', without the moral or military sanctions possessed by exploiting classes in prior types of society, becomes particularly important. In other types of class-divided society, the dominant class has normally had direct possession of the means of violence, and hence of disciplining recalcitrant labour where necessary. But in capitalism (a) regularised labour discipline is more integral to work than in most contexts (especially that of the peasant producer) of production in earlier forms of society, and (b) the chief coercive sanction employers possess to ensure the compliance of the workforce is that the latter is propertyless, and hence compelled to find employment in order to make a living. It is quite right, I think, to argue that the significance of these phenomena can best be analysed in terms of the capitalist labour contract. But the contractual encounter between capital and wage-labour has to be seen as providing axes of chronic struggle in which the working class is by no means always and inevitably the loser.

There are, I consider, two connecting axes or 'sites' of class struggle in the capitalist societies. One is class struggle in the workplace, the main focus of Braverman's attention. As I have argued, I do not think Braverman adequately acknowledges the significance of such struggle on the level of day-to-day practices on the shopfloor. Braverman's work can here be usefully complemented by studies such as that of Friedman.[18] Friedman argues that not only Braverman but Marx himself, in anticipating the progressive homogenisation of labour through the undermining of skill differentials, fail to give sufficient weight to the influence of worker resistance at the level of the firm, and the need of employers or managers to incorporate the fact of such resistance into their own strategies. Friedman distinguishes two principal types of managerial strategy that are commonly used to control the labour force. One such strategy is that of 'responsible autonomy'.[19] Workers in these circumstances are allowed considerable independence of activity in the work situation, so that they are encouraged to co-operate in accepting technological changes in ways which conform to the overall aims of management. This can be contrasted with the strategy of 'direct control'. Such a strategy approximates to that which Braverman takes to be prevalent throughout industry. Here managers attempt to obtain the compliance of the labour force by close supervision of the labour process, and the sustaining of discipline by minimising worker responsibility through Taylorist techniques. Braverman, says Friedman, exaggerates the scope and the effectiveness of the second of these strategies. This over-emphasis follows from 'a failure to appreciate the importance of worker resistance as a force provoking accommodating changes in the mode of production', a mistake which 'leads to a technological deterministic view of capitalist development'.[20] Part of the importance of distinguishing different types of managerial strategy in this way is that it becomes possible to connect the analysis to the study of dual or segmented labour markets. Those in weak positions in segmented labour markets are probably usually less able to resist incorporation within managerial strategies of 'direct control'. Such workers include particularly ethnic minorities – and women.

The second site of class struggle involves the pitting of labour movements against the organised power of employers and of the state. Here we have a prime example of the operation of the dialectic of control. In the early years of the development of capitalism, as Marx showed, the capitalist labour contract was a medium of bolstering the power of the emerging entrepreneurial class. By dissolving feudal bonds of fealty and obligation, the capitalist labour contract allowed for the 'freedom' of employers to buy, and workers to sell, labour power, at its exchange value. By making the relation between employers and workers a purely economic one, abstract 'political' rights were confined to a separate sphere of the polity, a separation first of all supported by property qualifications on the franchise. The capitalist labour contract, however, in the context of parliamentary government, allowed the creation of labour movements based upon the power generated by the threat or actuality of the withdrawal of labour. In my opinion, the struggles of labour movements to improve the general economic conditions of the working class, and to realise 'citizenship rights', have helped profoundly to alter the characteristics of the capitalist societies of the West.

Braverman is not directly concerned with such issues in his book, but again I do not believe they can be wholly separated from the problems he discusses. For the achievements of Western labour movements have undoubtedly acted to counter the kind of mono-lithic triumph of capitalism suggested by the style of analysis Braverman develops. Just as Braverman underestimates the signifi-cance of worker resistance in the work-place, many other Marxists have been dismissive of the part played by labour movements in transforming what C. B. Macpherson calls the 'liberal' state of the nineteenth century into the 'liberal democratic' state of the twentieth.[21] The worst of these analyses incorporate the flaws of both 'objectivistic' social science and of functionalism:[22] whatever citizenship rights the working class may have obtained are the result of 'adjustments' of the capitalist system protecting its source of labour supply. Consider the judgement of Müller and Neusüss on the welfare state: 'By establishing a minimum subsistence level (through workmen's protection and social security systems) the material existence of wage-labourers is ensured during the times when they cannot sell their labour-power on the market (sickness, old age, unemployment)'.[23] Such assessments not only ignore the long-term battles workers have had to conduct in most countries to attain political and welfare rights, but once more treat workers as mere dupes of the system. Evaluations of such a kind have about as much validity as contrary assertions of the sort often heard from conservative sectors of the British press, that 'the country is run by the unions'. At least this second viewpoint does accept that the organised working-class has achieved a considerable measure of power in the liberal democratic state, even if it wildly exaggerates the scope of such power.

Conclusion: agency and alienation

In this essay I have concentrated upon indicating that abstract issues of social theory do have a definite bearing upon concrete problems of social analysis. In emphasising the notion of the dialectic of control, I do not mean to imply that those in subordinate positions in social systems are chronically driven, or are able, to overthrow those who dominate them. I am not suggesting some sort of revised version of Hegel's master–slave dialectic. But I do think the critique of Weber's interpretation of the expansion of bureaucracy (directed against Marxist class analysis) and of works such as that of Braverman (written supposedly precisely from a standpoint of Marxist class analysis) allows a more satisfactory analysis of issues of the relation between class domination and authority systems than their writings provide.[24] In concluding this analysis, however, I want to return to a more philosophical plane.

If my arguments about human agency and power in the opening part of the essay are correct, they can be related, I think, to Marx's discussion of the alienated character of capitalist production. To be an agent is to have the capability of 'making a difference', of intervening in the world so as to influence events which occur in that world. To be a *human* agent is to be a highly knowledgeable and skilled individual, who applies that knowledgeability in securing autonomy of action in the course of day-to-day life. By 'alienated labour' Marx refers to work situations in which the worker becomes an appendage of a machine – Braverman's study is about 'alienated labour' in this sense, although he barely mentions the term itself. In my terminology the connection of alienation with the 'human-ness' of our 'species-being' can be expressed simply and coherently in a single sentence. The more a worker comes close to being an 'appendage of a machine', the more he or she ceases to be a human agent. As Marx puts it, 'The animal becomes human and the human becomes animal.'[25] The interest of this analysis for a philosophical anthropology of labour, however, should not make us forget that, precisely because they are not machines, wherever they can do so human actors devise ways of avoiding being treated as such.

References

1. See *New Rules of Sociological Method* (London: Hutchinson, 1976); *Studies in Social and Political Theory* (London: Hutchinson, 1977); *Central Problems in Social Theory* (London: Macmillan, 1979).
2. *Central Problems in Social Theory,* pp. 145 ff.
3. See *New Rules of Sociological Method.*
4. Harry Braverman, *Labour and Monopoly Capital* (New York: Monthly Review Press, 1974).
5. Max Weber, *Economy and Society* (Berkeley: University of California Press, 1978) vol. 1, p.223.
6. Weber, *The Methodology of the Social Sciences* (Glencoe, Ill.: Free Press, 1949).
7. Wolfgang Mommsen, *The Age of Bureaucracy* (Oxford: Blackwell, 1974).
8. Cf. Arthur Mitzman, *The Iron Cage. (*New York: Grosset & Dunlop, 1971).
9. Emile Durkheim, *The Division of Labour in Society* (New York: Free Press, 1968).
10. Peter M. Blau, *The Dynamics of Bureaucracy* (Chicago: University of Chicago Press, 1967); see also the important discussion in Martin Albrow, *Bureaucracy* (London: Pall Mall, 1970).
11. Michel Crozier, *The Bureaucratic Phenomenon* (London: Tavistock, 1964).
12. *Central Problems in Social Theory,* pp. 147 ff.
13. Cf. Reinhard Bendix, *Work and Authority in Industry* (New York: Harper, 1963).
14. Braverman, *Labour and Monopoly Capital,* p.27.
15. See Russell Jacoby's review of *Labour and Monopoly Capital,* in *Telos,* no. 29, 1976; and Gavin Mackenzie, 'The political economy of the American working class', *British Journal of Sociology,* vol. 28, 1977.
16. *The Class Structure of the Advanced Societies* (London: Hutchinson, 1973) p. 111.
17. Cf. Bryan Palmer, 'Class, conception and conflict: the thrust for efficiency, managerial views of labour and working class rebellion, 1903-22', *Review of Radical Political Economy,* vol. 7, 1975; H. G. J. Aitken, *Taylorism at Watertown Arsenal* (Cambridge, Mass.: Harvard University Press, 1960); Stanley Aronowitz, *False Promises* (New York: McGraw-Hill, 1973), and 'Marx, Braverman, and the logic of capital', *Insurgent Sociologist,* Winter 1978–9.
18. Andrew L. Friedman, *Industry and Labour* (London: Macmillan, 1977).

19. Cf. Michael Buraway, *The Manufacture of Consent* (Chicago: University of Chicago Press, 1980).
20. Friedman, *Industry and Labour,* p.7.
21. C. B. Macpherson, *The Real World of Democracy* (Oxford: Clarendon Press, 1966).
22. For a critique of functionalism, in the light of the conception of structuration, see 'Functionalism: après la lutte', in my *Studies in Social and Political Theory.*
23. Wolfgang Müller and Christel Neusüss, 'The "welfare-state illusion" and the contradiction between wage-labour and capital', in John Holloway and Sol Piciotto (eds), *State and Capital: a Marxist Debate* (London: Arnold, 1978) p.34.
24. For the elements of such analysis, see my *A Contemporary Critique of Historical Materialism* (London: Macmillan, 1981).
25. T. B. Bottomore, *Karl Marx: Early Writings* (New York: McGraw-Hill, 1964) p.125.

15

From Marx to Nietzsche? Neo-Conservatism, Foucault, and Problems in Contemporary Political Theory

A strong current of political conservatism has swept through the West in the past decade. Not only have conservative political parties come to power in a range of countries, but they have done so in a political climate that shows obvious tendencies towards ideological realignment. With the seeming dissolution of Keynesianism, which in the post-1945 period was in some degree accepted by conservative parties as well as by social-democratic ones, conservative parties have not only swept to power, they have done so under the aegis of a revitalised and radical conservatism. It is possible, I think, to exaggerate the long-term import of such a phenomenon. After all, it is only something over ten years since the days of the efflorescence of the New Left. If the New Left appears positively old hat, one must not forget the feelings of many at the time – both among those who held strongly hostile attitudes as well as among its supporters – that profound changes were occurring in the fabric of the industrialised countries. So we should be careful about over-generalising in the light of a few years' experience. In my opinion, the social sciences in the postwar period have been particularly prone to this tendency. On the basis of a decade and a half of rising growth rates, and relatively stable 'consensus politics' in the Western liberal democracies, the most grandiose 'theories of industrial society' were created, projecting an indefinite future of progressive expansion. Most such theories, including the so-called conception of 'post-industrial' society, seem to me to have lacked the detailed historical sense necessary to such ambitious generalisation – and have been exposed as having serious shortcomings.

With these reservations in mind, I do believe that, diffusely connected with conservative politics, there are important developments in political theory that it would not be wise to ignore. Rather than discussing these in the context of the Anglo-Saxon world, I shall concentrate upon certain aspects of the philosophical 'new conservatism' that has achieved a considerable notoriety in France. There is, I think, a distinctive difference between the most prominent new conservatisms of Britain and the USA, on the one hand, and the 'new philosophers' in France on the other. The former have been mainly centred upon the realm of civil society, especially as regards the influence of monetarism; the political implications have been, as it were, guided by economic theory. The new philosophers, on the other hand, have discovered the state, and they have discovered power. They are aptly called philosophers, and can hardly be said to be close to the centres of government. Their writings have, for the most part, a grandiose character, and they bear the hallmarks of a conversion experience. For the new philosophers are the disillusioned survivors of the 'May events' of 1968, who find themselves not in a world of liberated humanity, but instead in an age of barbarism. They have moved from Marx to Nietzsche.

Let us allow Bernard-Henri Lévy to speak for the new philosophers:

> I am the bastard child of an unholy union between fascism and Stalinism. If I were a poet, I would sing the horror of living and the the new Gulags that tomorrow holds in store for us. If I were a musician, I would speak of the idiot laughter and impotent tears, the dreadful uproar made by the lost, camped in the ruins, awaiting their fate. If I had been a painter (a Courbet rather than a David), I would have represented the dust-coloured sky lowering over Santiago, Luanda, or Kolyma. But I am neither painter, nor musician, nor poet. I am a philosopher, one who uses ideas and words – words already crushed and macerated by fools. So, with the words of my language, I will do no more than speak of the massacres, the camps, and the processions of death, the ones I have seen and the others, which I also wish to recall. I will be satisfied if I can explain the new totalitarianism of the smiling

Princes, who sometimes even promise happiness to their people. [My work] . . . should thus be read as an 'archaeology of the present', carefully retracing through the fog of contemporary speech and practice the outline and the stamp of a barbarism with a human face.[1]

Recognition that the barbaric world of today has 'a human face', really a mere superficial mask of humanity, represents an acknowledgement that the state today claims to act in the name of the people. But the 'human face' of the contemporary state (a) is more than counterbalanced by the increasing concentration of terror in an age of scientism, bureaucracy, and high military technology; and (b) is a shallow concealment of a universal institution, the state as co-ordinated power. Now the twentieth century is the century of two devastating world wars; the horrors of Nazism, even the excesses of Stalinism are hardly new. Why the shock of discovery? Why the wholesale abandonment of Marx and the clasping of Nietzsche in such a fervent embrace? No doubt there are reasons particular to France, or to sections of the European Left, which were reluctant to admit the realities of Stalinism; Solzhenitsyn's account of the Gulag had more shattering effects in French Leftist circles than, I think, has been the case in Britain or in the USA. But I think there are also deeper intellectual factors involved, to do with the intellectual traditions from which Marxism, and Marx's thought also, sprang.

Marxism is a creation of nineteenth-century Western Europe, developed via the critique of political economy. In formulating such a critique, Marx imbibed certain features of the forms of social thought he set out to combat: especially the conception that the modern (capitalist) state is primarily concerned with guaranteeing the rights of private property, against a backdrop of the national and international extension of economic exchange relationships. The classical Marxian texts not only lack an elaborated theory of the state, as even Marx's most close adherents now freely admit, they lack a satisfactory conception of *power* in a more general sense. Marx has, of course, an analysis of class power or class domination; but the accent here is on 'class' as at the origin of power. Both the state, and, as Marx sometimes says, 'political power', are to be transcended with the disappearance of classes in the anticipated socialist society of the future. There is therefore a certain antithesis between Marx (the radicalisation of property) and Nietzsche (the radicalisation of power) that provides something of an open door for the disillusioned. The door perhaps only tends to stand open one way – from Marx to Nietzsche – because Nietzsche offers a refuge for those who have lost their 'modernist' illusions without relapsing into complete cynicism or apathy. But it is probably more common to lose one's illusions, to recognise them as illusions, than to capture a faith in progressivism from nowhere. And there seem to be relatively few who are prepared to endure the mental burden of attempting to draw from both Marx and Nietzsche. Of those who have tried, Max Weber is perhaps the most illustrious example; and he seems, as Fleischmann has remarked, to have ended most close to Nietzsche.[2] Weber's sombre reflections on the state of the world in 1918-19 in 'Politics as a vocation', in fact, share some remarkable echoes with Lévy, even if they lack the flights of rhetoric of which the latter author is fond.

Reference to Max Weber, of course, reminds us that the influence of Nietzsche over social theory is by no means solely a contemporary phenomenon. Indeed there are those, such as Lukács in his book the *Destruction of Reason,* who have regarded Nietzsche as the baleful influence over a rising tide of irrationalism in German thought which precisely culminated in the triumph of fascism. But there is something novel about the resurgence of interest in Nietzsche today. Nietzsche has not before exerted the sway over French intellectual circles that he tends to do now; and ideas in some part borrowed from Nietzsche do not only fund a new conservatism. A number of groups of writers who regard themselves as being on the Left have come under the sway of ideas drawn from Nietzsche. And in parenthesis we must recognise that the stance of the new philosophers could not unambiguously be said to be 'on the Right'.

Rather than discussing the writings of the new philosophers in any detail, I propose to concentrate my attention upon Foucault. In 1977 Jean Baudrillard published a little book called *Oublier Foucault.* But in the English-speaking world there could hardly be any question of forgetting Foucault because I think it would be true to say that he has only just been discovered – the Foucault of power, at any rate, rather than the cryptic Foucault of metahistory. In this essay I shall discuss critically certain of the themes that have come to the fore in Foucault's work, returning at the end to the challenge posed by the new philosophers.

Foucault's more recent writings, those that are primarily preoccupied with power, do of course preserve some of the emphases of his earlier ones. His historical studies are informed by what he calls 'genealogy', by which he means 'a form of history which accounts for the constitution of knowledges, discourses, domains of objects, etc., without having to refer to a subject, whether it be transcendental in relation to the field of events or whether it chase its empty identity throughout history'.[3] Foucault is often bracketed to 'post-structuralism', in spite of his dislike of the term. And one can see some reason for this. Foucault continues, and indeed elaborates upon, the theme of the decentring of the subject that was introduced by Saussure and by Lévi-Strauss. In Foucault's work, the decentring of the subject becomes both a methodological and, in a certain sense, a substantial phenomenon. History is constituted in epistemes, or more latterly in fields of power, through which human subjects are disclosed; and, in the current age, we are moving away from an era dominated by a particular type of constitution of subjectivity. We are witnessing the 'end of the individual', a phrase which has a poignant contrast with that employed increasingly by Horkheimer and Adorno towards the ends of their lives.

To my mind, Nietzschean themes are strongly prominent in Foucault's later writings, although they are deployed in quite a different (and in some ways much more interesting) way from that of others of his contemporaries in France – even those with whom he has been closely associated, like Deleuze. These themes include not only the all-enveloping character of power, its priority to values and to truth, but also the idea that the body is the surface upon which power impinges. Power, for Foucault, is declaredly the opposite of that haunted and hunted spectre which it appears as in Marxist theory – a noxious expression of class domination, capable of being transcended by the progressive movement of history. Power, says Foucault, is not inherently repressive, not just the capability to say no. If this is all power were, Foucault asks, would we really consistently obey it? Power has its hold because it does not simply act like an oppressive weight, a burden to be resisted. Power is actually the means whereby all things happen, the production of things, of knowledge and forms of discourse, and of pleasure.

This theory of power forms the axis of Foucault's as yet only partly begun history of sexuality. 'Sexuality', as we understand that phenomenon in contemporary Western society, is a product of power rather than power being repressive of sexuality. Sex has a specific political significance in modern times because it concerns characteristics and activities that are at the intersection between the discipline of the body and control of the population. There are evident connections here with Foucault's account of the origins of the prison, which I find to be his most brilliant work, the focus of most of what he has to say of importance about power. I presume a familiarity with this work, and shall not seek to reproduce its arguments in any detail. According to Foucault, the widespread adoption of the prison in Western societies in the nineteenth century signals a major transition in fields of power. In the sphere of punishment, incarceration replaces public executions, torturing, or other 'spectacles'. A 'double process' of change is involved: the disappearance of the spectacle, and the elimination of pain in favour of the deprivation of liberty and correctional discipline. This epitomises the disappearance of one type of social order, based upon 'the representative, scenic, signifying, public, collective model', and the emergence of another, 'the coercive, corporal, solitary, secret model of the power to punish'.[4]

Discipline and surveillance are key aspects of the prison, according to Foucault; and in his view it is essential to see that these are not peculiar to prisons. On the contrary, they pervade a range of other organisations that also come to the fore in nineteenth-century industrial capitalism: factories, offices and places of work, hospitals, schools, barracks, and so on. Discipline, Foucault says, dissociates power from the body, the contrary of traditional practices, in which the body was marked – in the case of punishment, publicly branded in some way. At the same time, the emphasis is placed upon the 'interiorisation' of power. Disciplinary power, in Foucault's phrase, is 'exercised through its invisibility'; those who experience it acquiesce in this new technology of power, and their acquiescence is an essential part of that new technology. It is not difficult in such a context to see how these notions might connect to the analysis of authority that Sennett has developed in his work – and I mean here not just the book *Authority*, but earlier work also. By the 'hidden injuries' of class, Sennett means, I take it, not simply that the 'injuries' of class domination are 'hidden', but that it is in the nature of class domination in contemporary capitalism that it is 'exercised through its invisibility'.

But the invisibility of disciplinary power, Foucault allows, has a visible counterpart, and sustaining mechanism, in surveillance. The idea that individuals should be constantly 'under observation', he argues, is the natural correlate of discipline, once the latter is manifested externally in regularity of conduct by 'docile bodies'. Thus the type case of the layout of the prison is Bentham's plan of the Panopticon, with its central observation tower. But this is only an 'ideal' form of the physical layout that inevitably accompanies the discipline/surveillance relationship. For disciplinary power involves the specified enclosure of space, the partitioning of space according to specialised criteria of identification or activity. Such spatial sequestration is so much a part of factories, offices and the other organisations I have mentioned that we should not be surprised to find they all resemble prisons. Perhaps it would not be stretching things too far to say that, for Foucault, it is the prison and the asylum which above all exemplify the modern age, not the factory or place of production as it was for Marx. And this contrast, one might add, in turn expresses Foucault's particular version of the displacement of Marx by Nietzsche.

Now we should not miss the significance of Foucault's work, which in my assessment is perhaps the most important contribution to the theory of administrative power since Max Weber's classic texts on bureaucracy. None the less, it is equally important not to fall too easily under its sway: it is at this juncture I want to begin a series of observations that lead in the end to a rejection of the 'Nietzschean resurgence' in social theory. I want to make several major objections to what Foucault has to say about power, discipline and surveillance; and these will eventually lead us back to issues raised by the perorations of the new philosophers. I believe that the points I shall make both have relevance to social theory as a whole, as it currently exists, and to questions of politics.

1.   I think it very important to break with the 'post-structuralist' style of thought in which Foucault stands. Foucault seems to link the expansion of disciplinary power with the rise of industrial capitalism, but he does so only in a very general way. Like the 'epistemic trans-formations' documented in his earlier works, the transmutation of power emanates from the dark and mysterious backdrop of 'history without a subject'. Now I accept that 'history has no subject', if that phrase refers to a Hegelian view of the progressive overcoming of self-alienation by humanity; and I accept the theme of the decent-ring of the subject, if this means that we cannot take subjectivity as a given. But I do not at all accept the idea of a 'subject-less history', if

that term is taken to mean that human social affairs are determined by forces of which those involved are wholly unaware. It is precisely to counter such a view that I have developed the tenets of the theory of structuration.[5] Human beings, in the theory of structuration, are always and everywhere regarded as knowledgeable agents, although acting within historically specific bounds of the unacknowledged conditions and unintended consequences of their acts. Foucault's 'genealogical method', in my opinion, continues the confusion which structuralism helped to introduce into French thought, between history without a *transcendental subject* and history without *knowledgeable human subjects*. These are two very different things, however. We must disavow the first, but recognise the cardinal significance of the second – that significance which Marx expressed pithily in the famous observation that 'men make history, but not in conditions of their own choosing'.

2.   This first objection has concrete implications for the analyses that Foucault has produced of the prison and the clinic. 'Punishment', 'discipline', and especially 'power' itself, are characteristically spoken of by him as though they were agents – indeed the real agents of history. But the development of prisons, clinics and hospitals was not a phenomenon that merely appeared 'behind the backs' of those who designed them, helped to build them, or were their inmates. Ignatieff's work on the origins of prisons is in this respect a useful counterbalance to Foucault.[6] The reorganisation and expansion of the prison system in the nineteenth century was closely bound up with the perceived needs of state authorities to construct new modes of controlling miscreants in large urban spaces, where the sanctioning procedures of the local community could no longer apply.

3.   Foucault draws too close an association between the prison and the factory. There is no doubt that prisons were in part consciously looked to as models by some employers in the early years of capitalism in their search for the consolidation of labour discipline. Unfree labour was actually sometimes used. But there are two essential differences between the prison and the factory. 'Work' only makes up one sector, albeit normally the most time-consuming one, of the daily life of individuals outside prisons. For the capitalistic work-place is not, as prisons are, and clinics and hospitals may be, a 'total institution', in Goffman's term. More important, the worker is not forcibly incarcerated in the factory or office, but enters the gates of the work-place as 'free wage-labour'. This gives rise to the historically peculiar problems of the 'management' of a labour force that is formally 'free', analysed interestingly by Pollard among others.[7] At the same time, it opens the way for forms of worker resistance (especially unionisation and the threat of collective withdrawal of labour) that are not part of the normal enactment of prison discipline. The 'docile bodies' which Foucault says discipline produces turn out very often to be not so docile at all.

4.   In line with his Nietzschean 'hermeneutics of suspicion', by treating the prison as the exemplar of power as discipline, Foucault to my mind produces too negative a view of 'bourgeois' or 'liberal freedoms', and of the reformist zeal they helped to inspire. We are all well aware of the Marxian 'hermeneutics of suspicion', which sees liberal freedoms as an ideological cloak for coercive and exploitative class domination. No one can plausibly deny that the freedom of 'free wage-labour' in the early years of industrial capitalism was largely a sham, a means to the exploitation of labour power in conditions not controlled by the worker. But the 'mere' bourgeois freedoms of freedom of movement, formal equality before the law, and the right to organise politically, have turned out to be very real freedoms in the light of the twentieth-century experience of totalitarian societies in which they are absent or radically curtailed. Foucault says of the prison that 'prison reform' is born together with the prison itself: it is part of its very programme. But the same point could be made, and in less ironic vein, about various of the political and economic transformations introduced with the collapse of feudalism. Liberalism is not the same as despotism, absolutism or totalitarianism, and the bourgeois ethos of rational, universalised justice has the same double-edged character as prisons and their reform. With this major difference: prisoners are denied just those rights which the remainder of the population formally possess. Taken together, freedom of contract and freedom to organise politically have helped generate the rise of labour movements that have been both a challenge to, and a powerful force for change within, the political and economic orders of capitalism.

5.   There is a surprising 'absence' at the heart of Foucault's analyses – thus far at any rate – an absence shared with Marxism. It is what I have drawn attention to earlier: an account of the state. In Marx, as I have commented, this lack is in some part to be traced to his involvement with political economy. In Foucault, one suspects,

it is related to the very ubiquity of power as discipline. The state is what Foucault describes as the 'calculated technology of subjection' writ large, *the* disciplinary matrix that oversees the others. If Foucault does believe this, it is to my mind at best a partial truth. There can, in the contemporary world, no longer be a theory of 'the state', but only a theory of *states;* and this has implications both 'internally' and 'externally'. 'Internally', whatever the new philosophers may say or imply, it seems to me nonsense to claim that the very existence of 'the state' negates both liberal and socialist principles. Diffuse talk of the prevalence of power and the unchallengeable might of the state generates a quiescence which is every bit as weakly founded as glib Marxist chatter about the transcendence of 'the state'.

'Externally', it seems to me of the first importance to follow Tilly and others in emphasising the significance of the association between the rise of capitalism and the pre-existing European state system. Foucault writes as follows:

> If the economic take-off of the West began with the techniques that made possible the accumulation of capital, it might perhaps be said that the methods for administering the accumulation of men made possible a political take-off in relation to the traditional, ritual, costly, violent forms of power, which soon fell into disuse and were superseded by a subtle, calculated technology of subjection.[8]

But this analysis can very easily be misleading, like all talk of the state in general. There has never been a 'capitalist state', there have always been capitalist nation-states, in which the internal processes of pacification of which Foucault speaks have been accompanied by a fearsome concentration of the means of violence in the hands of the state. In a book I have recently completed, I have tried to show that there are direct relations between the capitalist labour contract, as a medium of class domination, and the appropriation of the means of violence by the state.[9] The capitalist labour contract begins as a purely economic relation, in which the employer possesses neither moral sanctions nor sanctions of violence to secure the compliance of the labour force in the work-place. This 'extrusion' of the means of violence from the labour contract meant that compliance was secured in substantial degree through the novel technology of power which Foucault describes. But one could hardly argue that 'costly, violent forms of power' were thereby done away with, in the context of the relations between nation-states. Rather, the twentieth century has seen an escalation of violence upon a level unparalleled in prior history.

What, then, of power, the state and the new conservatism? What relevance have these analyses for those who look to socialist traditions of thought in general, or to Marxism in particular, for some kind of sustaining principles that will further what Jürgen Habermas calls 'modernism'? My argument would be as follows, and has two principal strands – strands, I suppose, that I have been doing my best to unravel and recombine in most of my recent work. It seems to me that it is correct to speak of an exhaustion of Western social and political thought in current times: a vacuum which, as John Dunn has emphasised in his *Western Political Theory in the Face of the Future,* is particularly characteristic of liberalism and Marxism, which have mingled origins in late eighteenth-century thought.[10] A runner who is exhausted is not necessarily about to depart this world, however, but may after suitable refreshment be able to carry on with renewed energy. I don't want to pursue such an inept metaphor too far, but I think it valid to say that social and political theory is currently going through a period of transition, rather than terminal collapse. There is no need to release hold of 'modernism' yet, to renounce the ideals of the Enlightenment as false gods to be replaced by a brutish acquiescence in the reality of power.

One level of transformation concerns the analytical tools of social theory. Social thought was for a lengthy period dominated by empiricist models of natural science, which those in the social sciences strove blindly to follow. The result was the prevalence of the 'orthodox consensus', centred upon the twin poles of naturalism and functionalism. The orthodox consensus was largely a legacy of late eighteenth- and nineteenth-century thought, revitalised in the twentieth century by logical empiricism and systems theory. From its early origins it had a rival, a 'counter-tradition', that refused to accept natural science as a model for social thought and, via its basic opposition between *verstehen* (understanding) and *erklären* (explanation), emphasised the meaningful, purposive character of human conduct. Even though accepting language as its exemplar for explaining social forms, structuralism and 'post-structuralism' have been much more closely aligned with the orthodox consensus than with the counter-tradition. But I think it can be seen today that all these rival traditions of thought incorporate fundamental deficiencies. What is on the agenda at the present time is a reconstruction of social and political theory that breaks substantially with all three traditions. It is clear that by now familiar denunciations of 'positivism' barely touch the problems involved. On the one hand, there are basic questions to be tackled concerning human subjectivity in relation to the structural components of institutions formed in the 'long duration' of historical time. In my opinion, here it is necessary to accept the structuralist contention that the subject must be 'decentred'; but neither structuralist nor post-structuralist thought have proved able to cope conceptually with its implications. This includes Foucault; I refer back at this point to my earlier emphasis upon treating human beings as knowledgeable, capable agents, the products and the producers of history.

The importance of developing what I have called a theory of structuration is not confined to the social sciences. For, while seeking to rethink the nature of human action and institutions, we have at the same time to integrate this with an appraisal of the basic changes that have occurred in the philosophy of natural science. Both the orthodox consensus and the counter-tradition operated with a model of natural science – one fashioning social theory after it, the other contrasting the social and natural sciences – which now appears obsolete.

In this agenda, the concept of power certainly does occupy a basic role. I think it the case that not only Marxism, but many other forms of social theory too, lack a satisfactory theory of power. Here the interpretative sociologies generated by the counter-tradition share a good deal in common with the functionalism of Talcott Parsons. Both see meaning or norms as the most 'elemental' feature of social life. Power is a secondary phenomenon, to be added in at second reserve. Foucault, and those influenced in a more uninhibited way by Nietzsche, are right to insist that power is chronically and inevitably involved in all social processes. To accept this, I think, is to acknowledge that power and freedom are not inimical; and that power cannot be identified with either coercion or constraint. But I also think it quite wrong to be thereby seduced by a Nietzschean radicalisation of power, which elevates *it* to the prime position in action and in discourse. Power then becomes a mysterious phenomenon, that hovers everywhere, and underlies everything. I consider it very important to reject the idea that power has primacy over truth, or that meanings and norms can be explicated as congealed or mystified power. A reductionism of power is as faulty as economic or normative reductionisms are.

This brings me to the second strand of transformation in social and political theory in contemporary times. Here I should declare *parti pris,* and say that my political sympathies lie on the Left, and therefore I am probably not the proper type of person to give the new conservatism a fair hearing anyway. However, I do think the issues of power and the state brought into sharp focus by the new philosophers do constitute one major element in a reformulation of political theory that has to be every bit as far-reaching as the analytical reconstruction of social theory mentioned above. In my concluding remarks, I shall concern myself mainly with Marxism – not because I am, or have ever been a 'Marxist', but because Marxist thought in my view must be an essential point of departure for anyone wishing to defend an emancipatory politics. I have no doubt that a substantial core of what Marx wrote about industrial capitalism is correct, and should be sustained today. However, I can find little to commend in the commonly held view that Marx was right about nineteenth-century capitalism, but that his views need adjustment in the light of developments since his day. This *is* certainly correct, but does not go to the roots of the matter, which is that there are elemental weaknesses in Marx's thought at source. I should like to produce – and have made a first contribution to this in a book mentioned earlier – a 'contemporary critique of historical materialism'. But it would be one from the Left, not from the Right, and it is certainly a project to which Foucault's writings, themselves critically appraised, offer an important stimulus.

A contemporary critique of historical materialism must theorise socialism on two intersecting planes. Marx looked forward to the achievement of socialism as the overall transcendence of capitalism: there is no indication that he anticipated a world in which the capitalist 'heartlands' have not experienced a successful socialist revolution, and in which capitalism coexists with societies governed by groups claiming affiliation to his doctrines. Socialism is both an 'actually existing' reality, and a set of ideals that still seem capable of more profound development well beyond that achieved in any society to date. The twentieth century, as the new philosophers remind us if we could forget, is the century of the Gulag. Socialism no longer has its hands clean, and whatever ways one may choose to criticise the existing socialist societies, including taking the easy option of declaring that they are not really 'socialist' at all, there is no way of attributing all the evils of the world in some diffuse way to 'capitalism'.

No reworked socialist theory can be adequate that does not seek to come to terms with the major absences in Marxism: these include sexual exploitation and ethnic domination. Neither of these was invented by capitalism, although both have taken specific forms with the spread of capitalist industry. Particularly relevant to these themes are the shortcomings of the materialist interpretation of history. About this one can say several things. First, the idea that history can be fruitfully understood in terms of the expansion of the forces of production, or a dialectic of forces and relations of production, has to be abandoned.[11] Second, much of what Marx has to say about the non-European societies is both 'Europocentric' and factually wrong. One may think here of his comments on China and India, but we should also remember the very range of pre-capitalist civilisations that barely figure in Marx's writings at all – some of which he could not have written about in any case, since they were unknown at his time. Third, the elements of a 'universal history' of humankind, which Marx tried to integrate into his evolutionary scheme, must be radically revised. For Marx, capitalism appeared as the high point of a 'universal history', but in contradictory form; socialism was to be the culmination of human history as a whole. For this view to be plausible, capitalism has to be regarded as the summation of human history thus far, in alienated form. Such a conception could only be entertained, however, if we closed our eyes to the 'absences' I have mentioned in Marx, and to his Europocentrism.

Here we have to return again to the themes of power and the state. The absence of a theory of power, including the use of violence by individuals, collectivities and states, runs like a red thread (or perhaps one should say, a blue thread) through the writings of Marx and of Marxism subsequently. The implications of this, as I have mentioned previously, have to be traced out 'internally' and 'externally' in terms of state theory. Let me just mention very quickly what these implications are.

'Internally', we must take seriously the possibility that socialist theory is inherently connected with what might be called 'Left totalitarianism'. In analysing this phenomenon, and attempting to develop counter-possibilities, we can draw upon Foucault. 'Surveillance' is perhaps the core concept here, and can be said to concern two related activities of states. One is the collection and analysis of information about subject populations, employed to regulate or monitor their activities. The other is the direct supervision of tasks in the various institutional sectors of the state. Defined thus, surveillance is a characteristic of all states; it is not coincidental that the early origins of states were usually connected with the invention of writing. Writing originated as a mode of co-ordinating the administrative order of the state. But the advent of the modern state greatly expands the range of surveillance activities. Information control is a major mode of exploitative domination, but not one that classical socialist theories have been well equipped to analyse.

'Externally', socialist theory must seek to come to grips with the role of the state as the purveyor of violence, a phenomenon that has reached a terrifying peak in the contemporary world system of nation-states. The nation-state does not disappear with the advent of socialism, at least in its 'actually existing' form. If this is the era of the Gulag, it is also one of warlike confrontations between socialist states, of Pol Pot and something close to genocide in Kampuchea. Nothing, in my opinion, exposes more plainly the gulf between nineteenth-century political thought and the world we confront today; re-read what little Marx had to say about nationalism, re-read Bakunin on the peaceful international community of nations he presaged for the future. It would be merely foolish to be sanguine about the task of reconstructing Left political theory confronting these issues, as the world totters on the edge of nuclear confrontation. However, I for one have no intention of jumping from Marx to Nietzsche. Here permit me one final quote from Lévy. 'The individual comes into being,' he says, 'only as the lackey and prop of power'; hence 'we must get rid of the *worn-out and related concepts of oppression and liberation*'.[12] But I would say quite the contrary; nothing is more important than to defend and expand upon the use of those concepts in the face, not of power as such, but of the massive co-ordination of power and exploitation in the contemporary world system.

230   *Profiles and Critiques in Social Theory*

References

1. Bernard-Henri Lévy, *Barbarism with a Human Face* (New York: Harper & Row, 1980) p. x.
2. Eugene Fleischmann, 'De Weber à Nietzsche', *Archives européennes de sociologie,* vol. 5, 1964.
3. Michel Foucault, *Power, Truth, Strategy* (Sydney: Feral Publications, 1979) p. 35.
4. Foucault, *Discipline and Punish: the Birth of the Prison* (London: Allen Lane, 1977) p. 131.
5. *Central Problems in Social Theory* (London: Macmillan, 1979).
6. Michael Ignatieff, *A Just Measure of Pain* (London: Macmillan, 1978).
7. Sidney Pollard, *The Genesis of Modern Management* (London: Arnold, 1965).
8. Foucault, *Discipline and Punish,* pp.220–1.
9. *A Contemporary Critique of Historical Materialism* (London: Macmillan, 1981).
10. John Dunn, *Western Political Theory in the Face of the Future* (Cambridge: Cambridge University Press, 1979).
11. Cf. *A Contemporary Critique of Historical Materialism.*
12. Lévy, *Barbarism with a Human Face.*

Index